The Portsmouth Connection

Stories and Lives of Devon Villages and an Aristocratic Estate

JONATHAN CROFTS

'This is the immemorial, provincial England, stable, rocted deep
in the soil, unmoving, contented, and sane. Those are my forebears,
who have made me what I am whether I like it or not; and I have
enlarged upon them a little because they have really determined
what sort of book this is.'

W G Hoskins in his author's introduction to *Devon*, 1953

First Published 2024
by Richmond Bridge Media

A CIP record for this book is available from the British Library.
Paperback ISBN 978-1-8382510-1-7
First Edition

Edited and additional research by Monica Byles
Cover design by Annie Rushton
Page design by Alison Gardner

Printed in England by Pureprint Group on recyclable materials and using vegetable-based inks

Front cover: Photo of Eggesford House by Ed Howell, the architect owner since the 1990s

Back cover: Photo of the Portsmouth P and crest by Jonathan Crofts
Paintings of the 5th Countess and 5th Earl of Portsmouth
(photos by Jonathan Crofts, by kind permission of Viscount Lymington)
Photo of tractor and farmers working in the fields by kind permission of Yvonne Gerry

A proportion of the sale price of this book will be donated to the Friends of Eggesford
All Saints Trust, along with Chawleigh Parish Lands Charity

Contents

'It might well have been in the "Happy Valley" above which this Country House stands, among surrounding hills covered with wood, that Rasselas may be supposed to have meditated, "the world forgetting." It gives the perfect idea of peaceful seclusion, and the little old church below adds its quaint and becoming feature to the lovely picture.'

A reference to Eggesford House and Dr Samuel Johnson's only novel *The History of Rasselas, Prince of Abyssinia*, Rasselas being a young prince in his own pursuit of happiness.

An 18th-century watercolour by Reverend John Swete
showing the earlier Eggesford House and the Taw valley

(By kind permission of Ed Howell)

'Crossing the bridge and ascending through woods which spread themselves wide over the hills above, we soon came to a spot on the verge of a quick descent from the road, from whence I had a full view of a most delicious Valley – border'd on both of its sides by the richest woods – and enliven'd by the windings of the Taw, and the verdant pasturage which spread itself from the river to the Woods; at some distance in front of a range of larger trees, on the left stood the House – and almost contiguous to it, behind, was seen the top of the Church tower : the distant ground was well finished by gently rising hills, cultivated and woody.

The Landscape had nothing in it of the wild, or romantic, it was a sweetly-pleasing picture touch'd by the soft, the minute, the elegant pencil of Nature – Art did not seem to me to have used much of its interference in the embellishment of this little Paradise.'

The Reverend John Swete writing as he approached Eggesford House and the Taw valley, c.1797, in
Travels in Georgian Devon: The Illustrated Journals of the Reverend John Swete (1789–1800), Volume III

FOREWORD
by Julian Fellowes, Baron Fellowes of West Stafford, DL

Jonathan Crofts' book is a treasure trove of connections brought to light through people's lives and the places they live in. The letter 'P' and a crest over the front door of a Devon village farmhouse connect the 400-year-old building to the Wallop family, the Earls of Portsmouth, who owned the enormous local estate for over two centuries, along with three quarters of that village, and many others nearby.

There is a historical connection with my own family, the Fellowes, earlier owners of the estate, who married into the Portsmouth (or Wallop) family, and I am still friendly with the Portsmouths today. My own family claim descent from Thomas, of the original family of William Fellowes of Eggesford.

In the late nineteenth century, Eveline, Countess of Portsmouth, and her husband, the 5th Earl, were friends with Thomas Hardy, one of England's most prominent writers, who visited their Eggesford estate – although he was less than complimentary over his host's obsession with his hounds. I too have a strong connection with Hardy as President of the Thomas Hardy Society, and he was a regular visitor to my home, Stafford House in Dorset, Hardy's county of birth, to call on my great-great-aunt Gertrude Floyer. Thomas Hardy's story 'The Waiting Supper' references a waterfall in the grounds, and Tess of the D'Urbervilles ties the knot with Angel Clare apparently in our local church.

Of the great-grandchildren of William Fellowes, the early eighteenth-century owner of the Eggesford estate, Isaac Newton Wallop (5th Earl of Portsmouth) was the second great-grandson, and the sixth was George Herbert (8th Earl of Carnarvon). That brings us back to my most well-known screen work, *Downton Abbey*. The Carnarvons have owned Highclere Castle, the famous main location for the TV series and films, for over three centuries.

The connections (or perhaps coincidences?) run deep. For one episode of *Downton Abbey*, I dared to name one of the characters after the current Lady Portsmouth, Annabel. The son of my great-aunt, Isie, who helped bring my father up, is buried in the churchyard of the Eggesford estate, All Saints. Isie herself was the model for the late Maggie Smith's redoubtable Dowager Countess in *Downton*. And the great-grandmother of the current (10th) Earl of Portsmouth, Quentin Wallop, took care of my own great-grandmother when she was suddenly widowed in a carriage accident in the 1890s.

Jonathan's book tells the story of the evolution of the Eggesford estate, its owners and its principal seat, Eggesford House, through to the last Portsmouth owners in

Devon in the 1930s. He recounts tales of the buildings and inhabitants of Eggesford, a parish without a village. Historically and geographically close to Eggesford, the ancient village of Chawleigh bursts into life with tales from the past of buildings such as the church, parsonage/rectory, schoolhouse and traditional hostelries. Stories of its inhabitants reveal a rich social and agricultural history, dating back even before the Domesday Book to when forests were cleared by cattle herders.

In 1869, Chawleigh suffered a catastrophic fire, and the memory of the respected 5th Earl of Portsmouth who helped rebuild the village has been preserved in the name of the pub closest to the area of regeneration. His Countess, Eveline, who grew up at Highclere as a daughter of the Carnarvons, embraced not only her friends from the world of literature and traditional country pursuits, but was an early supporter of the suffragettes and active in charity work.

Snapshots of English life outside the towns and cities, especially in the Georgian, Victorian and Edwardian periods, show influences over recent centuries from people and politics, national and world events, the improvement of transport, arrival of electricity and other factors. Today, the legacy of my ancestors and family friends is overshadowed by transformations in agriculture, property ownership and technology which continue to affect the character of villages such as Chawleigh and Eggesford.

Jonathan's book is full of illustrations and will delight readers who know and love this part of Mid and North Devon, but others also who are interested to understand the historic counterpoint between aristocratic families and their estates, tenants and other occupiers, not to mention the connections with literature and screen. Although very different, usually on a smaller scale and no doubt not as rich, many original such estates and landowning families continue to thrive, especially in large rural counties such as Devon.

Julian Alexander Kitchener-Fellowes, Baron Fellowes of West Stafford DL is an actor, novelist, film director and screenwriter, and a peer of the House of Lords. He is the author of several *Sunday Times* bestselling novels, the screenplay for *Gosford Park* (Academy Award winner for Best Original Screenplay in 2002) and other films, and creator, writer and executive producer of the internationally acclaimed, multiple award-winning TV series *Downton Abbey*, together with its associated films. He also fulfils a range of charitable roles in Dorset and across the nation.

Julian Fellowes, photo by Alison Rosa Cohen (© Home Box Office, Inc.)

INTRODUCTION
Tales of Rural and Aristocratic Life

Today, Leaches House is a family-sized home, built primarily of cob and thatch, with four outbuildings on the site of structures which formerly served the surrounding farm, three of which relate to their original purposes: barn, piggery and privy (lavatory). The evolution of the house over the last four hundred years or so is not untypical of the story of English rural life across the nation.

Leaches House, formerly Leaches Farm (which has now moved down the adjoining Blackwalls Lane, and is home to a herd of South Devons cattle), is in the village of Chawleigh, a settlement named (as Calveleia) in the Domesday Book of 1086. Chawleigh itself represents one community amongst many which formed part of the enormous estate based around Eggesford House, Eggesford being a neighbouring parish – small, but with its own church and railway station and earlier, a school.

The estate at its peak covered more than 16,000 acres, first mentioned in the hands of the Anglo-Norman Reigney family (also known as Reigny or de Reini) in the early thirteenth century. It passed through the hands of a few of Devon's ancient landed families until it came into the ownership of the Earls of Portsmouth via the Fellowes family. The Fellowes married into the Portsmouths (whose family name was and still is Wallop), and the family line carried through until the Fellowes name was adopted once more in the late nineteenth century.

Historic Houses Association, which helps owners to conserve 1,650 houses, castles and gardens throughout the UK, estimates that almost five thousand large country houses existed in the mid-nineteenth century at the peak of the great country estates, only some three thousand of which remain today. Traditionally, the 'four Ds' have been the primary reasons for selling up: Death, Divorce, Debt and Disaster.

Often originating as the manor house at the heart of a large agricultural estate, in the seventeenth and eighteenth centuries, such properties typically supported hundreds of local staff and labourers, along with suppliers of food, fuel and services. Ben Cowell OBE, director general of the Historic Houses Association, explained in 2018: 'Owners made money from renting land to tenant farmers, but many also invested in industry, mining, or railways, which helped to replenish the family fortune and fund a country house way of life.'

'The decline started in the late 19th century', he continues: the agricultural depression of the 1870s meant farming rents were lower, death duties on landed wealth were introduced in 1894, then other legislation worsened finances and forced many to sell parts of their estates. 'Once the land was lost, the house itself became less and less viable.'

What happened next is better known: the political environment turned against the landed, often aristocratic, classes, and social changes accelerated by the First World War saw the start of the end for the old established order. Many houses were destroyed or fell into ruin.

In 2002, Devon author Rosemary Lauder wrote in her study of old *Devon Families* and their houses:

> 'We are lucky in Devon that we have managed to keep 25 per cent of our estates still in the same families… The trick, as several owners said to me, was to keep your head down and do nothing to attract attention until the troubles had blown over.'

In contrast, a focus on national politics and other family estates by the 6th Earl of Portsmouth, Newton Wallop, helps explain why the challenging economics of running large rural estates overwhelmed the Eggesford estate, even before the First World War, while others survived.

A *Country Life* columnist wrote in September 2022, following the transition from one monarch to her son, of the 'centuries-old balancing act in this kingdom: ancient genealogy providing an intricate tapestry of history and continuity, a tangible and useful reminder that political lives are more temporal than royal reigns'.

As the death of Queen Elizabeth II and the accession of King Charles III have shown, there remains a role for landed estates and the sometimes anachronistic titles associated with them: the significance of inheritance in the UK persists, whatever the politics of those involved. That of course may change over time, but at the very least, the commercial relationships between landowners and tenants seem likely to continue.

This book is not intended as a comprehensive account of the characters of the village of Chawleigh and the Eggesford household and estate, but to offer some vignettes of some of those lives, and to reflect how people lived at different points over the last four centuries in rural England; its scope is a social history as much as anything. Part of that history is the role played by the Church of England and other religious groups, by the spread of education, and by global conflict. Much of the story ends with the Second World War, and the impact of the First World War is clear.

The book also describes some of the architecture of key buildings in that history, and how communities were connected by developing transport links in this deeply rural part of England. There is a persistent theme of charity and helping those who have fallen on hard times, not just from the aristocratic families, but within these small communities themselves. Often church-based at the outset, some of these local charities have endured beyond their religious origins, even if their evolution has at times been controversial.

Although most periods of history were largely dominated by men, socially and politically, women featured in charitable and creative endeavours, and not only amongst the wealthy. Hunting and fishing were primarily leisure pursuits for men of the monied and farming classes, but women led local interests in the arts: a surprising number of high-profile literary figures arrived as guests at Eggesford House in its heyday.

While there is no 'great family and household' now at the centre of the area covered by the old Eggesford estate, many smaller country houses originally owned by the estate do still offer Open Gardens for charity, host or help organise similar fundraising events, or provide some community benefit. A sense of public duty is still prevalent across British society, evident in the breadth of the 'third' or 'charity' sector in the life of the UK, offering a helping hand where the state often does not.

A detailed history of agriculture in Devon is not included here, although farming has necessarily always been a significant economic and social force in this Mid / North Devon community. Agriculture in the UK once again finds itself at a turning point in 2024, as the fallout from Brexit impacts on government subsidies, and Defra clarifies what EU payments will be replaced with and how that process will work. Labour is limited in many places as European seasonal workers have been constrained from entering the UK or simply decided to return to their native countries. Feed, fuel, vet and fertiliser costs have suffered from significant inflation since the Covid pandemic and conflicts in Ukraine and the Middle East, and the unstable weather resulting from climate change have not helped.

Similarly, the whole environmental debate is having a major effect, as farmers decide which of 'wilding' or 'rewilding', organic farming, regenerative farming or traditional mixed farming is both sustainable and financially viable. Science and technology may help, but farmers here have huge decisions to make about their futures, and that of the Devon countryside.

Many people will have welcomed the demise of the Eggesford estate up to the 1930s, as some tenants were able to buy their farms, homes and land, and the power and influence of a family with significant inherited wealth and status dwindled – even if the later Earls in Devon continued to commit themselves to public works. But perhaps the estate and the family name provide a valued continuity and sense of history, long after their departure.

The legacy of the Portsmouths and their estate on Eggesford, Chawleigh and other villages locally cannot be underestimated: past generations of many families were

Chawleigh street with pony and trap, when motorised transport was rare (c.1917). The house on the right is Forn Court, now replaced by the social housing next to the village shop.

(Photo by kind permission of Daphne Cockram)

9

employed in the big house and around the estate as housekeepers, cooks, domestic staff, groundsmen, gardeners and grooms. Portsmouth tenants could earn a living through farming, hunting, working at the sawmills, quarries, and other occupations. And the Portsmouths improved schools, churches, roads and railways, along with pubs and other community facilities, visiting and supporting those suffering ill health or who had fallen into poverty. In part this was all to support their own lavish lifestyles, but there was no doubt a benefit to the wider population, even if inequality of opportunity and income was clearly apparent.

In the time of the 6th Earl, the last in Eggesford, telegrams were well established, telephones were becoming more common, Louis Blériot was wobbling across the Channel in his fragile monoplane, Zeppelin airships had emerged and huge naval ships like the dreadnoughts were being built. The 6th Earl had his own relatively fast cars, which were not always favourably viewed in Devon. Technological change continued as it always does.

The retail showroom for hatmakers and dealers Gamble & Gunn in The Royal Oak, a sixteenth-century pub in Chawleigh

(Photo © Gamble & Gunn)

A sixteenth-century pub in Chawleigh these days houses a successful business as 'Hat Makers & Dealers in Vintage Headwear', enabled by the internet. If more were known about all the characters who have lived here over the centuries, there would be a myriad of stories and anecdotes to tell. No doubt the houses, the farms, the villages and beyond will produce rich new tales in the future, as rural Devon continues to evolve. A tale of rural West Country life in a twenty-first-century, digitally connected world could have many outcomes.

CHAPTER 1

THE ORIGINS OF A GREAT ARISTOCRATIC ESTATE

In the twenty-first century, Eggesford is a relatively small settlement, probably best known for its railway station on the Tarka Line (formerly the North Devon Line), with a farm shop and café alongside. Positioned along the Taw valley, it was clearly of strategic interest from Norman times.

Eggesford Castle and Heywood Castle

Transactions of the Devonshire Association 95 (1963) by ET Vachall, MA, considered the origins of the Eggesford site and the existence of two castles, Eggesford and Heywood. Eggesford was described as the lesser of the two:

> 'the work comprises only earthen banks and ditches, and is of unusual shape. It consists of a roughly circular enclosure surrounded by a formidable bank, to which is appended a somewhat larger enclosure defended on its northern and western sides by a rather slighter hook-shaped bank. The eastern side of the larger enclosure is defined by an abrupt and steep erosion scarp cut by the Taw in the local Culm rock. On the side away from the scarp the whole earthwork is surrounded by a ditch of considerable depth and width. The siting of this work is also somewhat unusual...
>
> ... even if it is not in a military commanding position, the small fort does control movement along the river valley, and there is no eminence within bowshot from which the circular inner work could itself be commanded, though at its north-west extremity this hook-shaped outer bank does get rather dangerously close to rising ground from which it could be overlooked. Neither in form nor in siting does this earthwork approach the military requirements of the Iron Age...
>
> The Taw valley probably formed a temporary frontier between the West Welsh and the West Saxons during the period in the first half of the 8th century when the latter were infiltrating and fighting their way westward from the Somersetshire flat-lands to the Tamar–Ottery line; but the layout at Eggesford does not suggest a Saxon work...
>
> What we do have seems to be a small and probably rather primitive Norman work of the ring-motte type, a variation of the more usual form known as the motte and bailey castle... the level of the central area has been built up a little, if at all, above the original natural level of the ground, and here the size of the enclosure is only sufficient to contain perhaps a log-built tower but not habitable buildings... Its purpose therefore was presumably primarily defensive. ... it seems therefore that the only artificial defence considered necessary on this side was a timber stockade along the brink of the scarp...
>
> The approach to this stronghold appears to have been from the western side, where a track under close command from the motte leads down to the outer bank of the ditch to the site of a gateway, which was presumably constructed of logs, as there are no traces of any masonry.'

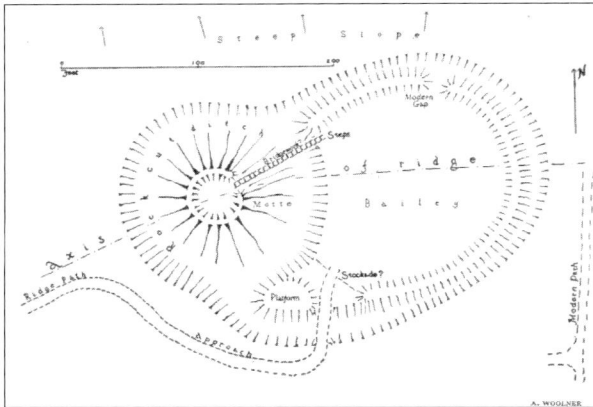

Sketch plan of Heywood Castle
by A. Woolner

Taken from *Transactions of the
Devonshire Association*, vol. 95
(1963) by ET Vachall, MA.

Heywood Castle was however more significant:

'These earthworks are the remains of a typical Norman stronghold of the ring-motte type and consist of a small but impressive mound surrounded by a formidable rock-cut ditch, with, beyond this ditch, a bailey of rather more than ⅓ acre protected by a bank and an extension of the ditch round the motte. The motte is some 25 feet high, and round its upper edges a ring-bank which still stands in places to a height of about 12 feet. The depressed central area within this bank is too small to have been intended to contain living quarters and must have been merely the 'arx' – the stronghold for ultimate defence if the outer work should be carried during an attack.

The bailey is sufficiently commodious to accommodate the normal dwelling quarters for the Lord and also hutments for his retainers. Adequately defended by a ditch cut in places some 5 ft. into the solid rock and by a bank which presumably originally carried a timber stockade. There is no longer vestige of any masonry in the defences of the Bailey, or, what is more significant, in those of the motte either. Nor are there any signs of the holes or trenches which are the usual indications that masonry has been robbed.

From the military engineering aspect the siting is perfect for this type of stronghold and utilises the natural topographical features to the best possible advantage. ... Strategically it is excellently placed to control the Taw obstacle within striking distance of the point where it was crossed by one of the few ridgeway tracks which lead right through this hilly region from the east into Cornwall.'

The layout of the castle appears relatively clear:

'The castle is now approached from the south-west along a spur by a farm road which carried down to the river. This seems to represent the ancient trackway, and from it a diversion appears to have passed, within close missile range from the defences on the motte, to a wooden drawbridge which crossed the bailey ditch of the southern side. The drawbridge led into the Bailey through a gateway which was defended on its western side by a small raised and stockaded fighting platform (of which vestiges remain) and on its eastern (bailey) side by the bank of the bailey itself. There may have been another, inner, gate between the bailey bank and the motte ditch to make access to the bailey more difficult.

The motte seems to have been approached from the bailey in the normal manner by means of a sloping wooden bridge-work leading from the northern corner of the bailey to the existing depression in the banks of the ring-work. This depression presumably marks the position of the innermost gatehouse or gateway.

The absence of any masonry in these defences, or of any evidence of masonry having been robbed even from such tactically critical points as the gateways, indicates that this stronghold was of a primitive type and that it never developed into a masonry fortress.

Heywood Castle, however, seems to be larger than the usual adulterine [without royal approval] castle, and there seems to be no historical reason why such a large one should be built in this position at this period. ... this castle was built during the early Norman period and probably not much, if at all, later than the time of William II. It may have been used during the Stephen wars [the twelfth-century civil wars between Stephen and Matilda], but after that at latest it went out of commission and never developed into a masonry fortress.

If this deduction is correct, Heywood Castle would be closely analogous, in both form and date, to the first castle at Bampton – the Lord of which, Robert De Bampton, caused Stephen so much trouble at the beginning of his reign – and to Dunster Castle, which in its original form, Stephen besieged in person. It would be slightly older than Court Castle at Winkleigh (only 4½ miles away), which the writer deduces to have been built by Robert, Earl of Gloucester, against Stephen.

… The usual explanation of the existence of two Norman forts so close together is either that one was a 'counterwork' used during a siege upon the other, or that the occupants of the more primitive work subsequently moved to the other, which was either more commodious, better sited or more suited to later concepts of military engineering. Heywood Castle is so ably cited and is so commodious that it seems clear that this was the more important work. Eggesford Castle can hardly have been a counterwork against Heywood, for they are too far apart.

… Eggesford Castle was the original Norman stronghold in this neighbourhood. It is not mentioned in Domesday and therefore could not have been constructed earlier than late in the reign of William I. Its object seems to have been to control north–south traffic along the Taw valley and east–west traffic along one of the main ridgeways. After a brief occupation it was abandoned in favour of the greatly superior and more commodious Heywood site.'

Writing in his *Illustrated Journals* circa 1797, the Reverend John Swete refers to a 'passage underground' between Heywood House (see below) and Castle. This was first referenced by historian Tristram Risdon (circa 1580–1640).

Eggesford Castle was listed as a Scheduled Monument in 1928. In 2023 Historic England confirmed:

'… Eggesford Castle, a ringwork castle situated above a ford to the west of the River Taw at Eggesford. It lies to the south west of a second motte and bailey castle called Heywood Castle… The monument survives as an oval mound... Part of the ringwork has been levelled by 19th century ornamental gardening. The bailey, which lies to the NNE, … is surrounded by a bank … Surrounding the whole is a ditch … on the north eastern side; at this point steps have also been cut to facilitate

access to the river. The history of the castle is not clear, although a date of 1130s to the 1140s seems most likely.'

Eggesford Castle, just northeast of Eggesford House, is now listed as Heritage At Risk by Historic England, with 'Extensive significant problems; Principal Vulnerability: Scrub/tree growth; Trend: Declining'.

Heywood Castle was also listed in 1928, and the Historic England description in 2023 confirms much of the 1963 analysis:

'… a motte and bailey castle known as Heywood Castle which is situated in a commanding location overlooking the valley of the River Taw. The monument survives as a circular motte, rock-cut ditch and crescent shaped bailey with an outer bank... On top of the motte is a ring bank... The central enclosed area has a small linear bank running from north to south within it … and runs across the top of the mound… The crescent shaped bailey lies to the north east of the motte … bounded on all sides by a bank...

On the eastern side there is an entrance... From the entrance and across the ditch there is a causeway which extends to the outer bank. On the northern side of the bailey a more modern entrance has formed... From the bailey to the motte on the north eastern side there is the possibility of a bridgeway. An outer bank surrounds the motte and bailey... The monument lies relatively near another contemporary castle which lies a short distance to the south... The castle is thought to date to the 1130s and 1140s and the fact that two are so close together may reflect civil war antagonism or replacement of one by the

14

other. The timber steps and walkways are excluded from the scheduling, although the ground beneath them is included.'

While under the ownership of Newton Fellowes Wallop, 4th Earl of Portsmouth, an extraordinary plan was proposed to build an elaborate tearoom with a quaint tower on top of the original Heywood motte and bailey, with views of Eggesford House and the Park. Two cottages would be built behind a wall. The ornamental 'folly' remained only in the imagination, and was never constructed.

These days the public have access to what remains of Heywood Castle, which lies on Forestry Commission (Forestry England) land. The Eggesford Castle site remains in private hands in the grounds of today's Heyswood House.

The Eggesford Estate

The story of the estate centred around Eggesford can certainly be traced back to the early thirteenth century. Prior to that, Baldwin the Sheriff was recorded as the largest landholder in Devon at the time of the Domesday Book (1085–1086), holding land from the Crown as Tenant-in-Chief, with lands here and around Chawleigh, formerly in the hands of the Saxon lord Siward of Hemington.

The Victoria History of the Counties of England: A History of Devonshire (William Page, 1906) confirms Baldwin the Sheriff as landowner of the Honour of Okehampton (the Honour was a group of estates with the castle at Okehampton at its heart):

Sketch of the Proposed Folly for Heywood Castle ('Haward Castle'), 1804

(Photo by Jonathan Crofts)

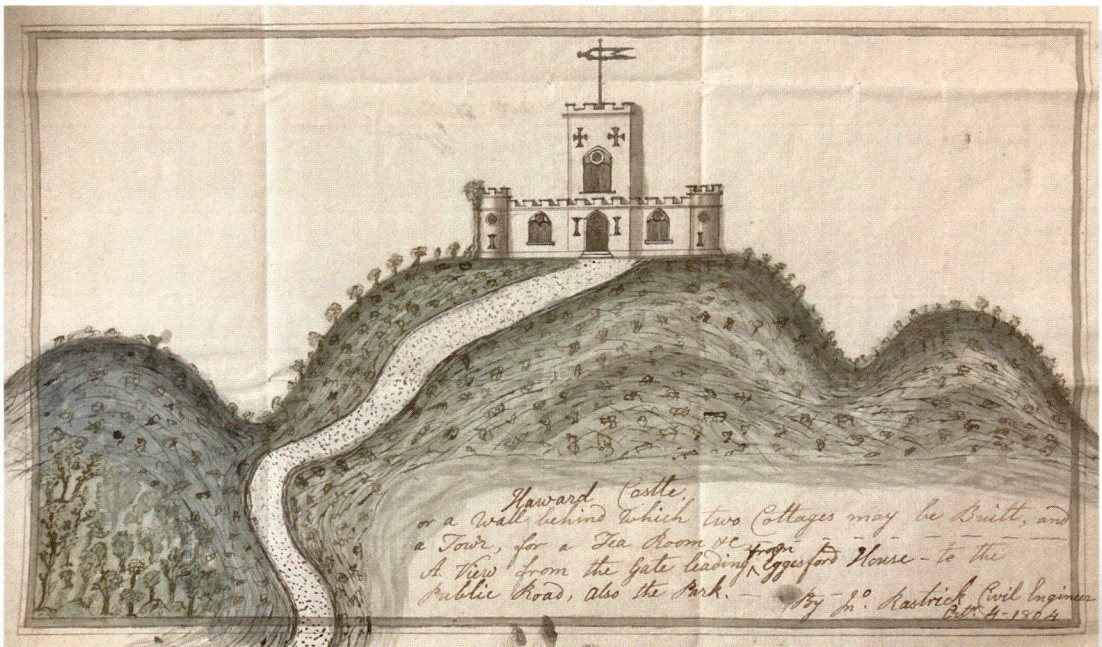

Haward Castle, or a Wall behind which two Cottages may be Built, and a Tower, for a Tea Room &c from a View from the gate leading Eggesford House - to the Public Road, also the Park. — By Jn.º Rastrick Civil Engineer Feb.r 4. 1804

Coats of arms of aristocratic and landed families associated with Chawleigh, drawn by Algernon Pepperell / F W Hillman, c.1963.

Chawleigh Notes, c.1970.

(Photo by Jonathan Crofts)

1. Courtenay of Devon   Or three torteaux.
2. Stafford Or a chevron gules.
3. Reigny . Gules 2 falcons' wings in lure ermine (quartered by Copleston & Monk)
4. Copleston. Argent a chevron engrailed between three leopards heads or.
5. St. Leger. Azure fretty argent a chief or.
6. Chichester of Devon Chequy or and gules a chief vair
7. Fellowes. Azure a fess indented ermine between 3 lions heads erased or murally crowned argent
8. Wallop, Earls of Portsmouth. Argent a bend sable
9. Affeton of Affeton. Argent a chevron engrailed between 3 fleur-de-lys sable
10. Stucley of Affeton Azure three pears pendant or.
11. Bury of Colleton. Ermine on a bend engrailed azure 3 fleur-de-lys or
12. Hrrey-Wyke of Chawleigh Week Ermine three battle-axes sable
13. Cheney of Chenson. Azure powdered with stars 2 lions passant or.
14. Radford. Sable three man-tigers in pale argent.
15. Wood. Argent & sable barry on a canton gules a demi-woodman holding a club.
16. Pollard of Way & Horwood Argent a chevron sable between 3 escallops gules
17. Tonpish of Tonpish in Crediton. Argent a bend cotised within a bordure engrailed sable

16

'The largest landholder in Devon at the time of the Domesday Survey was Baldwin de Brionis, son of Count Gilbert de Brionne, in Normandy, called also Baldwin de Molis, from the castle of Meules where he was born, or de Clare, but usually, Baldwin the sheriff. He owned 177 manors assessed at 146 hides [a unit of land], and comprising roughly 100,000 acres under cultivation in the county...

Baldwin was twice married, (1) to Albreda the Conqueror's niece or cousin, and (2) to Emma, and had issue three sons, William, Robert, and Richard, and a daughter Adeliza, and possibly another, Emma... William succeeded his father as sheriff in 1090, and was succeeded by his brother Richard, who held that office together with the honour of Okehampton in 1129. Richard died without issue [childless] on 25 June 1137, when the sisters became his heirs. The elder one Adeliza was married to William, son of Wimund, and died in 1142 after founding Ford Abbey.

The exact descent of the honour now … appears to have passed through the Avenel family to Maud d'Avranches, whose second husband, Robert, a natural [illegitimate] son of Henry I, was in possession of it in 1166. Upon the death of Robert in 1172 and that of his widow in the following year the honour came into the hands of Reginald de Courteney, who appears to have availed himself of a grant of the wardship of the two daughters to marry his son William to Hawise, daughter of Maud d'Avranches by her first husband, and to himself marry Maud's namesake and daughter by her second husband, Robert the king's son.

The honour of Okehampton thus came to the Courteney family, in which it continued until Thomas Courteney was attainted in the first year of Edward IV.'

Edward VI reigned from 1461–1483, and Thomas was the 6th (or some historians say 14th) Earl of Devon. In the early Wars of the Roses, Thomas was loyal to Henry VI, but was eventually captured in the Battle of Towton in 1461, and beheaded in York. He was attainted by Parliament (condemned and deprived of his estates) in the November, leaving his heirs without any succession to the earldom of Devon, the barony of Courtenay and his lands at that time.

The de Reini (or Reigney or Reigny) family and the Coplestones

As for the more local Eggesford estate, early evidence shows that John de Reini held half a Knight's fee in Eggesford in 1242–1243. *Feudal Aids 1284–1431* (published by HMSO in 1899) indicated that in 1284–1286 Hugh de Courtenay, ancestor of the current Earl of Devon, held the manor of Chawleigh – then known as Chalvelegh – together with Dughelton (Dowland), part of the Honour of Okehampton. By 1316 Eggesford (Egeneysford) had been added to the list of holdings.

In feudal England at the time, a Knight's fee was a measure of land regarded as large enough to support the Knight, his family and servants, including provision for horses and armour to carry out his feudal duties to his overlord in battle. The de Reini family (later known locally as Reigny or Reigney) were an Anglo–Norman family whose various branches held lands in many parts of England and Wales. In 1303 Peter de Reigny was listed as still holding half the ancestral Knight's fee in Eggesford, while by 1346 Richard de Reigny had taken over the holding. 1428 saw John Reigny as their successor.

Reverend C A Cardale's notes on Eggesford House (and All Saints Church, Eggesford, see Chapter 4) circa 1975 added:

'The original House down by the Church was probably a Plantagenet building. The Estate belonged to the Reigney Family. Ibota of this family, at the end of the 15th century, founded an Almshouse in the parish. It was endowed with lands and valued at £4. 10. 6d. per annum in 1547.

Daniel & Samuel Lysons' *Magna Britannica* (*Devonshire*, volume 6) in 1822 confirms the Reigney lineage, referencing: 'Reigny of Eggesford… 9 descents below Henry III [reigned 1216–1272], marrying into the family of 'Coplestone'.'

The sixteenth century was a period when the wool trade was fuelling the wealth of Devon, and the population grew as a result. The Coplestones (with various spellings) were another significant Devon family of the time, with a number of branches across the county.

Historian Tristram Risdon's *Survey of the County of Devon*, published in 1811 but originally compiled 1605–1632, is used as a source in the 1881 Eggesford parish magazine, and explains the lineage further:

'In ancient times called Eglesford, of a passage through the river (ford) and goodly woods sometime there, wherein if tradition be taken for truth, eagles bred in our forefathers day. Sir John Reigney held Eggesford in 1233 and eleven Reigneys, called either John or Richard, succeeded in direct line. The last John Reigney had issue. Anne, wife of Charles Coplestone of Bickton, who had issue, John, who died in 1606. This John Coplestone married a daughter of Beeston of Cheshire and had issue, Anne wife of Edward Viscount Chichester of Carrickfergus.'

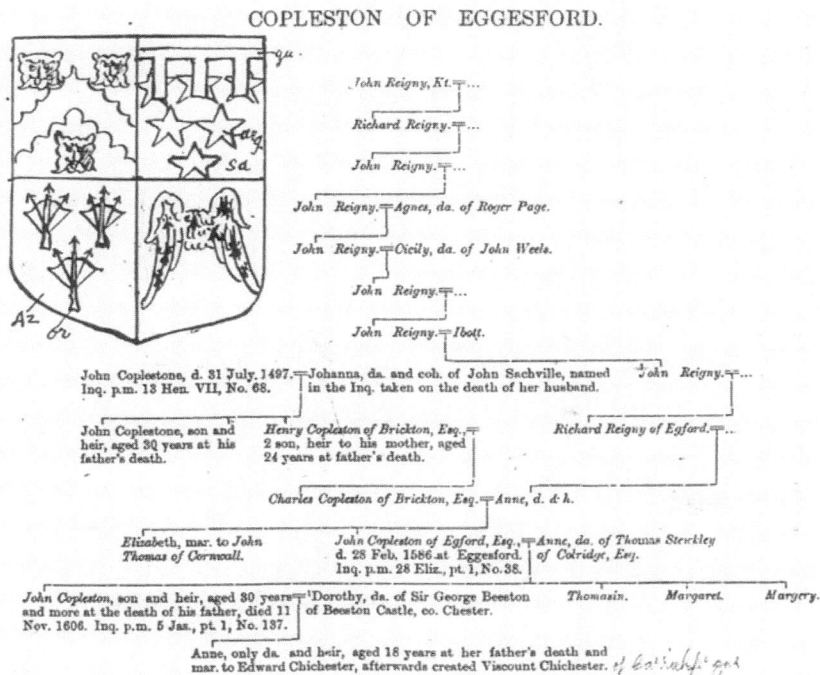

COPLESTON OF EGGESFORD.

The descendancy of the Reigny and Coplestone family, taken from *The Visitation of the County of Devon*, c.1564. The second Anne Coplestone shows at the bottom.

18

The Chichester family

The Chichesters number amongst the oldest families in Devon, with branches in North Devon best known in connection with the estates at Arlington (now National Trust) and Hall (near Bishops Tawton). The descendants connected with Eggesford were known as the 'Irish branch' and are prominent in Irish history.

Historian Tristram Risdon wrote of the 1st Viscount Chichester: 'This Lord Chichester hath builded a fayre house and dwelleth now at Egesford'. According to the 1881 parish magazine, 'Risdon also tells us that Lord Chichester rebuilt the manor-house in the reign of James I (1603–1625), and that there were two brothers, Sir Arthur and Sir Edward Chichester, the former becoming Baron Chichester of Belfast and the latter Viscount Chichester of Carrickfergus. When Sir Arthur died in 1624 [actually 1625] he left his great estates to his brother, Edward.'

In Irish history Sir Arthur is seen partially as a founder of Belfast (streets are still named after him) but also as the architect of the devastating English 'scorched earth' policies which suppressed Irish rebellion at the time. He is said to have harboured a grudge against the (Scottish) McDonnell family in Antrim who killed his brother John and reputedly used John's head as a football.

Anne Coplestone, married to Edward (later Viscount) Chichester, was born c.1583, in the year of the Spanish Armada. She died in 1616, he in 1648. Their effigies lie side by side in All Saints Church, Eggesford.

(Photo by Jonathan Crofts)

19

His nephew, also named Arthur, is portrayed by the *Dictionary of Irish Biography* as 'Arthur Chichester (1606–75), 1st earl of Donegall, soldier, and administrator, … born 16 June 1606, eldest son of Edward Chichester (brother of Arthur Chichester …) and his wife Anne (née Coplestone) of Devon. He was thus heir to the largest Ulster estate after that of the earl of Antrim.'

Reverend C A Cardale's notes on Eggesford added 'The Coplestone arms which Anne Coplestone brought to the Chichester family is described as 'Silver a chevron engrailed gules between three leopards' Heads azure'. She was Sir Edward Chichester's first wife, and she died in 1616. Edward then married Mary Denham who died in Belfast in 1637. The name of the first bell in Eggesford Church is no doubt a form of his surname and all three [bells] were hung in Chichester times.' (See Chapter 4.)

Anne's son, Arthur, the 1st Earl of Donegall, married three times. His first two wives appear with him on his memorial. His first wife, Dorcas Hill, had one daughter, Lady Mary, who later inherited the Eggesford estate. She married John St Leger of Doneraile in 1655 and had a son, also named Arthur, the 1st Viscount Doneraile.

The second wife was Lady Mary Digby, the daughter of the 1st Earl of Bristol. She had six sons and four daughters (although reports differ), who all died young.

Arthur's third wife was Letitia Hicks, daughter of Sir William Hicks or Hickes, 1st Baronet of Beverstone. Their six children also died young, except for Anne who married firstly John Butler, Earl of Gowran, and secondly Francis Aungier, Earl of Longford. There were no children. After Arthur's death in 1675 Letitia married again to Sir William Franklin of Bolnhurst (or Maverne) in Bedfordshire.

(Left)

The memorial to Arthur Chichester, son of Anne Coplestone, in All Saints Church, Eggesford, showing his first wife (left), Dorcas Hill, and his second wife (right), Lady Mary Digby, daughter of the Earl of Bristol. His third wife, Letitia Hicks, was the daughter of Sir William Hicks, 1st Baronet of Beverstone.

(Photo by Jonathan Crofts)

(Right)

Arthur Chichester, 1st Earl of Donegal, after Wenceslaus Hollar, etching, late 18th to early 19th century

(© National Portrait Gallery, London)

Arthurus Comes De Donegal

Vicecomes Chichester de Carickfergus Baro de Balfast.1661.

The above Inscription on the Original by Hollar. in the British Museum.

Arthur, the 1st Earl of Donegall, stood as MP for Antrim in 1627. On his father Edward's death, he became Governor of Carrickfergus and in 1643 Governor of Belfast. He was a Royalist supporter in the English Civil War, part of the strong Royalist base in the southwest. The Eggesford house is believed to have garrisoned soldiers under the command of Royalist General (Lord) Goring, but was taken by a Parliamentarian regiment of dragoons under Colonel John Okey in December 1645.

The St Leger family

Devon landowner, MP and historian Sir William Pole (1561–1635) wrote in his *Collections Towards a Description of the County of Devon* (published 1791) of Sir Edward Chichester, 1st Viscount Chichester: 'Edward survived until 13 July 1648. His eldest son Arthur had been created, in vita Patris, Earl of Donegal … but the estate of Eggesford had been settled on the Lady Mary, the only daughter of Sir Arthur Chichester, 1st Earl of Donegal, by his first wife Dorcas Hill.'

According to the Chichester family history of 1871, Lady Mary 'was married in 1655 to John St. Leger, of Doneraile, County Cork, and bore him five sons and three daughters. The eldest son, Arthur St. Ledger, was created Viscount Doneraile in 1703. His male issue failed, but his grandson, Mr. [St Leger] Aldworth, was created Viscount Doneraile, in 1785, and took the name of St. Leger [thus becoming 'St Leger St Leger']. On the death of his aunt Anne [daughter of Letitia Hicks], the 1st Lord Doneraile succeeded to Eggesford. In 1718 he sold it to William Fellowes, Esq., a Master in Chancery…' (See Chapter 2).

The Le Speke (or Speke) family

The 1881 parish magazine (quoting historian Tristram Risdon, 1811) suggests there have been at least three iterations of a great house at Eggesford over time. The first Eggesford House:

'… was rebuilt by William Fellowes who died in 1724 and the Hon. Newton Fellowes [Wallop, 4th Earl of Portsmouth] had it pulled down and the present Eggesford House built on the site of Heywood, the ancient seat of the Speke family…

Wembworthy, a tything [sub-division of a parish or manor] adjoining Brushford belonged to the family Le Speke, where they have a house called Heywood, furnished with fair woods, in which the compass of a castle is to be seen between which and the house (as some say) was a passage underground.

This family was notable after the conquest as appears from their deeds 'To all their men, French, English or Norman...' Sir John Speke (circa 1442–1518) of Whitelackington, Somerset, and of Heywood and Brampford Speke in Devon, was Sheriff of Devon in 1517 and a Member of Parliament. He has a monument, the Speke Chantry, in Exeter Cathedral.

Sir William Pole, the early Devon historian, remarks that:

'Wembworthy was the ancient dwelling of Speke who have had it from the time of the Conquest. In Henry II's reign, Richard de Espek held five fees. Sir Geoffrey Speke was Lord of Wembworthy in 1620 and about this time he leased Heywood to Sir John Dodderidge, a Justice of the King's bench [and MP for Barnstaple from 1589; he was also known as 'the sleeping judge' for closing his eyes while concentrating on the case].

The Manor was sold about 1695 to a Mr. Foote of Tiverton, who left five daughters as co-heiresses. Mr. William Fellowes purchased two shares in 1718, one of which included Heywood. Lord Portsmouth by 1881 had all five shares. The name of Speke still remains at Wembworthy in the crossway, not far from the church, known as Speke's Cross.'

This latter structure was listed as a Scheduled Monument in 1970:

'Wayside crosses are one of several types of Christian cross erected during the medieval period, mostly from the 9th to 15th centuries AD … The monument includes a medieval standing cross known as Speke's Cross situated 500m north east of Eggesford House. The cross is located on a triangular island between three drives within the landscaped grounds which originally formed part of the Eggesford Estate. It stands in a square socket stone on a modern two-stepped pedestal. The cross is roughly carved from a single piece of granite. One face is flattened and smooth; this faces north west. The other faces are roughly tooled and dressed. The cross is a simple 'Latin' cross which tapers slightly upwards and is roughly square in section … This type of cross is typical of those thought to date to the 15th century, and … was allegedly moved to its present location by the Portsmouth family.'

Devon author and historian Rosemary Lauder (*Vanished Houses of North Devon*, 1981) positions the original Eggesford House on 'reputedly the level ground in the grass meadow adjoining the church'. Investigations by local residents in the 1990s placed it to the west of the church. Richard Polwhele's *The History of Devonshire* (1797) describes it as 'a brick house built in 1718, and much improved by the present possessor, who also laid out the grounds under the direction of Mr Richmond.' (For more on Nathaniel Richmond, see Chapter 3.)

Rosemary Lauder continues:

'Did William Fellowes himself build a new house in 1718, or did he add to and alter the much older Eggesford, home of the Reigney and Chichester families? If Risdon is believed, Lord Chichester rebuilt his home between 1603 and 1620, but again this could refer to improvements and additions. Whatever the age and fascinating history of the old house, all records appear lost forever, for it was pulled down around 1824 after the new Eggesford was completed... The former walled garden remains, and close by Eggesford Barton incorporates the stabling and grooms' quarters belonging to the original house.'

(See Chapters 3 and 24 for more on the different incarnations of Eggesford House.)

The connection with the Fellowes family was significant in later establishing the estate, through marriage, as the Devonshire seat of the Earls of Portsmouth (whose family name was Wallop). It was this 'new' Eggesford House which positioned them as the grand aristocratic family at the heart of their vast farming and sporting lands in southwest England.

CHAPTER 2

THE FELLOWES CONNECTION

The Eggesford estate's connections with the Fellowes family span three centuries, from the early eighteenth right up to the twenty-first. Dr Elizabeth Foyster's account of John Charles Wallop, 3rd Earl of Portsmouth (see Chapter 6), shows the origins of the Fellowes' acquisition of the estate in the 1700s, revealing a focus on position and wealth not untypical of aspiring families of the early Georgian period.

William Fellowes' father, a London merchant, married the sister and heir of Thomas Coulson, MP for Totnes, and a director of the East India Company. William Fellowes' older brother, Sir John Fellowes, 1st Baronet, was deputy governor of the South Sea Company when the 'South Sea Bubble' burst, losing many of its protagonists' fortunes in what was later seen as a gamble in stocks, shares and overseas trade. William (1660–1723) had avoided trade and commerce and become a lawyer, called to the Bar in 1686, and was later Senior Master in Chancery.

His fortune came from his uncle and his marriage to Mary in 1695, an heiress who inherited £60,000 in 1718, with a stipulation on where to invest it. The Eggesford estate was purchased from the St Leger family and its main house rebuilt as a red-brick and fashionable Palladian-style country house. Deeds held by Norfolk Record Office confirm the will of William Fellowes' father-in-law, Joseph Martyn, which stipulated that his daughter should invest in landholdings in Devon:

'Deeds re £30,000 for purchase of estate for William Fellowes, his son-in-law, left by will of Joseph Martyn 1715; manors of Eggesford, Chawley, Borriston, Cheldon, Cudlip, East Worlington, Witheridge, Drayton; hundred of Witheridge; capital messuage called Eggesford, and farm and advowson, Devon, and manor of Mountsey and estates, Somerset, Lord Doneraile to William Fellowes 1718.'

A portrait of Gulielmus Fellowes de Eggesford in Com Devon...
William Fellowes, father of Coulson Fellowes, 1723;
print made by John Smith, the mezzotinter
After John Vanderbank.
(© National Portrait Gallery, London)

William (1660–1723) owned the Eggesford estate and bequeathed it to his son Coulson Fellowes, whose daughter Urania (named after her mother) married John Wallop, the 2nd Earl of Portsmouth on 27 August 1763.

William Fellowes died on 19 January 1723 (also recorded as 1724) and was buried at Eggesford. His heir erected an imposing neo-classical monument to his memory, for which the north aisle of the church was expanded to the east, and an extra window created for lighting. The monument fills the entire eastern wall, and has space for an urn, now missing. William was apparently very attached to his new manor of Eggesford, as the Latin inscription on his monument suggests:

'M(emoriae) S(acrum) Gulielmi Fellowes Arm(ige)ri almae curiae cancellariae Magistri quo officio tenente summa legis et aequitatis cura decessit 19.mo (und-evicensimo) Jan(uar)ii 1723 aeta(tis) 64. Mariam Josephi Martyn de London mercatoris viri integritate insignis filiam et haeredem duxit; liberos quinqe ex ea genitos viz (videlicet) tres filios et duas filias reliquit. Familiam diu hic permanere cupiens ossa sua hoc in loco deponi voluit'

'Sacred to the memory of William Fellowes, Esquire, Master of the Court of Chancery in holding which office in the highest care of law and equity he departed on the 19th of January 1723 of his age 64. He married Mary the daughter and heir of Joseph Martyn of London, merchant, a man outstanding in integrity; he left five children born from her, namely three sons and two daughters. Desiring his family long to remain here he wished his bones to be deposited in this place.'

Mary's will requested that she be buried with her father Joseph at St Mary-at-Hill, a church in the capital near London Bridge. She died in 1759, aged 87, and her will does not mention her two sons Martin and John who had died previously.

William and his two brothers, John and Edward, appear not to have traced a sufficiently satisfactory line of descent, and had to apply for a new grant from the College of Arms to use the coat of arms and crest to which the family had been accustomed. This was granted in 1713 and the brothers continued in the old family

The monument to William Fellowes in All Saints Church, Eggesford: reputedly made in Italy, it originally included four kneeling figures at the base, since lost.

At the top, in a heraldic escutcheon, are the arms of Fellowes quartered with the arms of Martyn, his wife's family: Argent, a pair of dolphins hauriant proper.

(Photo by Jonathan Crofts)

traditions: their arms can be seen on the vault they built at the St Michael Paternoster Royal church in London, in which their maternal uncle Thomas Coulson was interred.

William Fellowes had two remaining sons: William, of Shotesham Park, Norfolk, and the eldest, Coulson Fellowes. Coulson Fellowes (1696–1769) was educated at Christ Church, Oxford, and became a lawyer like his father, called to the Bar in 1723. He inherited Eggesford from his father, and went on to marry Urania Herbert in 1725, daughter of Francis Herbert of Oakley Park, Shropshire, and sister of Henry Herbert, 1st Earl of Powis (1703–1772).

WILLIAM FELLOWES, of Eggesford, co. Devon, Senior Master in Chancery, b. 4 Oct., 1660; d. 19 Jan., 1724. = MARY, only dau. and heiress of Joseph Martin, of London: b. 1662; m. 8 Oct., 1695; d. 28 Dec., 1759.

Coulson Fellowes, of Ramsey Abbey, co. Hunts., and of Eggesford, co. Devon, b. 12 Oct., 1696; d. 23 Feb., 1769. = Urania, dau. of Francis Herbert of Oakley Pk., co. Salop, m. 20 April, 1725; d. 6 Feb., 1779.

Martin Fellowes b. 20 July, 1702; d. s.p. 19 July, 1732. = Jane, dau. of ——— Clarke, who m. 2ndly Charles Bowles, of N. Ashton, co. Oxon.

William Fellowes of Shotesham Park, co. Norfolk, b. 28 July. 1706; d. 30 Jan., 1775. = Elizabeth, dau. of ——— d. 2 Aug., 1784.

Mary Fellowes b. 3 March, 1705; m. 2 Mar., 1725; d. 24 Oct., 1762. — Robert Eyre of New House, co. Wilts, d. 14 Dec., 1752. (issue extinct).

William Fellowes of Ramsey Abbey, co. Hunts, and of Nacton, co. Suffolk, M.P. d. 4 Feb., 1804. = Lavinia, dau. and co-h. of James Smyth of St. Audries, co. Somerset; m. 17 May, 1768; d. 6 Dec., 1827.

Henry Arthur Fellowes, of Eggesford, co. Devon, d. unm. 29 Jan., 1792.

Urania, b. 18 Jan., 1743; m. 27 Aug., 1763; d. 29 Jan., 1812. = John, 2nd Earl of Portsmouth, b. 29 June, 1742; d. 16 May, 1797.

William Fellowes of Danbury, co. Essex; d. 8 Mar., 1778. = Elizabeth, dau. of Samuel Harris, d. June, 1772.

Robert Fellowes of Shotesham Park, Norfolk, M.P.; b. 1742; d. 8 April, 1829. = Ann, eldest dau. of Jno. Berney, of Bracon Ash, co. Norfolk, b. 1751; m. 27 Dec., 1776; d. 21 Feb., 1794.

I.   II.   III.   IV.

The marriage settlement of 1725 required Coulson to transfer land in Devon and Somerset to trustees following the male line of descent:

'Manors of Eggesford, Chawley also Chawleigh, Borrington also Burrington, Cheldon Cudlip East Worlington Witherigges also Witheridge and Drayford, the Hundred of Witherigges, the capital messuage called Eggesford in Eggesford parish and Chawley, other lands in parish of Eggesford, Wembworthy, Chawley, Borrington, Winkley Rings Ash Dowland Rose Ash Crediton, South Tawton, Great Torrington, Cholmley Cheldon Cudlip East Worlington Witheridges and Drayford, parts of the Manor, borough, hundred, rights and lands of Northtawton, the Manor, borough, hundred, rights and lands of Brampton [probably Bampton], the Manor of Hollacomb Parramore in p. of Wynkley, lands in Winkley and Winkley Town, messuages in Goldsmith Street and Keylane by Key Gate, Exeter, parts of messuages in Moreton Hamstead and Chagford and the advowsons of the churches of Eggesford, Chawley, Cheldon, and East Worlington, Devon, and the Manor of Mountsey also Mounyseaux and lands in Mounseaux and Dullverton, Somerset'.

Lines of descent from William Fellowes and Mary Martin, from 'Some Notes on the Family of Fellowes' in The Family & Descendants of William Fellowes by the Reverend Edmund Horace Fellowes (1910)

Urania Fellowes, 2nd Countess of Portsmouth

(Photo by Jonathan Crofts, by kind permission of Viscount Lymington)

Sir Isaac Newton 1643–1727, mathematician, physicist, astronomer, alchemist, theologian and author

Painting by Sir Godfrey Kneller

(Photo by Jonathan Crofts, by kind permission of Viscount Lymington)

Urania was only seventeen but brought £10,000 to the marriage. Two sons, William and Henry Arthur, followed, as well as three daughters, Mary, Urania and Dorothea. From August 1729, the month of Mary's birth, the family's presence at Eggesford became more frequent, even though Coulson was acquiring land in West Ham, Essex, and in 1737, Ramsey Abbey and Abbots Ripton near Huntingdon in Cambridgeshire. (The Fellowes name persists at Ramsey Abbey and Abbots Ripton today: in 1993 John Ailwyn Fellowes became the 4th and current Lord De Ramsey.)

Coulson's land brought him into politics, and he stood as MP for Huntingdonshire from 1741 to 1761, as well as a Sheriff of Devon for two years. When in London he resided at St James' and in Hampstead. By most measures, he was a wealthy man.

An aspiring family of the period (and for centuries to follow) prized easy access to the aristocracy, and Coulson was pleased to secure his middle daughter Urania's marriage to the 2nd Earl of Portsmouth, John Wallop. The Wallops had been connected to Georges I, II and III, and their family history dated back to Norman times: Mathew de Wallop held lands in Hampshire, Dorset and Somerset during the late twelfth to early thirteenth centuries (for more on the Wallop family, see Chapters 6 and 8).

The son of the 1st Earl, another John, became Viscount Lymington, and provided the family connection to the famous mathematician, physicist, astronomer, alchemist, theologian and author, Sir Isaac Newton: he married Catherine Conduit, Newton's great-niece and joint heiress. The names Isaac and Newton persisted down the family line for decades. Sadly the 1st Earl outlived his son, and the Viscount never inherited the role or the lands, which instead passed to his son, also a John.

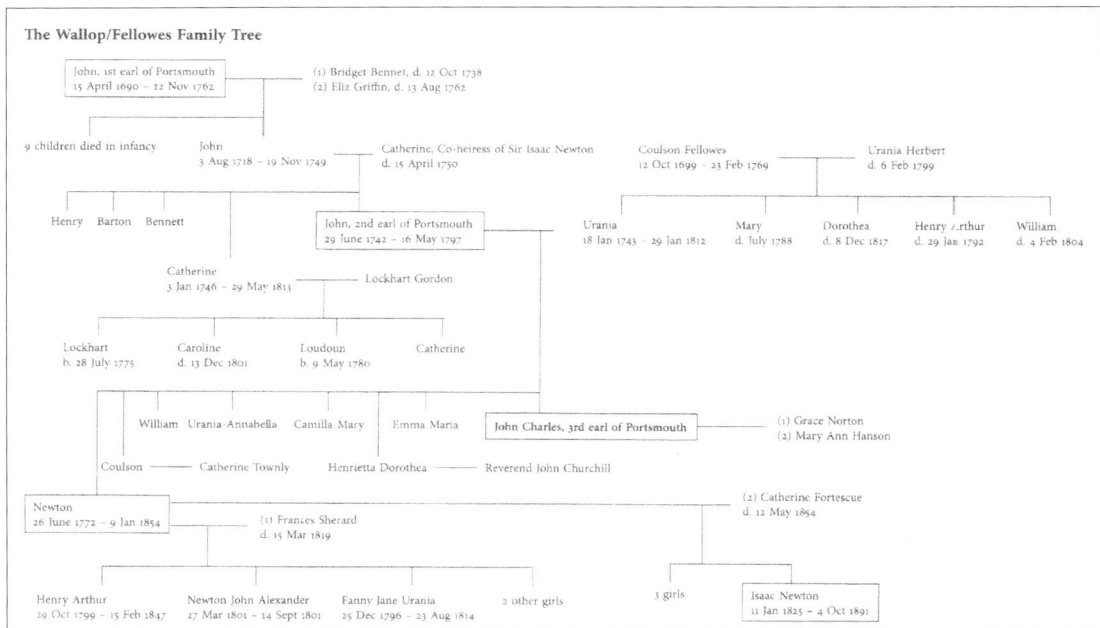

The Wallop/ Fellowes family tree, showing the first five Earls of Portsmouth (© Elizabeth Foyster)

Coulson's entry into the aristocratic world was achieved by offering a dowry to accompany his daughter Urania, which he paid as an annuity of four per cent. He died in 1769, leaving his one-year-old grandson, John Charles, as Lord Viscount Lymington, the future Earl of Portsmouth.

Of Coulson's two sons, William Fellowes (died 1804), the elder, was elected as MP for Ludlow in 1768, Andover in 1784, and Sudbury and High Sheriff of Cambridgeshire and Huntingdonshire in 1779. He married, in 1768, Lavinia Smyth, daughter of John Smyth of St Audries, Somerset, and his eldest son William Henry Fellowes (1769–1837) became MP for Huntingdon and then Huntingdonshire between 1796 and 1830. William Henry's second son was Edward Fellowes, 1st Baron de Ramsey (1809–1887).

Coulson had earlier settled all his lands on his elder son William, but in his will dated 1766 (two years before William's marriage) he bequeathed his lands in Devon, Somerset, Huntingdonshire and Cambridgeshire to his second son Henry Arthur, should William die childless. Although William went on to have children, and Henry Arthur eventually died without offspring, it was Henry Arthur Fellowes who acquired the Eggesford estate from his elder brother. Henry Arthur became High Sheriff of the County of Devon in 1775, and died unmarried in 1792.

Architectural historian James Rothwell wrote in 2007 for the Society of Architectural Historians of Great Britain:

> 'William was furious, believing his sister Mary to have poisoned their father's mind against him, but eventually confirmed the will, claiming that he did so only out of affection for his brother and a desire to save him the cost of a lawsuit. This was the first of a whole series of rancorous family disputes that were ultimately to have a fundamental impact on the architecture of Eggesford House.'

It was Coulson's daughter Urania, through her marriage to John, 2nd Earl of Portsmouth, who brought together the Wallop and Fellowes names, a bond which endures after nearly three centuries.

Their son Newton (later the Hon. Newton Fellowes) married into the prestigious Devon family of Fortescue, taking Catherine, daughter of 1st Earl Fortescue of Castle Hill, Filleigh, as his second wife. He went on to succeed his maternal uncle Henry Arthur Fellowes to the Eggesford estate, and took the name of Fellowes in place of Wallop by royal licence on 7 August 1794. He eventually became 4th Earl of Portsmouth, succeeding his brother John Charles, the 3rd Earl, for a year only before he too died.

Newton and Catherine's son Isaac Newton Fellowes became 5th Earl in turn, prolonging the Fellowes name in Devon into the late nineteenth century.

Henry Arthur Fellowes (1799–1847), Newton's son by his first marriage to Frances Sherard, followed in his father's steps by becoming MP for Andover, but was recorded as being inconsistent in his parliamentary duties, according to *The History of Parliament* (historyofparliamentonline.org):

> 'Fellowes was a nephew of the simple-minded 3rd Earl of Portsmouth, who was certified by a commission of lunacy in February 1823. The proceedings, which were widely reported, revealed his obsession with bellringing, his compulsive attendance at funerals and, most notably, the fact that his wife's lover had shared their marital bed. It appears that this Member may have been the nominal petitioner, though his father, the earl's brother, was undoubtedly behind the suit. As Member for

Andover, 1802–20, his father had generally aligned himself with the Whigs, and he was classed as a Liberal when he resumed his parliamentary career in 1832 as Member for North Devon, where his principal residence lay. Until 1835 he remained steward of Andover, where the family had long possessed an interest, but he was so lax in the execution of his corporate duties as to be accused of deserting the borough. This did not prevent his son standing at the general election of 1831, after the sitting Members had retired in the face of the corporation's conversion to parliamentary reform. On the hustings Fellowes claimed that he had always been a 'strenuous advocate' of this cause and pledged his 'firm and unflinching' support for the Grey ministry's bill. He was returned unopposed.

Fellowes evidently missed the early part of the [parliamentary] session, perhaps through illness, and is not known to have uttered a word in debate. …

Fellowes was returned unopposed for Andover at the general election of 1832 and was subsequently described as a 'moderate reformer and in general a supporter of ministers'. He retired at the 1834 dissolution. His existence is not even mentioned in the family history, and he died intestate at Eggesford in February 1847, 'after a long and lingering illness'. His father never troubled to lay claim to his estate, administration of which was eventually granted in August 1854 to Fellowes's half-brother, Isaac Newton Fellowes, who had succeeded their father as 5th Earl of Portsmouth that January.'

Although the next Earl of Portsmouth, the 6th, who started the breakup of the Eggesford estate in the early twentieth century (see Chapter 22), was known as Newton Wallop, the Fellowes name in Devon lingered on into that century with the 7th Earl of Portsmouth: John Fellowes Wallop (1859–1925) (see Chapter 22) is commemorated in St Mary's Church, Morchard Bishop, the village neighbouring the Wallops' last property in Devon.

Even now, connections between the Portsmouths, the Fellowes and Eggesford are manifold. The 5th Countess of Portsmouth, Eveline Alicia Juliana Herbert (1834–1906) was the daughter of Henry Herbert, 3rd Earl of Carnarvon and his wife Henrietta, whose family seat (where Eveline grew up) was Highclere Castle in Berkshire, principal location for the filming of the highly successful TV series *Downton Abbey*.

Best known as the creator of *Downton Abbey* and its associated films, Julian Fellowes – formally Julian Kitchener-Fellowes, Baron Fellowes of West Stafford, Deputy Lieutenant of Dorset – also fulfils a range of charitable roles in Dorset and nationally, including as President of the Thomas Hardy Society. Actor, novelist, film director and screenwriter, as well as a peer of the House of Lords, he continues longstanding family traditions of public duty and literary endeavour. The author Thomas Hardy was friendly with the 5th Countess and her husband and paid visits to Eggesford House (see Chapter 9).

Julian's family claims descent from Thomas Fellowes, relative of William of Eggesford, whose grand-daughter was Urania Fellowes, Countess of Portsmouth. Although a distant connection, the family remain friendly with the Portsmouths today. Julian named one of his minor characters in *Downton Abbey* after Lady Annabel, the (current) 10th Countess. His great-aunt Isie was the model for the formidable waspish ladies played by the late Maggie Smith in *Downton* and his 2001 hit, *Gosford Park*. Isie's son lies buried in Eggesford churchyard (see Chapter 4). Eggesford as a settlement hides many surprises.

CHAPTER 3

'THE FORD OF THE EAGLES' – EGGESFORD: A HOUSE WITH A PARISH

Eggesford is relatively unusual in being a parish without a village. Historically the earlier great house of the estate lay alongside the church. Visitors to the newer Eggesford House, built higher up the hill, required transport of the modern industrial age, resulting in the building of a railway station at the request of the estate owners, the Portsmouth family (also known as Fellowes or Wallop). The earlier site of the house and the remains of the walled garden currently lie in Eggesford parish; the later site now falls in the parish of Wembworthy.

Many of the houses in today's Eggesford community originally belonged to the estate. Heywood Wood and its motte and bailey castle are in Wembworthy parish, as are Heyswood House (not to be confused with Heywood House) and the site of Eggesford Castle, which is in private hands. The Little House is formed from part of the outbuildings of Eggesford House, now a separate dwelling. The Old Glebe, the former parsonage and rectory, is in Eggesford parish.

Flashdown Wood, a section of the larger Eggesford Forest, was the Forestry Commission's first plantation in 1919, to the south of where Eggesford House now lies. The River Taw runs through the whole area,

broadly following the A377 road, and there is a small airfield with a 600m grass strip to the south, based at Trenchard Farm.

The Reverend Richard Polwhele, Devon historian, in 1797 described Eggesford as:

'small, not exceeding 2 miles in length or breadth, its situation in general high and hilly. ... The parish is inclosed by common hedges, well wooded with all kinds of forest trees, the most flourishing of which are the beech and oak, embellishing the vales with a variety of beautiful scenes. The whole parish is in the manor of Eggesford, a considerable part of which is kept in hand by the lord of it, the rest distributed into small farms; the houses built chiefly with mud walls, a few with stone, and thatch'd, furnished with the usual appendages of gardens and orchards, and in a moderate state of cultivation.'

At its heart was 'one gentleman's seat ... built about the year 1718, of brick, much increased and improved by the present possessor, who also laid out the grounds about it with much elegance and taste, under the direction of the late Mr. Richmond: woods well interspersed, considerable plantations, and the river Taw contributing much to enrich and beautify the scene.'

Eggesford House

Hugh Meller, former National Trust curator for Devon, in his first volume of *The Country Houses of Devon* (Black Dog Press, 2015), believes there to have been five significant houses at Eggesford since the time of the Reigney family in the thirteenth century (whose name remains in the nearby village of Ashreigney). Their house persisted until the marriage into the Coplestone family, when Edward, Lord Chichester, rebuilt the house in its second incarnation around 1620.

33

A lintel later moved to nearby Eggesford Barton bears the year '1626', presumably dating to that rebuilding. In 1664 the Devon 'hearth tax' records refer to 18 hearths, indicating a house of some considerable size.

William Fellowes built the third house, near the church, around 1720, and some believe that architect Henry Joynes (who had worked for Sir John Fellowes, William's brother, at Carshalton in Surrey) was behind it.

There were plans for a 'fourth' house, designed by Thomas Lee (contemporary architect at Arlington Court in North Devon), which initially would have been a classical rival for Castle Hill, the childhood home of Newton Fellowes' second wife, Lady Catherine Fortescue.

Lee proposed a larger gothic building to absorb the current house, and plans evolved three times, before Newton and his family moved into the thatched Heywood Barton, originally the home of the Le Speke family (see Chapter 1). Newton preferred this site, which became the fifth house, the Tudor gothic building still familiar today in the metamorphosis of its ruins.

Architectural historian James Rothwell wrote in 2007 for the Society of Architectural Historians of Great Britain of the earlier House:

> 'Henry Arthur Fellowes ... first visited Eggesford after inheriting in August, 1769, and whilst back in London that winter he paid £100 to 'Mr. J. Meadows, Carpenter for work to be done by him at Eggesford'. This was the architect John Meadows for whom the commission, which may have been his first of any substance, was to prove immensely valuable. It led to virtually all his work thereafter, comprising a string of Devon commissions, including Hartland [Abbey] and [the earlier] Arlington...
>
> The remodelling of Eggesford started in the summer of 1770 and was completed two years later, payments to Meadows totalling nearly £3,000 [the equivalent of over £22,000 in modern currency, a considerable sum at the time]. Undated and unsigned plans for the addition of two-storey wings with canted bays on the river front may relate to this work but the additions ended up rising to full height as can be seen in the Rev John Swete's watercolour of 1796...
>
> In 1782–3 Fellowes had employed the accomplished landscape gardener, N. Richmond, to lay out the park. There is no archival evidence for what he did and according to Repton, who ranked him alongside Kent and Brown, Richmond never delivered any general plan. He must have been responsible, however, for the heightening of the river by means of a weir below the bridge over the Taw and the overall result of his work was sufficiently attractive to please both Swete and Polwhele, neither of whom were universal in praise.'

Nathaniel Richmond was a master surveyor and nurseryman employed as an 'improver' for some five years to oversee projects on behalf of Capability Brown, leaving the esteemed garden and landscape designer free to ride off and plan schemes for the next great estates. On going solo, Richmond's own practice quickly flourished in London and the shires beyond. With the cachet of his former master's name in his credentials, he offered a fine alternative to a landowner seeking quality at the best price. He died at around 64 in February 1784 as a result of a 'mortification' of his leg, which had slipped through a grating at work and presumably become infected.

Rev. Swete's view of Eggesford House and the Taw valley

(By kind permission of Ed Howell)

In 1999 the diaries of Reverend John Swete were published, having been rediscovered in the then Devon Record Office. He recorded his travels around Georgian Devon, including a visit to the first Eggesford House in 1796, describing the location as 'a little paradise'. He enjoyed the interior equally: '… a very good eating and Drawing room, and the tea room over part of the latter in which we sat, being a bow, took into the prospect, the chief of those beautiful views which the Valley afforded.'

Eggesford's link via the architect John Meadows and the Stucley family estate at Hartland Abbey was later strengthened as seen in another Stucley refinement at their nearby estate at Affeton Castle. Sir Hugh Stucley, the current (6th) Baronet, recalls that his 'great-grandfather, Sir George [1812–1900], used to stop off at Eggesford House when he rode from Hartland to inspect his properties at Affeton. I was always led to believe that the chimney stacks which he erected at Affeton, being all part of his 1870 restoration of the ruins, were copied from Eggesford House.'

Returning to his architectural account of Eggesford House, James Rothwell continued that Thomas Lee:

'was employed to make the best of Heywood Barton, a 16th-century thatched house in an elevated position overlooking the 18th-century parkland in the valley below. It was far better sited than the old Eggesford House which was low lying, hemmed in by the church on one side and north facing, and at some point between 1823 and 1826 the decision was taken to abandon it and the Neo-classical scheme in favour of building at Heywood, henceforward known as Eggesford House.

Professor Donaldson's memoir of the life of Thomas Lee (RIBA Library) suggested the old house at Heywood was incorporated but the remodelling, if such it was, must have been very comprehensive as there is little obvious evidence of older fabric in the surviving structure or in Lee's elevations for the new house. Construction, which was well underway by 1828, continued until at least 1832 and the end result, which drew on Lee's design for Priory Hall, Dudley (circa 1825) was predominantly Tudor domestic with a frenetic skyline of turrets, battlements, buttresses and elaborate chimney stacks and a combination of cusped 15th-century tracery, simply uncusped windows and, on the north wing, straightforward sashes with only the vaguest of Tudor airs. In combination with the play on different levels Lee was successful in giving the impression of an accumulative development, whether or not that was in fact the case.'

The site of Lee's new house exploited the picturesque views of Nathaniel Richmond's landscape to the east, but his 'notion for laying out' did not include formal gardens at this stage. Carriage drives, tracks and paths aimed to create a sporting estate for hunting, shooting and riding, and both of the earlier motte and bailey castles (see Chapter 1) were to be included.

Nearly 140 years later, much of that elegance, taste and beauty had fallen into rubble. Historian and publisher Eric R Delderfield wrote in *The Western Morning News*, 28 November 1963, of *The Glory that was Eggesford*:

'Very little is left of Eggesford House in Mid-Devon, near the Exeter–Barnstaple A377 road, except the ruin which rises above the skyline. It is just another of the mansions, which, in their prime, were kept up magnificently by the Lord of the Manor.

There was a mansion at Eggesford in the reign of James I, a house which was garrisoned for the King during the Civil Wars and taken by parliamentary troops in 1645. It was then situated much lower down nearer the church, and in 1718 it was demolished and another erected in its place.

Eggesford was the Devonshire seat of the Fellowes family (later through marriage the Earls of Portsmouth) and the 4th Earl … who inherited, was one of the many famous sporting squires of the 18th century. …

The house contained six lofty reception rooms, thirty bed and dressing rooms (excluding servant rooms), huge kitchens, a laundry, dairy, and stabling for forty horses. Three acres of kitchen gardens were in the valley a mile away and produce was carried to the house by pannier donkeys.

The main drive to the mansion was a mile long and the scale of things generally may be gleaned from the fact that two servants were kept fully occupied trimming, lighting, and attending to all the lamps in the establishment.

Like his father, the 5th Earl carried on the tradition and kept a pack of hounds. He was, in fact, Master of Hounds for thirty years and when he gave up in 1889, one of his prize packs was sold to the Duke of Beaufort. Lord Portsmouth's well-bred hunters were famous all over the country and his pack of hounds provided the foundation blood for many famous packs in Britain.

Again Eggesford was a meeting place for all and sundry, particularly the sporting types. Charles Kingsley and Parson Jack Russell shared a common birthday with Lady Portsmouth. It was always a day of celebration when they met for this special occasion at Eggesford House. Another frequent visitor was James Russell Lowell the American poet.

When his lordship died, in 1891, hunting was stopped in the district for some days as a tribute to his memory. On the first day after it was resumed, however, the fox found safety by running to earth in the freshly disturbed family vault in Eggesford churchyard. A fact which would have undoubtedly delighted such a sportsman.

The day of the great estates was gradually diminishing and … the 6th Earl caused the property to be put up for sale. It comprised about 3000 acres and the house, which stood in a separate 300-acre park. There were 700 acres of woodland, several large farms, the Fox and Hounds hotel, numerous small holdings, and six miles of salmon and trout fishing.

At the auction a figure of £100,000 was asked as a starting price, but it was eventually sold for £85,000. The house was withdrawn at £7000, but it remained empty except for a period when German prisoners of war were detained there, and in 1920 an unsuccessful attempt was made to persuade the County Council to take the building over as an isolation hospital.

Gradually the mansion decayed, it was stripped of all useful materials, and it is said that a room over the entrance was found to be papered with Penny Black stamps, which, of course, were beyond redemption and many of them, by today's standards, almost beyond price.

Today, just a ruin survives peeping above the magnificent trees of Eggesford Forest. Cattle graze contently around and about the park that was once a fitting setting for so fine a house, but only the crows and the rooks have any intimate knowledge of the shell which once abounded with life.'

Reverend C A Cardale compiled notes on Eggesford House (and All Saints Church, Eggesford) circa 1975, while Eggesford House still lay in ruins:

'Eggesford, the Ford of the Eagles... The ruins of Eggesford House stand out very clearly from the Tower as they do from the main road and from various vantage spots in the Forestry grounds. ...

It was sold in 1917 and has since fallen into decay. ... Still standing to the rear and almost out of view is the Tower. From the Church can be seen the front and behind it almost separate is the Lymington Wing, built as the nursery for the 5th Earl's numerous children.

The Tower is most interesting, despite the fact that it has lost his crenelation; remains of the parapet may be seen lying around the base of the tower. It is still possible to ascend the turret, although the floors are not to be trusted. There are no signs that any provision was made for bells despite the fact of the evidence of the louvred windows in the top storey. This tower is at one end of what was once the main entrance; the remains of an impressive porch are out to the right, nearer to the Church end.

It was a most impressive building and was a shining example of the glory of the Victorian age, just as now in its ruinous state it may possibly say to all of us 'How are the mighty fallen'. It is still private property, owned by a Winkleigh Farmer, and it is only right to say that there are notices up which clearly state that trespassers will be prosecuted.

Apparently there was a cricket ground in the area. I have yet to find out where. Also a tennis club. Matches were definitely played in 1884.

No doubt in time as with the first site only level ground will mark the site of the house.'

That 'shining example of the glory of the Victorian age' was best described in the 1913 sales catalogue, one of many sales of the estate which the 6th Earl had initiated some ten years previously. There was a local story that his father the 5th Earl had been a gambler, and there are references to 'certain mortgages and other incumbrances' in the sales particulars. The 5th Countess's (Eveline's) 1893 diary references a mortgage of £195,000. The rebuilding after a fire at their main Hampshire seat, Hurstbourne Park, in 1891 may, in fact, have been the principal cause.

The 1913 sale was possibly a reflection of the 6th Earl's preference for national politics, motor cars, and his recent acquisition of a sporting estate in Scotland, coupled with the changing financial and social environment for landed estates and their owners in Edwardian England. The effects of the First World War were soon to accelerate this upheaval, but pre-war the striking appearance of the house would have been clear to a prospective buyer:

'"Eggesford" is one of the most attractive Domains in North Devon … "Eggesford House" which is substantially built and of Elizabethan design, is a delightful County Seat, occupying a beautiful position some 415 ft. above sea-level, in the centre of a magnificently timbered Park of about 300 acres, with panoramic views over the valley of the Taw to the woodland heights beyond.

Wide Carriage Drives, some 2 miles in length, guarded by Lodge Entrances, wind their way through charming woodlands possessing every variety of ornamental shrub and forest tree of exceptional height and dimensions, Avenues of Chestnuts, and continuing through the Park terminate at the South-west entrance to the house.

Accommodation of House, Stables, etc. – The Residence is conveniently planned and contains:- Entrance Halls, Long Gallery, Suite of Six Lofty and Spacious Reception Rooms, 30 Bed and Dressing Rooms, exclusive of Men Servants Rooms, Two Bathrooms, Complete Domestic Offices. Stabling for 40 horses. Cottages. Men's rooms.

Gardens. – The Pleasure Gardens are attractively laid out in Lawns, Flower Garden and Terraces, relieved by clumps of fine Rhododendrons and Azaleas.

The Walled Kitchen Gardens, which extend to some three acres, are situated near the Site of the old Mansion.

Head Gardener's Cottage in Park, known as "Ivy Cottage".'

Billed as a 'Freehold, Residential, Sporting and Agricultural Domain', the property then for sale included the:

'Resident Agent's House… Woodlands of about 700 acres… six miles of the best Salmon and Trout Fishing in the River Taw. Good Shooting, Hunting with three packs. … attractive Country Residences …Village properties and licensed Premises – The well-known and full-licensed Fishing Hotel – "The Fox and Hounds," Eggesford, as well as the Cattle Market, Sawmills, and numerous Cottages… Agricultural. – … some of the best Land in the district… Responsible Tenants, and the Rents are moderate.'

The Total Rent Roll was cited as £3,564 19s 10d; the Outgoings (Tithe commutation Rent Charge) £247 6s 2d.

The Particulars detailed 'nearly 3,300 acres', and added:

'The New Lodge, thence through Heywood Wood, which is beautifully Timbered, and joining the Main Drive at the South-west side of the House.

From the North there is a Grass Drive, guarded by an Avenue of Stately Chestnuts, and another pretty Drive to the West Road leading to Wembworthy and the Kennels.

… charming Woodlands … through which there are some 7 miles of Private Walks, studded by finely grown Trees, including some of the finest specimens of Douglasii Glauca, Cedrus Deodara, Adrus Libanus Pinus, Strobus, Cupressus Lawsoniana, as well as many tropical plants, and banks of Rhododendrons

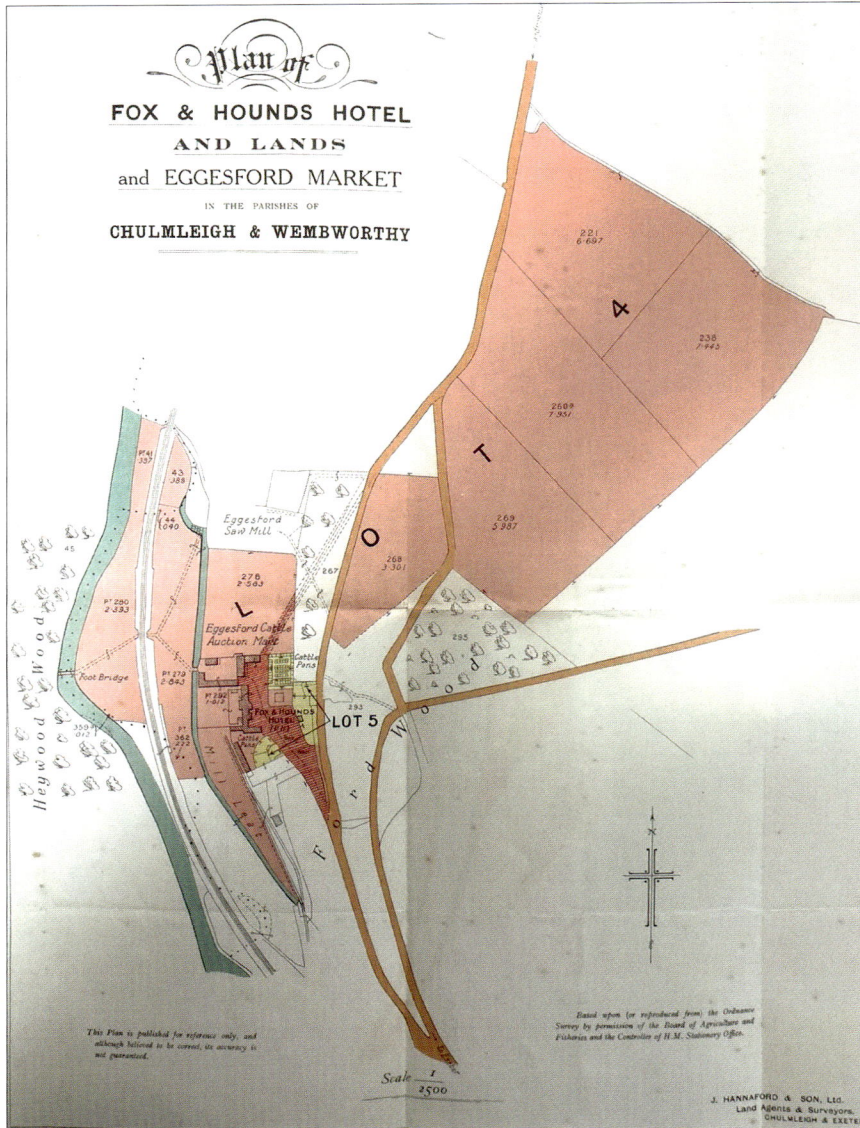

Plan from the 1923 sales particulars of the Fox and Hounds Hotel, the Eggesford cattle market and the Portsmouth sawmills

(Photo by Jonathan Crofts, by kind permission of Ed Howell)

Ponticum and Rhododendron Hybrids of almost every known variety, also famous species of Azalea Ponticum and Azalea Mollis.'

The interior of the house was imposing:

'… entered through a Massive Carved Door opening into the OUTER HALL, Granite Steps rising to an Oak Door giving access to Lofty STAIRCASE HALL, with Carved Plaster Work Ceiling, Stone Fireplace and Oak Floor. A flight of circular steps terminates at the foot of the wide Main Staircase with Carved Newell Figures, Heads and Balusters, lighted at Half Landing by a tall window. A pair of Massive Oak Glazed Doors screens the Long Gallery, leading from which all THE PRINCIPAL RECEPTION ROOMS, approached by Massive Oak Doors under Arched Doorways, the Gallery … lighted at the North end by a large window reaching to the ceiling, as well as side windows, and is fitted with Oak Polished Floor and Two Stone Fireplaces and fitted Cupboard.'

The main rooms were equally lavishly appointed, supported by an extensive household:

'… the artistically planned Drawing Room, a lofty apartment … Oak Floor. Walls partly panelled in Oak, representing figures and linen folds, the frieze rising to the ceiling carved in plaster panels, Oak Floor, Freestone Fireplace with Marble Base, Granite Upright Column and Stone Fireplace…'

'STATELY DINING ROOM', with 'Steel and Brass Mounted Stove', the 'Library … fitted with beautiful Carved Light Oak Bookcases … Granite Fireplace with Steel and Brass Grate … [the] SMOKING ROOM … [and] a Study…

The Domestic Offices, which comprise: Servants' Hall … a roomy apartment, fitted with large Steel Fireplace, surmounted by Carved Stone Overmantel and fitted with Wall Settle Seat. LINEN ROOM, DAIRY with Slated Floor and Shelving. COOK'S SITTING ROOM…, SPACIOUS KITCHEN, with Granite Floor, fitted with Open Range, Hot Plate, Charcoal Oven, Cupboards and Shelves and Store Cupboard adjoining. LARGE SCULLERY fitted with Stove for Scalding Cream, Copper and Sinks, Oven, Pump, Plate Racks, Boilers and Shelves. LARDER with Meat Racks and Hooks. Spacious Cellars under.'

The thirty bed and dressing rooms, including a State Bedroom and State Dressing Room, are further detailed, with stone and marble mantelpieces, and:

'At the end of the Main Corridor is a Room papered with postage stamps. … The Nursery Wing and Servants' Wing provide further sleeping accommodation.

Outside the House, there are Main Stables, a detached Cattle Yard, the 'Home Farmery, comprising: Stone and Slated Pig House, Implement Store, Shoeing Shed, Smith's Shop fitted with Furnace, Bench and Anvil, Carpenter's Shop, Mason's Shop, Cart Shed and Stable, Butchery, Five Loose Boxes and Stable with Four Stalls, Granary over, Range of Cattle Houses with Loft over.'

In spite of its rambling corridors, Eggesford House was the favourite home of the 4th and 5th Earls of Portsmouth, who preferred it to the principal family seat at Hurstbourne Park in Hampshire. The Lymington Wing was added to the north by the 5th Earl, possibly under Newmarket architects Clark and Holland, and a tower added in 1889, becoming effectively a sixth incarnation of the house, with further bedrooms (to accommodate a family of twelve children), a new kitchen, and with the tower offering laundry and stores as well.

The house fell out of favour in the time of the 6th Earl and his wife Beatrice Pease, who felt it was cold – a sentiment shared by the novelist Henry James, one of several literary figures to visit the house (see Chapter 9). This may have been due to the 5th Earl, Beatrice's father-in-law, banning fires in the sitting room hearth, having endured smoke-filled rooms from green and damp logs as a child. Beatrice was however a fan of the gardens, which she referred to as a 'paradise of bloom'.

The gradual demise of the estate under the 6th Earl (see Chapter 22) saw the house and its widespread village properties sold off in a series of sales. The social benefits of this redistribution are clear: many tenants were able to buy their farms and houses, and some of their descendants remain in situ today.

The seventh and most recent reincarnation of the house, reinvigorated in the 1990s, is described in Chapter 24. The visible legacy of the Portsmouths and earlier owners of the estate can still be seen in the fine monuments of Eggesford's secluded Church, some distance off in the valley below.

Early coloured postcard of Eggesford House, c. late 19th or early 20th century

(By kind permission of Ed Howell)

Eggesford House

CHAPTER 4

EGGESFORD: CHURCH, SCHOOL AND FOREST

ECCESFORD CHURCH.

Sketched and Drawn on Stone by W. Spreat
Printed by C. Hullmandel

Despite the relatively small community in Eggesford, and corresponding lack of facilities by modern standards, Eggesford's church and forest give it a recognisable place in regional and national history, notable for its aristocratic estate owners and its significance in post-First World War forestry.

All Saints Church, Eggesford (1842), lithograph by William Spreat

(Photo by Jonathan Crofts)

All Saints Church, Eggesford

The Reverend C A Cardale's notes on the church, compiled in the 1970s, describe its position as:

> 'highly picturesque and pleasing … surrounded by a luxuriant growth of venerable timber, where elm, oak, chestnut, cedar, and other trees of the forest unite in forming one of those spots which are the pride of our country.

There is a West Entrance beneath the Tower. This Tower is original 14th century. It is embattled, low and square. It has three bells which are named and dated.'

A 1986 report on the bells offered more detail than Cardale on the inscriptions:

'Sir Edward Cheches Knight, A M 1618; Humphry Beare + Hugh + Maunder 1652; and the third has the inscription 'Given to the glory of God alone' 1652 (Soli Deo Detur Gloria T P 1637, favourite motto of the 17th century founder). The three bells were supplied by Penningtons of Barnstaple [whose earliest dated bell is 1607].

In the 15th century the Church had a tower, nave, chancel and the Reigney chantry. By the 17th century, the chantry became a mausoleum with 2 Chichester family monuments, and the north chapel was added. In the 18th, the mausoleum was extended to include the Sir William Fellowes monument. In 1867 the £1000 restoration funded by the 5th Earl of Portsmouth added the aisle and the north door, removing the south door, and moving the Earl of Donegall (Chichester) monument to the south wall of the nave.'

Cardale adds that the altar's sculptor was 'a man called Bushell, of Down St. Mary', inscribed as 'W. H. B. Sculptor' with 'A. W. OWEN, Rector. Anno 1892', although a date of 1889 is shown in *The Deanery Magazine*; it was 'designed by Mr. Vickery, and made by Mr. Richard Trigger, of oak. The Brass Altar Cross was presented by the Hon. Edward Wallop, and the Pulpit Desk and lights were given by the Rector's wife, Mrs. Welsh Owen'. Cardale also lists an Elizabethan chalice and paten with the Tudor rose, undated, and a 1718 chalice with the Fellowes coat of arms, donated by that family.

There is an ornate nineteenth-century brass chandelier and a Norman font, Cardale suggests possibly from another church: 'An earlier font was described as marble and given by the Hon. Newton Fellowes on the occasion of the Baptism of his first daughter, with a basin of elegant form…' Stained-glass windows commemorate Isaac Newton, the 5th Earl in the south wall. The chancel has nineteenth-century stained glass, with Cardale recording three stained-glass windows in total, and the two south windows being 'plain but for two coats of arms on each. The window in the tower is interesting because in it are tiny fragments of an Elizabethan window; dare one imagine that they were ruined in Cromwellian days or just rotted with age?'

The 4th Earl of Portsmouth (who held the title for only a year, following the death of his brother the 3rd Earl) is commemorated in the church along with his second wife Catherine, daughter of Devon's 1st Earl Fortescue. Other monuments include those of Fellowes and Wallop family members, and their Portsmouth family vault, plus the grand memorial to the earlier Chichesters, Arthur, 1st Earl of Donegall, and his wives (see Chapter 1).

The monument to Edward Chichester of Eggesford (later 1st Viscount Chichester of Carrickfergus) and his wife Anne Coplestone (see Chapter 1) was erected in 1649 by their son. As architectural historian James Rothwell described in 2007:

'It is of alabaster with vestiges of the original decoration and consists of two excellent recumbent effigies on a massive sarcophagus, the latter strewn with the heraldic shields of the couple's children and their wives. Above are memorial tablets and armorials and the whole is set in an arched recess in the north wall of the Reigny Chapel.'

Dr George Oliver in his *Ecclesiastical Antiquities of Devon* (1840) noted:

'The Church is small, and at present has little to recommend it, except the costly and splendid monuments of the Chichester Family. Our readers are aware that Edward Chichester (the fifth and youngest son of the Sir John Chichester, of Ralegh, Knight, who died 30 November, 1569, by his wife Gertrude Courtenay [daughter of Sir William Courtenay of Powderham Castle, later seat of the Earls of Devon]) married Anne, sole daughter and heiress of John Coplestone, of Eggesford, Esq. by his wife Dorothy, daughter of Sir George Beeston, Knight.'

Twentieth-century Devon historian W G Hoskins enthused about the Chichester monuments: 'These two monuments are among the finest of their kind in Devon: only the Tawstock monuments of the Earls of Bath are comparable with them.'

Monument to Catherine, 4th Countess of Portsmouth, daughter of 1st Earl Fortescue, in All Saints Church, Eggesford

(Photo by Jonathan Crofts)

In 1867, the respected 5th Earl, Isaac Newton Fellowes, contributed £1000 for the restoration of the Church. The fourteenth-century tower remained, but the rest was largely rebuilt. The monument for Henry Arthur Fellowes (died 1792), heir to the estate after his brother William, was moved from the chancel.

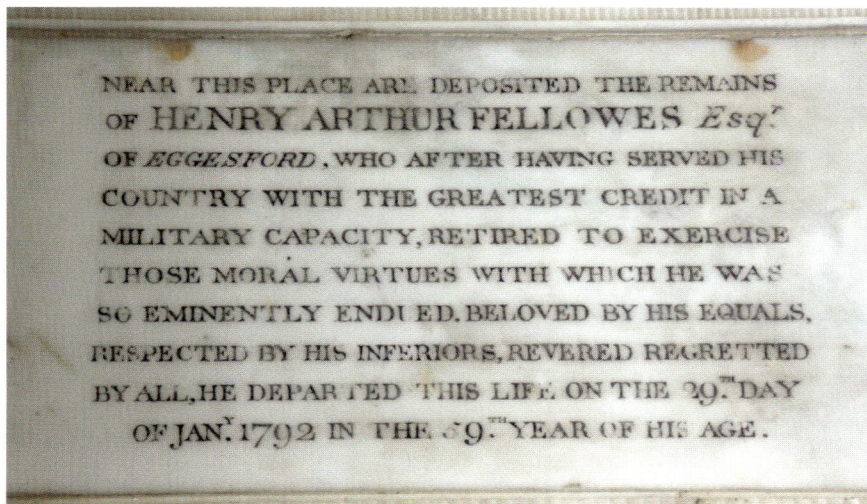

NEAR THIS PLACE ARE DEPOSITED THE REMAINS OF HENRY ARTHUR FELLOWES *Esqr.* OF *EGGESFORD*, WHO AFTER HAVING SERVED HIS COUNTRY WITH THE GREATEST CREDIT IN A MILITARY CAPACITY, RETIRED TO EXERCISE THOSE MORAL VIRTUES WITH WHICH HE WAS SO EMINENTLY ENDUED, BELOVED BY HIS EQUALS, RESPECTED BY HIS INFERIORS, REVERED REGRETTED BY ALL, HE DEPARTED THIS LIFE ON THE 29th DAY OF JAN. 1792 IN THE 59th YEAR OF HIS AGE.

Monument to Henry Arthur Fellowes, brother of Urania, 2nd Countess of Portsmouth, and William, in All Saints Church, Eggesford

(Photo by Jonathan Crofts)

Architectural historian James Rothwell added:

'The arch between the chancel and the Reigny Chapel was opened up ... and before that the magnificent tomb on the south wall of the nave stood here, opposite that to Viscount Chichester. It commemorates the first two wives (died 1630 and 1648) of his son, Arthur Chichester, first Earl of Donegall (died 1674) and the deceased children of his second marriage. His first wife died before her husband was a peer and is hence without a coronet and her daughter is absent because she was still living when the monument was erected in 1650. Lord Donegall is standing, dressed in armour and wearing a cape, a gilded Earl's coronet on his head. His wives flank him, perched rather uncomfortably on the slopes of an open pediment and seemingly only prevented from sliding off by the arch into which the monument is set. The effect would have been all the more impressive when seen hard-up against the tomb to his parents. Mrs Esdaile attributed the tomb to William Wright of Charing Cross in her 1935 article (*Associated Architectural Societies Report*) on the sculptor.

At the far end of the Reigny Chapel and placed with Protestant presumptuousness where the altar should be is the final piece in this impressive composition of three tightly packed and oversized monuments (as originally arranged). This one is to William Fellowes...' (see Chapters 1 and 2).

The Earls of Portsmouth's family pew in All Saints Church, with private heating from a cast-iron stove, now occupied by the organ, a Lieblich by Thomas C Lewis of London, installed in 1948.

(Photo by Jonathan Crofts)

Elsewhere in the Church, the seating mainly takes the form of box pews, with the most prominent being that of the Earls of Portsmouth, equipped with private heating to keep the family and guests warm in the cold Devon winters (from a so-called 'tortoise' stove, because it had a slow steady burn and was economical with fuel). The organ was later sited there.

The Reverend H Fulford Williams summarised 'The Patrons and Rectors of Eggesford, Devon' in *Devon and Cornwall Notes and Queries*, vol. 29 (1963), explaining that 'The parish of Eggesford has always been in private patronage. The Manorial Lords of the Reigney family presented until 1514. Copplestone, Chichester and St Leger succeeded by marriage to the Manor to 1718, when the last named sold to William Fellowes, whose heirs the Wallop family, Earls of Portsmouth, hold it.'

Private patronage meant that the lords of the manor nominated the Rector, and the 'living' that went with it, under the Anglican law of 'advowson', the right to recommend or appoint a clergyman for a vacant benefice. This was a guaranteed home and income for the clergyman, often the younger son of a wealthy family, his profession generally regarded as 'gentlemanly' and therefore socially acceptable. In practice, the role of a servant of the Church was very often a sinecure, and rectors and vicars had ample time in which to pursue their own interests. Records at All Saints go back to William de Bismario, who resigned in 1257. He was succeeded by William de Wembeworthy (the name of the neighbouring parish) in 1258, with John de Reigney as patron. The Norman names after the Conquest (such as those with 'de') persisted into the fourteenth century. One of the last of those was Richard de Bikelegh, in post in 1341, who died of the Black Death ('the plague') in 1349.

The parishes of Eggesford and Chawleigh have been linked in some way for centuries. John Ford of Chawleigh was recorded as Chaplain of Eggesford while Edwards Halls (or Halle) was in post from 1429–30.

In 1548 the Patron was 'William Cornall Esq. by grant of Charles Coplestone, husband of Anne, cousin and heir of William Reigney', marking the switch to the Coplestone era. William Stewkley however was patron for some twenty years from circa 1549; his first rector, Bartholomew Corde, was 'ejected by Mary [I] and restored by Elizabeth [I]' during the tumultuous years of England switching back to Roman Catholicism and then again to Protestantism. Corde was also Vicar of Coleridge, today's Coldridge. Corde's successor after his ejection was Richard Wuthers in 1554, although Wuthers was ejected in turn when Corde was reinstated in 1559.

Anne Wood became patron circa 1599, as widow of John Coplestone, but she had remarried Richard Wood of Ashridge, North Tawton: William Finchett and John Leigh were her rectors.

By 1643 Arthur Chichester, Baron of Belfast and Earl of Donegal, was patron, succeeded by Letitia, Countess of Donegal by 1687. Her rector, Matthew Nicholas, was one of twelve 'non-juror' incumbents in Devon. Following the 1688 Glorious Revolution, with James II and VII exiled, clergy had to swear allegiance to their monarch; clergy refusing this to the royal successors Williams II and III and Mary II were known as 'non-juring'.

By 1691–1700 Anne, daughter of the 2nd Earl of Donegal and Countess of Longford, was patron, to be followed by Arthur St Leger.

George Paddon became rector 1734–43, when the Fellowes were in evidence as lords of the manor and patron: in this case, Coulson Fellowes, son of William Fellowes. Lewis Greenslade, rector 1734–1743, was also rector of Mariansleigh, a village to the north-east of Chawleigh, although there were 'No services at Eggesford in winter from the badness of the roads & the shortness of the days'.

Pelham Fellowes Clay (1796–1879), nephew of the 4th Earl of Portsmouth, Newton Fellowes, was a longstanding rector of All Saints (and of St James' in Chawleigh) from 1819–1879. Pelham's father is believed to have been Reverend Benjamin Clay, rector of East Worlington for a period. (See Chapters 18 and 19 for Pelham's controversial role in Chawleigh.)

He was succeeded by Biscoe Hale Wortham, a 'musician of some note'. The Reverend was brother-in-law to Oscar Browning, the prolific but controversial educationalist, historian and author. Besides his tenure as rector of All Saints, Eggesford, Wortham served as headmaster of the English College, Bruges, and later vicar of St Margaret's, Ware, and rector of Dunton Waylett. Both Eggesford and Wembworthy parishes came under his care during his period as rector. In his non-liturgical life, Wortham produced translations of Sanskrit literature.

The Countess of Portsmouth became patron circa 1910 until the patronage returned to the male earls.

Kelly's Directory of 1923 describes the church in the early years after the First World War:

'The church of All Saints is an ancient building of stone in mixed styles, consisting of a chancel, nave, north aisle, north porch, and an embattled western tower containing 3 bells. ... The church was restored in 1867 by the Earl of Portsmouth at a cost of £1000 and has 150 sittings. The register of baptisms and burials dates from the year 1592; that of the marriages from 1586. The living is a rectory annexed to that of Wembworthy, joint net yearly value £502, including 11 acres of glebe, with residence, in the gift of the Countess of Portsmouth, who has two turns, and the Bishop of Exeter and Captain L. G. Cruwys, JP, who have one turn each, and held since 1920 by the Rev. Charles Ernest Treadwell who resides at Wembworthy. There is a charity of £30, left by the Rev. John Churchill, the interest of which is paid to the poor. The trustees are the Rector and a local committee appointed by the Charity Commissioners.'

Captain Lewis George Cruwys, a professional soldier, was from 1904 to 1957 owner of Cruwys Morchard House and its estate in a village to the east, married to Margaret, President of the Devonshire Association and of the Devon and Exeter Institution, and a Fellow of the Society of Antiquaries of London. The Captain was also patron of Cruwys Morchard's Church of the Holy Cross. John Churchill was the rector when The Old Glebe was built (see below).

In the churchyard at All Saints, the Reverend C A Cardale reports a date of 1761 for the oldest tombstone, and refers to a Wallop family wedding held there: 'Interesting account of the Wedding in 1886 of Lady Dorothea Wallop to Mr R N Rycroft at Eggesford. The decorations must have been superb mostly done by Mr Vickery, Polly and Clara Vickery. Mr Vickery and Mr Geary also made some arches over the road and a covered way at the Church entrance.' Sir Richard Nelson Rycroft, 5th Baronet (1859–1925) of Calton, Yorkshire, was also a Major and became High Sheriff of Hampshire in 1899. Lady Dorothea sadly died early in 1906.

The original English Heritage / Historic England listing for the church records a granite churchyard cross, probably 15th century. A chest tomb is dated 1788 in memory of Mary Fellowes, with a marble plaque recording the death of S Coulson Fellowes in 1769. Another chest tomb is dated 1818 in memory of the rector John Churchill, a fellow of Corpus Christi College, Oxford.

Cardale reported that the Portsmouth family vault had been last opened in 1932 for the burial of Lady Henrietta Evans, daughter of the 5th Earl.

On the north-east edge of the church graveyard, where the Fellowes tomb and related family graves are located, a headstone and cross marks the spot of another Fellowes descendant: 'Russell Lewis Stephenson, 6th Devon Regiment, only child of Hamilton Russell and Isie Madelene, née Fellowes. Drowned on Active Service July 18th 1940'. The mother in question, Isie, was commemorated by her great-nephew Julian Fellowes in his creation *Downton Abbey*, as he explained in a *Vanity Fair* interview on 8 November 2012 concerning his family background:

'His father, Peregrine Fellowes, was a civil engineer and diplomat who worked for the Foreign Office and later Shell International, the oil company. Julian, the

Eggesford Church in 1913, from the sales particulars for the Eggesford estate of that year. The Fellowes tomb is clearly visible in the north-east corner of the churchyard.

(With kind permission of Ed Howell)

youngest of four boys, was born while Peregrine was posted in Cairo. Peregrine had lost his own father to the Great War in 1915, when he was only three years old, and subsequently spent much of his childhood being shunted around to various great-aunts while his mother, "a fairly feckless character," in Fellowes's words, carried on with her romantic life. On the one hand, this instilled in Peregrine "a rather melancholic sense of exclusion from his own world," his son said. But, on the other hand, these great-aunts took good care of him and hung around long enough to become a big part of Julian's childhood. The eldest of them, Isie, is the model for Maggie Smith's dowager characters in both *Gosford Park* and *Downton Abbey*. "Aunt Isie had this sort of acerbic wit, yet she was kind," Fellowes said. "Lots of those lines Maggie has, like 'Bought marmalade! Oh dear, I call that very feeble,' and 'What is a weekend?' — they came straight from her.'

The Fellowes tomb in the All Saints churchyard at Eggesford, uncovered after many years by FEAST trustees and volunteers in May 2024.

One inscription commemorates the death in 1769 of Coulson Fellowes, son of the original William Fellowes of Eggesford.

(Photo by Jonathan Crofts)

50

Below Stephenson's memorial is another stone commemorating his wife Karin, née Karin Freiin von Malortie, daughter of Hermann Freiherr von Malortie, married on 8 July 1937. Karin was from an aristocratic family in Germany, the Second World War swiftly bringing to an end an Anglo–German alliance on a personal scale. Karin never remarried, and the stone marks her death in 2005, sixty-five years after that of her young husband.

The church was deemed redundant by the Church of England in 1982 but kept open to visitors for nearly ten years by local residents. It then reopened as a site for Anglican worship in 1991, with the sanction of the late Queen Elizabeth II. The Friends of Eggesford All Saints Trust (FEAST) was established as a charity in 1990 'to promote or assist in for the benefit of the public the preservation, repair, maintenance, restoration, improvement and ornamentation of the fabric of the church … and to provide or assist in the provision of articles for use in worship there'. FEAST flourishes to this day with trustees and volunteers fundraising and helping maintain the church, inside and out.

Set in rolling countryside, All Saints Church in Eggesford as it appears today

(Photo by Jonathan Crofts)

Eggesford School

Recognising the need to educate the children of his workforce, the 5th Earl of Portsmouth built a new school for the community in 1869. Technically it lies in Wembworthy parish, roughly halfway between Eggesford and the village of Wembworthy. Known first as Eggesford School, but soon after Wembworthy and Eggesford School, the original name persisted into the second half of the twentieth century.

Initially owned by the Earl of Portsmouth, the school was maintained as a voluntary school by the County Authority after the 1902 Education Act, and in 1909–1910 it became a council school, eventually purchased by the County Council in 1914 as parts of the Eggesford estate were auctioned off.

In 1938, the older students moved to a newly built senior school in nearby Chulmleigh, at which point the name was changed to Wembworthy Council Infants and Junior School, later Wembworthy County Primary School. It finally closed in 1972 and the students were relocated to a new school in Winkleigh.

The building reopened as an outdoor centre in 1974 but this subsequently closed circa 2011. Bought as a private residence, the new owners acquired 42 beds with the purchase. Today it retains the large windows of typical Victorian school architecture.

Eggesford Forest

The wider area around Chawleigh and Eggesford was visited by the late Queen Elizabeth II, together with Prince Philip, Duke of Edinburgh, in 1956: she unveiled a plaque to commemorate the Forestry Commission planting its millionth acre, and the royal couple planted a tree each too, in celebration of the Commission's first ever plantation.

The Commission had been founded to restore woods and forests following their depletion over the course of the First World War, timber having been in huge demand during that conflict, and in 1919 the first saplings were dug in at Eggesford Forest, all coniferous in place of the original mixed broadleaf trees.

A plaque records the occasion: '8th December 1919; Lord Clinton, Commissioner; H. Murray, Assistant Commissioner; C.O. Henson, Divisional Officer; T. Brown, Forester.'

On 4 October 1963 *The Western Morning News* contained a short history of the Commission: 'Forestry changing Western skylines … the first tree planted by the Commission was in Devon, at Eggesford Forest. The Scottish chairman, Lord Lovat, had arranged for the first tree to be planted in his country, but Lord Clinton, a member of the Commission, hurried to supervise the planting at Eggesford,

The late Queen Elizabeth II unveiling a plaque commemorating the first Forestry Commission plantation of 1919, Eggesford Forest

(Photo © Forestry England)

sending a telegram to Scotland which arrived just before the official ceremony was to take place. By the time the Second World War broke out there were forests in Devon at Eggesford, Exeter, Halwill, Hartland and Dartmoor, representing 11,000 acres of planted land. Since the war new forests have grown at Bampton, Bovey, Charmouth, Honiton, Malton and Plym, while the older forests have increased in size until now they are nearly 25,000 acres of woodland in the county under the Commission's control.'

Hidden among the trees of the forest and the local woodlands are other impressive buildings originally connected with the Portsmouth estate, each with its own story to tell. Today they have evolved into individual homes, but previously they played a part in the functioning of the estate and the small settlement around the big house.

CHAPTER 5

EGGESFORD: FINE HOUSES AND A WARSHIP

The beauty of the Taw valley, the social and economic benefits associated with the 'Big House', and the improving transport connections have all encouraged owners to produce other fine buildings in the Eggesford settlement. Unusually, there was also a maritime spin-off.

The Churchills and the Old Glebe

The Chantry Certificates for Devon and Exeter of 1546 show that 50 acres of glebe land were gifted by William Reigney (named as Raynye) to provide a stipendiary (regular income) for the rector: 'for the contynuall ffynding of A pryste to celebrate dyvyne s'vyce for the sowle of the sayd Wyll'm Raynye and all xpen sowles wt in the parysshe churche of Eggesford…'

The Chantry Certificates also reference the almshouse founded by Ibote Raynye: 'to the entent that … poor people should be from tyme to tyme thereby relevyed and susteyned so to continue for ev'.'

The original Eggesford parsonage was built later, around 1610, as a cob and thatch building. In 1613 the terrier (an inventory of the glebe lands and property in the parish which supported the rector and the church) described a glebe house with 'A hall, a parlour, three little chambers, and two little parlour rooms. A kitchen and a barne with a shippen'.

The Hearth Tax records for 1664 show the parsonage with two hearths, but a total of eighteen at the Chichesters' Eggesford House. The 1680 terrier described the parsonage house with '5 under rooms viz Dairy, Hall, Parlour, Dish house, Buttery. 3 chambers and a study. One Barne and one Kitchen adjoining it and one hogs stie.' All the 'under rooms' were 'rafted, plastered and whited overhead', and all rooms had earth floors. The attached land was 'Eighty acres bounded on East & North by the Bartn grounds of Eggiford. On the South side with the lands of the Right Honble Countess Dowager of Donegall on the West with the lands of the Worshipfull George Speak Esq.'

This was probably a reference to Sir George Speke, 2nd Baronet (1653–1683), the second and only surviving son of Sir Hugh Speke, 1st Baronet. The Speak / Speke family were the landowners in the manor of Wembworthy and resided at the earlier Heywood House (see Chapter 1), but later withdrew to their other base at Whitelackington in Somerset.

With Henry Fellowes as patron of the church and its living, John Churchill (1741–1818) became rector from 1773 to 1818 and also served as rector of Chawleigh. He died in post and was buried at Eggesford, leaving a bequest to Chawleigh and to Eggesford in his will.

This tradition of sharing rectors across multiple parishes continues to the present day, although Chawleigh has had a curate attached from time to time and the rector is now based in Chulmleigh. Today's rectors probably work considerably harder than most of those from a privileged background in the eighteenth and nineteenth centuries, for whom the post was often little more than a sinecure.

Today's Glebe Farm is next to the Grade II listed house, The Old Glebe. The listing states:

'formerly rectory. Medieval origins, may include some C17 walling much-altered between 1782–7 for the Reverend John Churchill by the architect John Meadows, and extensively refurbished circa 1840; mid C19 extension. …The owner's research shows that the site is documented back to C13. Accounts exist for the renovation of the house between 1782–7 for the Reverend John Churchill by the architect John Meadows.'

A 1777 statute exists for rebuilding part of the parsonage house and buildings belonging to the living. In 1782 plans and estimates were drawn up for the repairs,

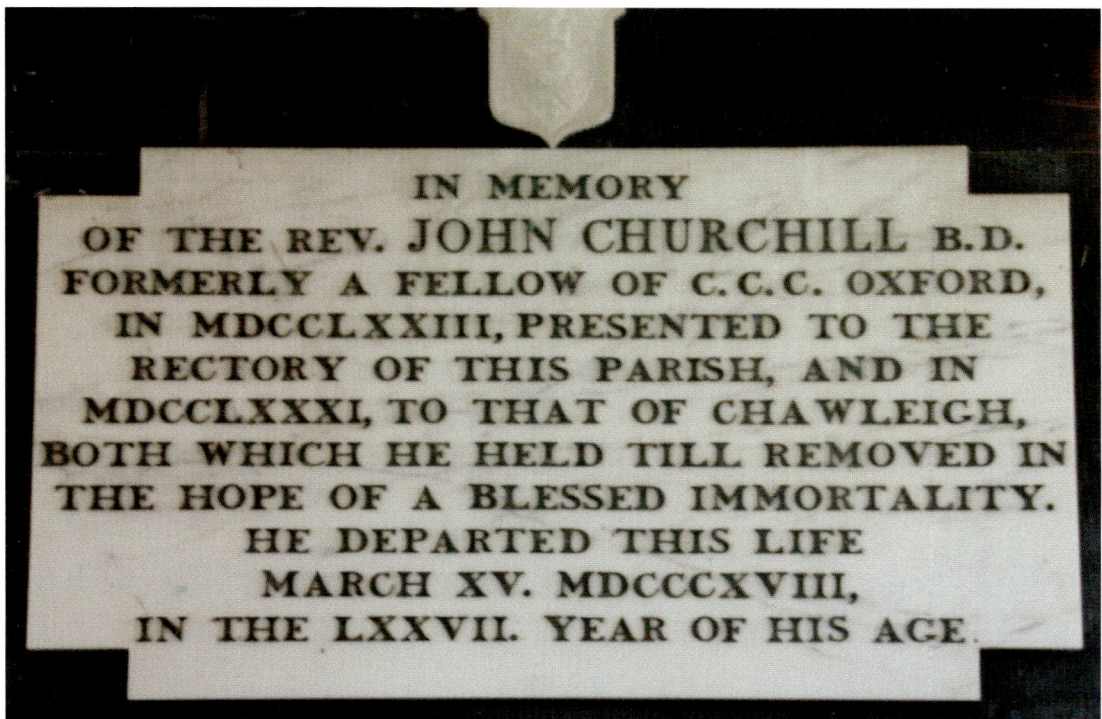

IN MEMORY
OF THE REV. JOHN CHURCHILL B.D.
FORMERLY A FELLOW OF C.C.C. OXFORD,
IN MDCCLXXIII, PRESENTED TO THE
RECTORY OF THIS PARISH, AND IN
MDCCLXXXI, TO THAT OF CHAWLEIGH,
BOTH WHICH HE HELD TILL REMOVED IN
THE HOPE OF A BLESSED IMMORTALITY.
HE DEPARTED THIS LIFE
MARCH XV. MDCCCXVIII,
IN THE LXXVII. YEAR OF HIS AGE.

Plan
OF

"THE OLD GLEBE"

EGGESFORD
NORTH - DEVON

For Sale by Auction by Messrs.

Hannaford, Ward & Southcombe, Ltd.

2nd OCTOBER, 1936

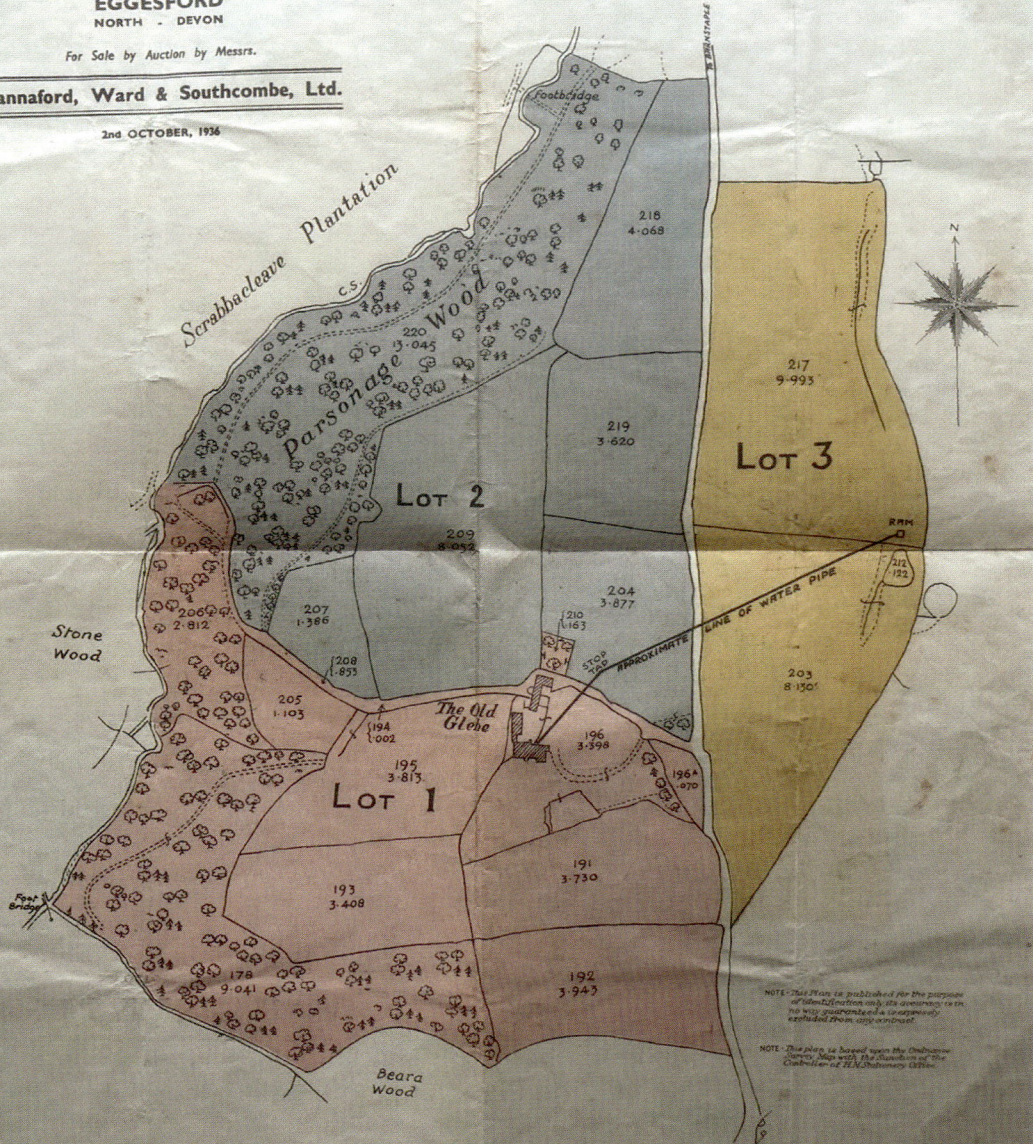

Scrabbacleave Plantation

C.S.

Parsonage Wood

Footbridge

TO BARNSTAPLE

218
4·068

217
9·993

Lot 3

220
3·045

219
3·620

Lot 2

N

209
8·052

204
3·877

RAM

212
·132

Stone Wood

207
1·386

210
1·163

STOP TAP

APPROXIMATE

LINE OF WATER PIPE

208
1·855

206
2·812

205
1·103

194
1·002

The Old Glebe

196
3·398

196A
·070

203
8·150

195
3·813

Lot 1

191
3·730

193
3·408

Foot Bridge

178
9·041

192
3·943

Beara Wood

NOTE:- This Plan is published for the purpose of identification only, its accuracy is in no way guaranteed (as expressly) excluded from any contract.

NOTE:- This plan is based upon the Ordnance Survey Map with the Sanction of the Controller of H.M.Stationery Office.

Scale $\frac{1}{2500}$

HANNAFORD, WARD & SOUTHCOMBE, LTD.
Auctioneers,
Chulmleigh, Exeter, Barnstaple & Torrington.

56

and in 1787 accounts show 'the taking down and rebuilding of a kitchen and other offices with chambers over them, & also a barn, stable, cow house and Linhay according…'

John Meadows, Surveyor, certified that the old buildings had 'become so decayed and worn as to be very unsuitable to the Residence and Decent Accommodation of a Clergyman's Family'. The result was a rectory built as a fine Georgian house for Churchill, and it continued as such until it passed into private hands in the early twentieth century.

The 1881 census records the inhabitants of the 'Rectory House' while Reverend Biscoe H Wortham was in residence. Apart from himself and his wife Malvina, there were 3 children, recorded as 'scholars', 6 pupil 'scholars' (one from the Pyrenees in France), and 4 servants: the nurse and domestic servant Maximilienne was also from France, and the cook, parlourmaid and housemaid were all of English nationality.

Later residents of the house included, from 1917 to 1935, Sir Henry Sullivan Hartnoll, Kt., who according to the *Indian Biographical Dictionary* (1915 by C Hayavadana Rao), was 'Judge of the Chief Court, Lower Burma, in 1914; educated at Extra Grammar School and Trinity College, Oxford; called to the Bar, 1898; joined service as Assistant Commissioner, Burma, in 1883; Deputy Commissioner, 1890: Commissioner, 1902; Judge, in 1906; Officiating Chief Judge, 1911'. He was based in Rangoon, Burma (today's Myanmar).

Extensive correspondence shows Lady Hartnoll taking a great interest in the Messenger & Company greenhouse (with Pilkington Brothers glass) for the garden, which she commissioned in 1929, is still in use today.

As with so many Devon families, their son, Lieutenant Hugh Peter Hartnoll, of the 1st Battalion, Worcestershire Regiment, was killed in action on the Western Front in the First World War, in December 1914 near Neuve Chapelle, France, aged twenty-one.

The eldest son of Sir Henry, Eric Stewart Hartnoll, became a Trooper in the King Edward's Horse in 1913, was commissioned into the 1/70th Burma Rifles, and served during the First World War in Egypt and Palestine. He then worked as an Assistant Conservation Officer with the Indian Forest Service. During the Second World War, when the Japanese invaded in 1942, he was Conservator of Forests, and was evacuated to the United Kingdom, where he was

(Left:)

Map of the grounds from the sales particulars of The Old Glebe, 1936

(Photo by Jonathan Crofts, by kind permission of Joanne and Peter Court)

Gravestone for Sir Henry Sullivan Hartnoll and his wife Grace, in the churchyard of All Saints, Eggesford

(Photo by Jonathan Crofts)

VACANT POSSESSION of the Residence and Grounds on completion.

NORTH DEVON

Half-mile from Eggesford Station, 3 miles from Chulmleigh, 12 miles from Crediton, about 20 miles from Exeter and Barnstaple and an hour's run from the well-known Golf Courses of Westward Ho ! and Saunton.

THE DELIGHTFULLY SITUATED FREEHOLD

RESIDENTIAL, AGRICULTURAL and SPORTING ESTATE

known as

"The Old Glebe"

comprising

THE WELL-APPOINTED RESIDENCE

surrounded by well timbered Grounds and approached by a Carriage Drive containing :—Lofty Entrance Hall, 4 Reception Rooms, 8 Bed and Dressing Rooms, Bath Room, 3 Servant's Bedrooms and the usual Domestic Offices.

Electric Light, Constant Hot Water, Telephone,
:: Stabling, Garage and other Buildings. ::

FLOWER, FRUIT & VEGETABLE GARDENS, LAWN, MEADOW, PASTURE, ARABLE AND WOODLANDS extending in all to about

84 acres   2 roods   21 poles

Hannaford, Ward & Southcombe, Ltd.

instructed by the Representatives of the late Sir Henry S. Hartnoll, will offer the above Property for Sale by Auction (as a whole or in lots) at

THE ROUGEMONT HOTEL, EXETER,

On FRIDAY, 2nd OCTOBER, 1936, at 3 p.m.

(unless previously sold privately).

For viewing apply at the RESIDENCE or to Mr. JAMES, Fourways. Eggesford (where a plan and Schedule may be seen).

For Particulars, Plan and Conditions of Sale, apply to the Auctioneers at Chulmleigh, 80, Queen Street, Exeter, Barnstaple and Torrington, or to the

Solicitors :—Messrs. SPARKES & CO., Crediton and Exeter.

"EXPRESS & ECHO," PRINTERS, EXETER.

58

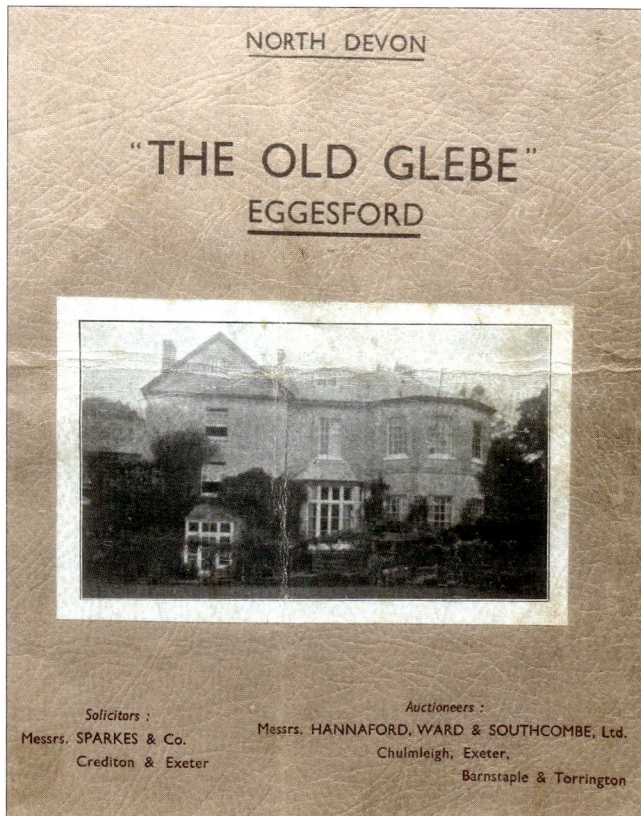

NORTH DEVON

"THE OLD GLEBE"
EGGESFORD

Solicitors :
Messrs. SPARKES & Co.
Crediton & Exeter

Auctioneers :
Messrs. HANNAFORD, WARD & SOUTHCOMBE, Ltd.
Chulmleigh, Exeter,
Barnstaple & Torrington

Sales particulars of
The Old Glebe, 1936,
still owned by the
Hartnoll family at
that time

(Photos by
Jonathan Crofts,
by kind permission
of Joanne and
Peter Court)

commissioned into the Royal Air Force, serving at home as a Captain. He once again survived and died, aged seventy-seven, in Hampshire in 1970.

Another son, Commander Henry James Hartnoll, RN, DSO and Croix de Guerre, put the Old Glebe up for sale in 1936. Sadly he was killed on active service in November 1940, aged fifty. His own son, Lieutenant Henry Digory Hartnoll, DSC of the Royal Marines, died only a year later in December 1941, aged twenty.

The Hartnolls were not the only Eggesford family to suffer heavily from the World Wars. Reverend Francis Henry Baring (1848–1914) was Rector at Eggesford from 1899 to 1900, and had seven children with Amy Stamper: only the eldest of five sons, John Theodore Baring (1887–1967), survived the wars, having served as Lieutenant in the Royal Engineers. Four other sons all died in the so-called Great War, 1914–18:

Private Charles Alexander Baring, Australian Imperial Force (1893–1916)

Lance Corporal Ernest Baring, Australian Imperial Force (1889–1917)

2nd Lieutenant Christopher Cecil Baring, Royal Kent Regiment (1897–1916)

Lieutenant Reginald Arthur Baring, RAF (1899–1918).

From 1940–1959 the Old Glebe was occupied by Sir George Moss KBE (formerly Consul-General in Hankow, China).

Research by a past owner of The Old Glebe uncovered the close links between the Churchill and Wallop (Portsmouth) families: a Reverend Henry Churchill was rector at nearby Morchard Bishop in 1719, and died in 1751, having had eight children by his first wife including a daughter, Jane, and three sons by his second wife, Grace Comyns: Henry Churchill of North Tawton, 'gentleman', John Churchill (of The Old Glebe) 1741–1818, and Peter Churchill of Dawlish.

EGGESFORD ROLL OF HONOUR.

James Trigger.	Reservist	1st Hampshire Regt.	Prisoner of War.
John Vernon.	Royal Navy.	H M S "Indefatigable."	†
Fred Cole.	Territorial	6th Batt Devon Regt	
Lieut H J Hartnoll. D.S.O.		Royal Navy.	
Lieut H P Hartnoll		Worcester Regt.	†
Lieut A V Hartnoll. M.C.		Royal Field Artillery.	—

John Piper	9th Lancers.	
William Leaman	8th Batt. Devon Regt.	†
Frank Trigger	9th Batt. Devon Regt.	— †
Thomas Peper	3rd Batt. Devon Regt.	†
Harry Trigger.	Somerset Light Infantry.	— †
William Luxton	6th Batt. Devon Regt.	
Percy Quick	6th Batt. Devon Regt.	
Percy Sampson	6th Batt. Devon Regt.	
Alfred Luxton	2nd Batt. Devon Regt.	—
Percy Manning	11th Batt. Devon Regt.	†
Herbert Manning	11th Batt. Devon Regt.	—
William Palmer.	11th Batt. Devon Regt.	— †
Lieut W. J. Hartnoll	West Yorkshire Regt.	═ ═
William Sandford. M.M.	2nd Batt. Devon Regt.	
George Snell	Royal Engineers (Transport)	
William Manning.	Royal Marine Light Infantry	†
William Trigger.	Royal Engineers (Road Construction)	
Robert Manning.	35th Training Reserves.	Prisoner of War.
John Cockerham.	Royal Field Artillery.	
John Harding.	Royal Naval Division.	
Charles Snell.	Royal Field Artillery.	→
Wyndham Hazelden.	Worcester Regt.	
Stoker P. A Hughes.	Royal Navy.	
Lieut E. Hartnoll	Indian Army.	
William Vernon	Royal Engineers.	
Frank Snell.	Tank Corps.	
Henry Snell	Royal Navy.	
Arthur Gill	1/6 Devon Regt.	†

GOD SAVE THE KING.

Those marked — have been wounded.

Those marked † have sacrificed their lives for King and Country.

60

Peter Churchill was sole executor of the last will of Ann Comyns, most likely his aunt, of Morchard Bishop in 1770. He was still resident in Morchard Bishop in 1780. Ann's husband, Peter Comyns, had died in 1770, and Ann died in 1779. Peter Churchill's wife was Margaret Weston Churchill, eldest daughter of Richard Inglett, collector of customs, of Dawlish (who took the additional name of Fortescue in 1776 when he succeeded to the Buckland Filleigh estate in Devon). Peter died at Dawlish in 1822.

The Reverend John Comyns Churchill (1778–1831) of Barton House, Morchard Bishop, married Lady Henrietta Dorothea Wallop (1780–1862) in 1816, daughter of the 2nd Earl of Portsmouth (making her the sister of the unstable 3rd Earl). Their son of the same name was born in 1817 but died in 1855, aged only thirty-eight. Henrietta Dorothea lived with serious hearing difficulties, not unlike Catherine, Countess to the 4th Earl (see Chapter 9).

The Morchard Bishop estate eventually descended to the 7th Earl of Portsmouth, John Fellowes Wallop (1859–1925), and was the last major holding of the Wallop family in Devon (see Chapter 22).

Sir George Sinclair Moss KBE (former Consul-General in Hankow, China), owner of the Old Glebe from 1940-1959

by Walter Stoneman bromide print, 1939

(© National Portrait Gallery, London)

(Left)

The Roll of Honour in All Saints Church, Eggesford, showing those who lost their lives or were wounded, plus those who served and survived.

Apart from the Hartnolls, there are other families with four or more names, including the Triggers, the Snells and the Mannings. The roll is not comprehensive: James Ernest Archibald Cornall is buried in the churchyard but is omitted from the Roll of Honour and from the War Memorial at Four Ways, Eggesford.

According to Historic England: 'The War Memorial lists 10 members of the local community who lost their lives in the First World War. A further 24 men also served but had returned from the conflict.'

(Photo by Jonathan Crofts)

Heyswood House

Not to be confused with the original Heywood House (precursor to the Victorian incarnation of Eggesford House) nor the contemporary Heywood House, Heyswood House is a Grade II listed house built circa 1850, with extensions added in around 1930, and further refinements at the start of the twenty-first century.

According to Historic England, it comprises:

> 'Originally a small 3-room plan cottage facing south-east with an L-shaped plan, 2 rooms in the main block and the third at right angles projecting forward from left (south-west) end. ... To the left a circa 1930 3-room extension continues the line of the main block into the hillside with the end room single storey with terrace at first floor level. ... To the right and set back slightly from the front is another circa 1930 extension with end stacks and under a separate roof. 2 storeys. Elizabethan Gothic style and circa 1930 extensions finished sympathetically in the same style. ... Heyswood House was once in the grounds of Eggesford House ... and according to the owners was built for a valetudinarian son of the 4th Earl of Portsmouth. His style is very similar to Eggesford House which was built by Thomas Lee of Barnstaple, particularly with its impressive show of Elizabethan-style brick chimney shafts.'

The middle chimney stacks are more ornate, whereas the outer ones are plainer but retain the tall stature. Located on a private drive, the garden around the house has now been beautifully enhanced, and the grounds and farmland are extensive. The current owners guard their privacy carefully.

Rose Cottage and Higher Ford House

Various other properties in Eggesford were once closely connected with the Portsmouth's estate. Rose Cottage, erected in around 1860–70 in Victorian Gothic style, is sited close to All Saints Church. Its Grade II listing from 1986 notes its main range with arched windows and a gabled porch, built from mustone rubble with Hatherleigh stone ashlar quoins and detail, on a 2-room and central staircase plan with a service block to the rear. Adjoining it to the south, the associated stables and coach house are constructed from roughly squared sandstone blocks with narrow windows with diamond-shaped panes of leaded glass to either side of the stable door.

Another nearby former Portsmouth property which has been transformed into a comfortable modern home is Higher Ford House, just over the River Taw and the A377 road. This was the hunting lodge for the Portsmouths and at one stage also an estate office; it has not been listed by English Heritage / Historic England. The owners believe that the original house on the site dated back to 1640 or earlier, along with the well in the grounds. Higher Ford is also listed in the 1618 will of Anthony Snell (see Chapter 17).

HMS *Eggesford*

Eggesford was also honoured in the name of the Royal Navy ship HMS *Eggesford*, which served as a Hunt-class Type III escort destroyer in the Second World War and was the first Royal Navy warship with this name. Funds raised in North Devon parishes supported the construction of the vessel as part of a successful Warship Week National Savings campaign early in the war.

HMS *Eggesford*'s initial missions in 1943 accompanied other military craft to and from Scapa Flow. Much of her battle engagement later that year took place in the Mediterranean on the run from Gibraltar via Malta to Algiers, and then around Sicily and Salerno, and in the Adriatic and off southern France in 1944. She was deployed back to UK waters and later arrived in Ceylon following VJ Day. After the war she joined the Rosyth Training Flotilla and was then given reserve status at Portsmouth. Eventually sold for service in the (West) German navy, she was refitted at Pembroke Dock as a weapons training ship in 1959. Ten years later she was removed from active service and scrapped in Germany.

In honour of her vital service, website Plymouth Military Gifts sells an HMS *Eggesford* fridge magnet.

Eggesford's national prominence, relative to the modest scale of the settlement, initially came from the Wallop family, Earls of Portsmouth, appointed some two hundred years before this ship was commissioned. The Wallops had figured on the royal circuit for some four centuries: it was Elizabeth I who had put the family on the map long before their connection to Eggesford was established.

HMS *Eggesford*, Type III Hunt-class destroyer

(By kind permission of South Molton Museum)

John Wallop, 1st Earl of Portsmouth, Painting by Sir Joshua Reynolds

(Photo by Jonathan Crofts, by kind permission of Viscount Lymington)

CHAPTER 6.

EARLS ONE TO FOUR:
A 'GOOD' MARRIAGE AND A 'LUNACY' TRIAL

'It is an early autumn day in 1591. A long procession of carriages and carts makes its way along the narrow Hampshire lanes, astonishing the bystanders with its colour and magnificence. At its head is a red leather coach carrying the impressive figure of Queen Elizabeth. Now in her late fifties, she is still intent on enjoying a progress in the company of her chief ministers. They have spent the previous night at Wield with William Wallop, and are to stay for two nights and a day with his brother Sir Henry Wallop. The Queen has been travelling for six weeks through Surrey, Sussex and Hampshire before arriving at Farleigh Wallop, and has been entertained in great houses along the way in a style to suit her holiday mood. Sir Henry is in his early fifties and has had a long career in public life in Hampshire and in Ireland. He has been in poor health for many years and is spending time at his English home, where he and his wife Katherine are preparing to meet their royal guest. The Wallop family name is already nearly 500 years old.'

This scene was set by Alison Deveson in the prologue to her history of the Earls of Portsmouth and the Wallop family, *En Suivant la Vérité*. It positions the family in England since the Norman Conquest of 1066, a year that saw another William, Duke of Normandy, crowned as King of England on Christmas Day in Westminster Abbey. Nearly a thousand years later the Hampshire home, now in the guise of Farleigh House in Farleigh Wallop, remains in the ownership of the family, and the coronation of another King, Charles III, has recently been celebrated in the ancient Abbey.

Other Wallop family estates were to follow those in Hampshire and Ireland, including in Scotland from 1905. Their Devonshire holdings, centred around Eggesford, came into the family via marriage, and lasted some three hundred years until early in the twentieth century.

The Wallops, who became the Earls of Portsmouth in 1743, have a colourful history, some of it tarnished by inheritance squabbles, scandal and ill health – perhaps to be expected with a family of such long standing and wealth. Mathew de Wallop is the earliest known ancestor, warden of Winchester Castle from 1204, who held land in what is now Hampshire, Dorset and Somerset in the late 1100s and early 1200s. The family's origins are linked with the Wallop villages between Andover in Hampshire and Salisbury in Wiltshire.

Sir John Wallop (died 1551), sailor, soldier and diplomat in the time of Henry VIII, was responsible for the origins of the verb 'to wallop', having led a number of ships which 'walloped' French coastal towns in 1512–1515, partly in retaliation for their attacks on Sussex. But it was a later John Wallop (1690–1762) who was given the title 1st Earl of Portsmouth in 1743, having been appointed to the House of Lords in 1720 as 1st Viscount Lymington and Baron Wallop.

Portsmouth and Lymington are retained as local placenames in Devon three hundred years later (such as The Lymington Arms in Wembworthy, next to Eggesford, and Portsmouth Arms on the Tarka railway line).

His eldest son and heir, another John (1718–49), became Viscount Lymington on his father's rise to earldom, and started a parliamentary career, as MP for Andover. It was this John who established the family link with Sir Isaac Newton, the famous physicist and mathematician, marrying his great-niece Catherine Conduitt, whom the unmarried Sir Isaac had appointed as an heir. John and Catherine's tale ends tragically, Lord Lymington dying aged thirty-one in 1749, and Catherine in 1750 having given birth to their sixth child. She is buried in Westminster Abbey with her father Sir John Conduitt and her great-uncle Sir Isaac Newton.

The 2nd Earl: John Wallop (1742–97)

The Wallops' Devonshire story really starts with the 2nd Earl, another John (eldest grandson to the earlier Sir John), who inherited the title in 1762 in the absence of his father Lord Lymington. John also inherited from his mother all of Sir Isaac Newton's papers, and one or both of the latter's names persisted throughout the Wallops' time in Devon. John later married Urania, daughter of Coulson Fellowes, who had inherited his father William's estates in Eggesford and secured this 'good marriage' which originated the Fellowes–Wallop connection with Devon (see Chapter 2).

Urania inherited his Eggesford estate to pass on to her second son Newton in 1792, provided he take Fellowes as his surname.

At the behest of Urania, John, the 2nd Earl, built a new Wallop home at Hurstbourne Priors in Hampshire. Three of their children died young, and the eldest son, John Charles Wallop, was to emerge with a mental health disability, for which Urania was unsuccessful in finding a 'cure'. He managed to pursue some education, but his parents eventually appointed trustees to run the estates and his affairs on his behalf.

The 3rd Earl: John Charles Wallop (1767–1853)

Elizabeth Foyster of Clare College, Cambridge, has published a full and sympathetic account of the tribulations of John Charles, the 3rd Earl, in *The Trials of the King of Hampshire* (Oneworld, 2016). Dr Foyster's presentation of the story characterises how mental disorders and disabilities were regarded in Georgian England, especially amongst the upper and supposedly educated classes. Although John Charles himself had little contact with his brother's estate at Eggesford, the tale of his life is both extraordinary and sad.

In June 1773, aged five, John Charles spent time with the family of the novelist Jane Austen, at her childhood home Steventon Rectory, tutored by Reverend Austen, and was then sent by his mother, Lady Portsmouth, to a 'specialist' called Mr Angier in Soho, London, regarding his perceived problems with speech – an early indication of his later mental health issues. Educated initially at Odiham School in Hampshire, then by a private tutor in Hammersmith, London, like many young men of his class at the time John Charles travelled abroad on the 'grand tour', eventually meeting a Frenchman called Jean Seilaz in 1790, who was to become his valet.

When his father died in 1797, John Charles Wallop became 3rd Earl, but two years later was 'abducted' by Jean Seilaz, who took him from Hampshire to London and then on to Yarmouth. He was 'rescued' by his brothers at midnight on 24 July, and by November a marriage to the Hon. Grace Norton was arranged by his brothers Newton and Coulson. One report described her as a 'pleasant and agreeable lady, but of an age which did not promise prolific consequences' – she was years older, chosen so that John Charles would not produce a son and heir.

John was clearly unusual, but tried to lead a typical aristocratic life, even giving a ball in 1800 attended by the novelist Jane Austen, who wrote in her letters that she may have 'drunk a little too much'. More threateningly, however, Jean Seilaz was to write from Hamburg in 1801 accusing John Charles of sodomy, and blackmailing the family for money. This culminated in a series of public court cases and Seilaz eventually being deported back to Hamburg.

Assisted by a medical attendant, John Draper Coombe, described to the servants as 'a company keeper for My Lord', John Charles and his Countess maintained an acceptable social life at Hurstbourne Park from 1808 to 1811, when Coombe left the household to get married. John Charles's mother, Urania, died in 1812, followed by his wife Grace in 1813.

The story took a darker turn again when John Hanson, the family solicitor and a trustee for John Charles, systematically abused his position. Having installed his own family at the Wallops' property, Farleigh House, Hanson arranged for John Charles to be brought to London when his wife died, and arranged a rapid second marriage to his own daughter Mary Ann. The Romantic poet and satirist Lord Byron, who had first known Hanson as the Wallop family solicitor, but then later saw Hanson as something of a father figure (referring to him as 'pater'), knew the Hanson family well and gave Mary Ann away.

John Charles's brothers Newton and Coulson had to resort to legal proceedings to challenge the validity of their brother's marriage, petitioning the Lord Chancellor to issue a Commission of Lunacy for him. Initially, in 1815, this was refused. Meanwhile, John Charles suffered at the hands of Mary Ann and family, enduring regular violence to control his behaviour (which today we might attribute to some level of autism), and probably exacerbating it. Mary Ann even blatantly took a lover, William Rowland Alder, giving birth to a child by him in 1822.

In the summer of that year, Newton Fellowes and William Norton, 2nd Lord Grantley (the brother of Grace, John Charles's first wife, and a John Charles trustee), wrote to Coombe to authorise him to remove John Charles from Edinburgh, during a tour of the North. Coombe and Fletcher Norton (another of Grace's relatives) drove him to Wonersh, the home of William, Lord Grantley. Newton Fellowes issued a writ of habeas corpus and John Charles was taken to a London judge who decided John Charles should be freed.

The family resorted once more to petitioning for a Commission of Lunacy, this time on behalf of his nephew, Henry Arthur Fellowes, elder son of Newton, and on 16 January 1823 this was issued, followed by a nineteen-day hearing in February in the Freemasons' Hall in London.

There was extensive press coverage and society gossip about John Charles's increasingly eccentric behaviour. In aristocratic circles at the time this was not entirely unusual, perhaps a reflection of inheritance squabbles, perhaps down to a limited understanding of mental health. The Commission's purpose was to decide whether he was of 'unsound mind, and when he became so'. Foyster recounts that more than one hundred aristocrats, domestic servants and agricultural labourers gave statements: some

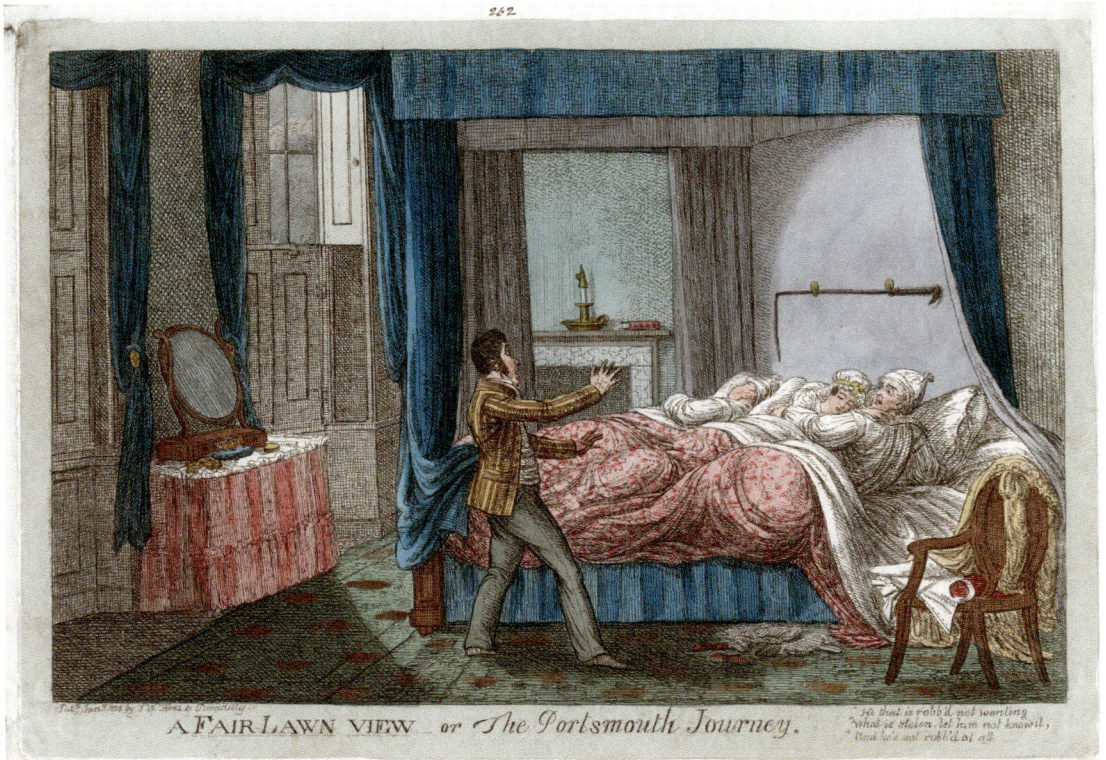

A FAIR LAWN VIEW _or The Portsmouth Journey._

related John Charles's 'sexual pleasure from blood-letting… humiliating humble villagers by turning up and even officiating at family funerals [which he called 'black jobs']', that he 'was routinely cruel to his servants, and allowed his wife to commit adultery in his own bed' and had 'delusions that he was the King of Hampshire, having ordered a throne to be built from which he intended to rule' (technically, this would have counted as traitorous to the monarch).

Others saw him as 'weak-minded' but 'civil and well mannered … performed his public duties well, and regularly held and attended social functions'. Mary Ann's family, the Hansons, helped provide a case in favour of John Charles's sanity, seeking to preserve her position as Countess of Portsmouth and the future inheritance for her baby daughter.

Eminent specialists in 'mad-doctoring', as mental health treatment was known at the time, provided no consensus on John Charles's state of mind. Nonetheless, the jury of twenty-four 'gentlemen', its foreman an MP, and including banker Sir Thomas Baring and the famous architect (later Sir) John Soane, voted unanimously that 'John Charles Earl of Portsmouth is a man of unsound mind, and incapable of managing himself or his affairs'.

A fair-lawn view, or, The Portsmouth journey, by Charles Williams, active 1797–1830 as a printmaker, published January 1823 by SW Fores, 41 Piccadilly, London.

One of the many satirical images published on the sad story of the 3rd Earl, which caught the attention of the press and the public in the early 19th century.

(Courtesy of The Lewis Walpole Library, Yale University)

The annulment of the marriage with Mary Ann was finally decreed in 1828. Mary Ann and Alder married, emigrating to Canada, and some thirty years later she wrote a begging letter to the Fellowes–Wallop family, claiming her means were 'not sufficient to buy my daily bread'.

John Charles spent the last thirty years of his life freed from aristocratic commitments in Hurstbourne Park, living out his delusions as 'the King of Hampshire'. He died on 14 July 1853 at the age of 86 after some years of ill health. Despite planning his own 'black job' some thirty years earlier, his funeral was simple and although reported in local newspapers, most readers had apparently forgotten him and his trial. He was buried in an unmarked grave, seemingly without, as would have been the custom, any portrait having been painted during his life.

John Charles's contact with the house and estate at Eggesford was minimal, but he appeared to have a close relationship with Lady Catherine (née Fortescue), Countess to the 4th Earl, sharing relatively intimate letters with her about his life and its events (see Chapter 9). Ironically, however, court witness statements and letters about him, along with his own letters, were kept at Eggesford rather than in Hampshire, and so survived the fire at his Hampshire residence in 1891. As a result, his wretched and eventful story can be told today.

The 4th Earl: Newton Fellowes Wallop (1772–1854)

It is against this background of John Charles's life that Newton Fellowes would have been known in Devon as well as elsewhere. The in-depth press coverage of the Commission of Lunacy ensured the story was comprehensively and publicly documented in the 1820s.

Newton had inherited the Eggesford estate in 1792, taking the Fellowes name as his uncle Henry Arthur wished, although the will was contested. He also inherited a fortune, boasting to a relative, 'I came into ten thousand a year and £200,000 ready money, and didn't I make it fly.' He split his public life between Devon and Hampshire, elected four times as MP for Andover (1802–1820) and twice for North Devon in the 1830s. His Devon offices included Captain in the South Devon militia in 1795, and in East Devon in 1820.

He married firstly, on 30 January 1795, Frances (who died in 1819), daughter of Reverend Castell Sherard of Glatton, Huntingdonshire, having two sons and three daughters, and secondly, on 27 June 1820, Lady Catherine Fortescue, daughter of Hugh Fortescue, 1st Earl Fortescue, of Filleigh, Devon. His second marriage produced one son and three daughters.

Having waited most of his life, Newton Fellowes Wallop inherited the title of (4th) Earl of Portsmouth only in his last year, as his brother John Charles Wallop lived on in Hampshire until 1853. Of his nine children from his two marriages, the only son to survive was Isaac Newton Fellowes (1825–1891), who became 5th Earl in 1854 on his father's death.

During John Charles's last years, newspapers reported that his successor would be Newton Fellowes, 'one of the relics of a class nearly extinct, that of the "old English gentleman".'

Like his son, Isaac Newton Fellowes, horses and hounds were part of the appeal of a country estate for the 4th Earl, and he also showed much interest in farming, enjoying the outdoor life. He had a favourite coach 'of original design' which he himself drove from Eggesford to London.

V J Watney's account of the Wallop family history tells the same story as historian Eric R Delderfield (see Chapter 3):

'When he died, the hounds, out of respect for his memory, were stopped from hunting for some days. At their next meet they had an exceptionally great run; and the fox found safety by running to earth in the freshly disturbed family vault at Eggesford. The local suggestion was that his lordship's shade [ghost or spirit], wishing to give his friends good sport, had temporarily inhabited the body of the fox.'

Delderfield in *West Country Historic Houses And Their Families* (David & Charles, 1968) wrote of the 4th Earl as:

'one of the many famous sporting squires of the eighteenth century. Though a JP, he claimed, even if he did not exercise, almost feudal rights, and dispensed justice in the main hall of his house seated in an enormous chair made from elm trees grown on the estate and shaped exactly to fit his posterior. He was a great character, a fine horseman and a coachman of no mean ability.

A story is told that while the family were travelling abroad in their own four-horse coach, they stayed awhile in Paris, and when about to leave the city, found the elder son was missing. 'Never mind,' exclaimed his lordship, 'I'll soon get him,' and seizing the coach horn, he amazed everyone in the Place Vendôme by blowing long blasts until the missing member of the family hurriedly rejoined the party.'

Newton Fellowes was not to everyone's taste. The Reverend Sabine Baring-Gould, well-known Devon antiquarian and composer (amongst many other talents), while writing about vicar of Knowstone John Froude, related:

'… there were some with whom he could not associate. Such was the Hon. Newton Fellowes, afterwards Earl of Portsmouth, but at that time a young man with a love of sport, which he maintained to the last, and then without much token of brains, but he developed later. Him Froude detested, mainly because Newton Fellowes busied himself to improve the roads, so that, when at Eggesford, he could drive about the country in his four-in-hand; partly, also, because he was never invited to cross the threshold of Eggesford. He revenged himself with his tongue. One day he was dining at the ordinary at the George Hotel in Southmolton when Newton Fellowes was there as well. The latter was telling the assembled farmers how he had fallen over a hurdle in a race a few days earlier. "And as the mare rolled," added he, "I thought I had broken my neck," and he put his hands to his throat to emphasize the remark. Whereupon Froude, speaking loud enough to command attention, explained: "No, no, Newton, you will never break your neck; we have scriptural warrant for that."

"How so?"

"The Lord preserveth them that are simple."

The story stuck to Lord Portsmouth for life.'

Newton had stabling for some forty horses at Eggesford House, as well as significant dog kennels. The 4th Earl had a longstanding relationship with the Exeter-based iron foundry, Garton & Jarvis, later Garton & King, who produced metalwork for the stables and kennels. This relationship with Garton &

Newton Fellowes Wallop, afterwards Newton Fellowes, 4th Earl of Portsmouth

Painting by Richard Livesay

(Photo by Jonathan Crofts, by kind permission of Viscount Lymington)

King was continued by the 5th Earl, Isaac Newton Wallop, and the foundry's archives reveal he ordered in 1863 a Turkish Bath for the house, with an 'iron galvanised boiler and a copper bath some 6 foot long and 2 foot wide, japanned inside and a painted marble effect outside… with all the necessary pipework' at a cost in the region of £44 – equivalent to more than £4,600 in today's money. A large 'Arnott' Ventilator was included.

Other orders included iron rabbit wire fencing, galvanised iron to replace lead pipework, and iron fencing to cap a stone wall for the dog kennels. The archives suggest four compounds in the kennels, 14 feet in diameter, with a wooden door for each. In June 1864 a 6-foot wide 'Oxford Range' was installed in Eggesford's 'new wing' for £25, together with its wrought-iron galvanised boiler.

The equipping of the stables facilitated the evolution of the 'Portsmouth Latch' (see next page) – apparently a joint effort between the 5th Earl and the company to design a latch to prevent intelligent horses escaping their stable doors. Registered under the number 4169 at the Designs Office, a registry under the then Board of Trade (precursor of today's Intellectual Property Office), it was offered with different finishes and a version with lock and key. The Earl was keen to recommend the latch to his friends and acquaintances, including suggesting his grandfather Lord Fortescue at Filleigh as a customer. The Earl also purchased enamelled mangers and gratings for the stables, and a saddle room stove.

The bond between Devon and the 5th Earl went much deeper than his interest in the house and its fittings, and he was at his happiest there in later years, a fact marked by the enormous local attendance at his own 'black job', his funeral in 1891 (see Chapter 8.) The time of the 5th Earl was probably the Portsmouths' heyday in Devon. Meanwhile, the long-lasting legacy of both 4th and 5th Earls were the major improvements in transport links which they encouraged and helped to be built.

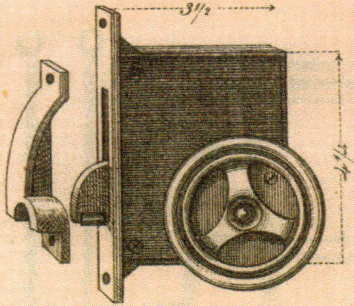

The Registered Portsmouth Latch.

	£	s.	d.
Japanned iron case, handles, and catch, gun metal wards, &c.	0	6	0
Japanned iron case, burnished brass handles and catch, gun metal wards, &c.	0	9	6
Brass case, burnished brass handles and catch, gun-metal wards, &c.	0	13	6

The Registered Portsmouth Lock and Latch combined.

	£	s.	d.
Japanned iron case, handles and catch, gun-metal wards, &c.	0	8	6
Japanned iron case, burnished brass handles and catch, gun metal wards, &c.	0	12	6
Brass case, burnished brass handles and catch, gun-metal wards, &c.	0	16	0

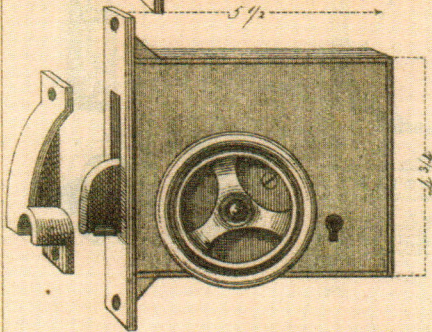

The Registered Portsmouth Lock and Latch combined.

Made in sets with master key.

	£	s.	d.
Japanned iron case, handles and catch	0	11	0
Japanned iron case, burnished brass handles and catch	0	15	0
Brass case, burnished brass handles and catch	0	18	6

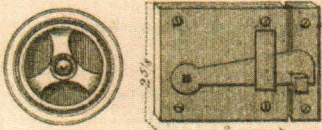

	£	s.	d.
Brass roller latch for cupboard doors	0	3	0
Ditto with brass flush handle	0	5	0

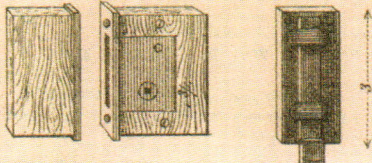

	£	s.	d.
Brass mortice latch with key for sliding doors	0	3	0
Self acting roller bolt for cupboard doors, with plate to fasten	0	2	0

Garton and King's catalogue showing the Portsmouth Latch, created with the 5th Earl of Portsmouth

(By kind permission of Ed Howell)

CHAPTER 7

TURNPIKE TO TARKA: ROADS AND RAILWAYS

An antique map of 1675 by John Ogilby shows the village of Chawleigh (known at that time as 'Chawley') on the main Exeter to Ilfracombe road. This road remained the main route from Exeter (with connections to London) until today's A377 was built as a turnpike road in the 1830s. Eggesford is not mentioned as it was not on this main route at the time, being down in the Taw valley. The turnpike road was followed by the North Devon Railway line alongside, which opened in the 1850s, and was eventually renamed the Tarka Line (after the otter in Henry Williamson's well-known book) in 1989.

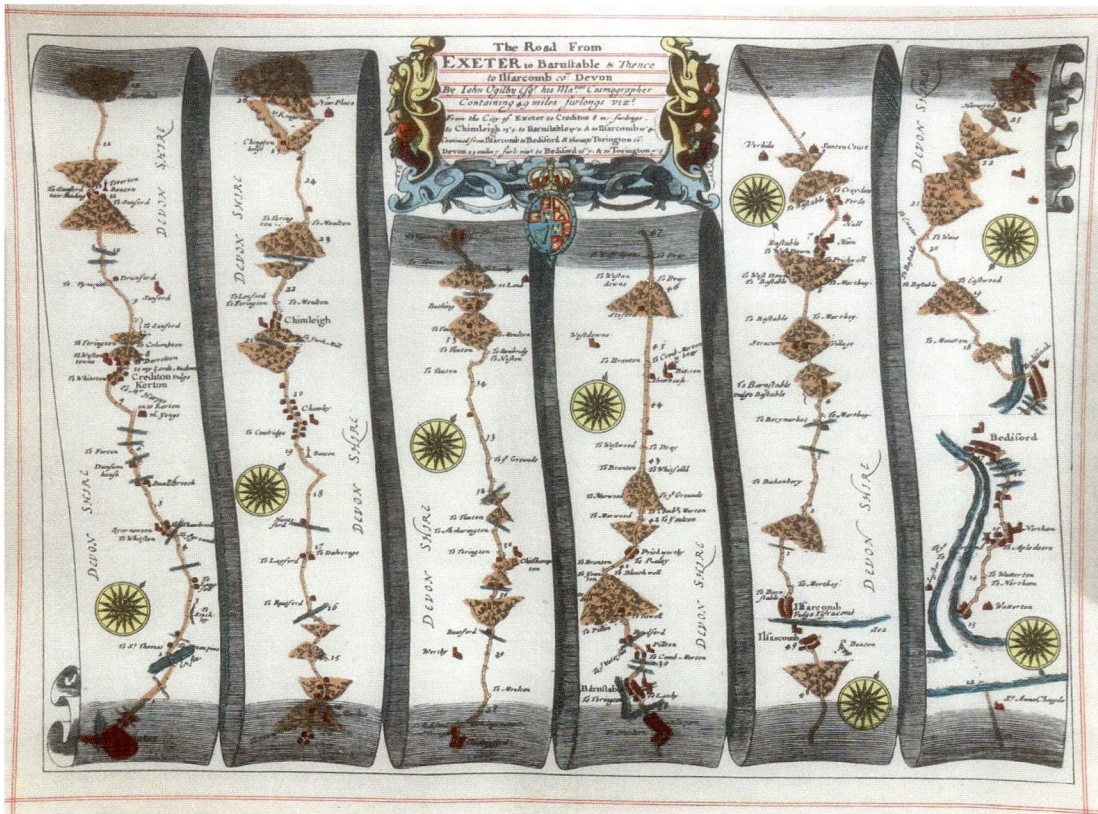

The antique ribbon map by John Ogilby (1675) shows the village of Chawleigh, marked as 'Chawley', on the main Exeter to Ilfracombe road – second ribbon from the left. The road, now the B3042 through Chawleigh, fell out of favour when the A377 turnpike road down in the valley was commissioned.

(Photo by Jonathan Crofts)

Legislation in the sixteenth century made local parishes responsible for maintenance of their roads, electing surveyors as overseers, and supported by larger landowners providing some labour and equipment. This was problematic, depending on the size of the parish and the extent of its roads, density of population, availability of labour, and local topography and geology which affected the quality of materials involved. Justice Trusts emerged in some areas in the seventeenth century, charging tolls, and run, like their successors the Turnpike Trusts, by local gentlemen and landowners.

The main road from Exeter to Barnstaple used to follow the ridgeway through what is now Mid and North Devon, so serving the hamlets and villages of Newbuildings, Morchard Bishop, Chawleigh and Chulmleigh. This helps explain the preponderance of coaching inns called The London Inn along the route (such as in Morchard Bishop and – later renamed – in Chawleigh). Once the turnpike road opened in the Taw valley, stagecoaches and then horse-drawn freight traffic started to use this faster route, with subsequent damage to the trade and populations of the settlements higher up.

Tolls were collected at tollhouses along these roads. In his gazetteer *Devon Tollhouses*, John Kanefsky explains the history of the Chawleigh Moortown and Chulmleigh Bridge tollhouses:

> 'These two buildings … are a puzzle. The first, on the NE side of the old (pre-1831) main Exeter-Barnstaple road, ¾ m NW of Chawleigh, near Moortown is "Turnpike Cottage", a plain thatched house of considerable age, now with eaves bedrooms. The Chawleigh toll gate was recorded in 1781 (Parliamentary Committee) and 1812 (EFP) and this is very likely a pre-existing cottage, given its position away from the road junction. Also shown on the 1" Greenwood Map …'

The Exeter Turnpike Trust's section of the road, south of Chawleigh, ceased to be turnpiked in 1831, but this gate remained active until at least 1846.' *The Toll-houses of North Devon* (Jenkinson & Taylor, 2010) provides further clarification:

> 'This two storey grade II listed traditional cob and thatch cottage … was once involved in the collection of tolls along what was originally the main Exeter to Barnstaple route prior to the 1830s… By 1871 it is recorded as 'Toll Bar' but was no longer being used by the Barnstaple Turnpike Trust.'

Kanefsky continues:

> '"Savourys Cottage" is a two storey rectangular cottage on the S side of Chulmleigh Bridge. The Chawleigh Tithe Map and Apportionment record this as a tollhouse (incorrectly, owned by the Tiverton Trust), and the Moortown tollhouse … is also shown but not named. A toll gate was marked near here on the 1809 OS map, although the more detailed Surveyor's Drawing shows this was further S, on the bend of the road. Neither house was included in the Trust's sale deeds of 1882. Possible explanations are that the collection point was moved between the two, perhaps more than once; or that the Moortown house was not a [tollhouse] and incorrectly marked by Greenwood; or the OS and Tithe Maps are in error – Savourys Cottage does not look to be an eighteenth century building…' [The listing shows many features still dating back to the 1600s.]

Jenkinson & Taylor add: '… it could have been operated by an independent Bridge Trust at this point on what was originally the main Exeter to Barnstaple road…'

There are other toll-houses nearby in the Chulmleigh area, and down in Chenson (near Eggesford) for the later turnpike road, today's A377.

Turnpike Trusts were empowered by Act of Parliament to take over main roads, establishing gates and tolls for maintenance and improvement, and in Devon the early 1750s saw the start of the transition from traditional packhorse trains as roads improved and four-wheeled carts became more practical. Turnpike Trusts were not for profit, but benefited the trustees more widely by improving roads for trade and personal travel.

The Earl of Portsmouth was a key protagonist in the development of the Exeter to Barnstaple turnpike road, which followed the Taw, Yeo and Creedy valleys. His name had many manifestations in local placenames: not to be confused with The Earl of Portsmouth pub in Chawleigh, the Taw valley featured the Portsmouth Arms pub in the hamlet of the same name, which is served by a station also known as Portsmouth Arms on today's Tarka (railway) Line.

In 1827–28 an Act of Parliament (7&8 Geo4 c14) laid out the creation of the new road along the 'Taw Vale', today's A377, and the two trusts involved agreed that it would meet at Eggesford Bridge: 'A new road through the valley of the Taw from New Bridge to Eggesford Bridge in the parish of Chawleigh, there to unite with the turnpike road about to be made by the trustees of the Exeter turnpike to lead to Exeter – the present Exeter Rd.'

The Barnstaple Turnpike Trust (1763–1880) eventually stretched as far as Bideford, Hatherleigh, Chulmleigh, South Molton and Ilfracombe. It oversaw the construction of the north-western end of the Taw Vale road, and the Exeter Turnpike Trust (1753–1884) saw the Exeter portion open in 1831. New branches to Torrington were made in 1835 and to South Molton in 1844.

In Chenson, Old Tollgate Cottage (or Old Toll Cottage or Old Toll House) originally belonged to the Earl of Portsmouth. He leased the cottage to the Exeter Turnpike Trust when it built the 'new road' until tolls were no longer collected. A metal toll bar blocking access across the road until travellers had paid their dues was inscribed simply 'Chenson'.

Tim Jenkinson's and Patrick Taylor's books examining *The Toll Houses of South Devon* and of *North Devon* provide more detail:

'An Act of Parliament was passed in 1826 (7 Geo 4 c25) to build a new road out of the city towards Barnstaple as far as Eggesford Bridge on what is today the A377. Built by the Exeter Turnpike Trust in c1829 as the road neared completion, this house was used to collect tolls in the hamlet of Chenson some 19 miles from the city. Of the traditional octagonal design built to the road edge, there is now a window inserted in the front wall where a door was once positioned with possibly a porch and gate extending across the road... A triangular Turnpike Trust milestone still stands beside the house showing a distance to Exeter that is recorded in Roman Numerals (XIX) and using the Medieval Latin name of EXON. The house retains its elegance on this once busy road that until 1989, upon completion of the North Devon Link Road, had been the main route from the city towards the town for around 170 years.

Census returns from the mid to late 19th Century reveal that in 1841 the house at 'Chenstone Gate' was occupied by forty-year-old Maria Sage and her seven daughters. By 1871 William Hunt and his wife Grace were employed by the Trust as 'toll-collectors' living at the house with their six children. The couple were still in residence at the 'Turnpike House' in 1881 but William is recorded as an 'agricultural labourer', a mere three years before the Exeter Trust disbanded and either dismantled or sold off all its toll-houses.'

The Earl of Portsmouth also built the bridge over the Taw at Chenson, for the benefit of farmers and others heading to and from the former Chenson Mill.

The demise of the turnpike trusts was largely caused by the success of the emerging steam railways as passengers migrated to these, which in turn reduced revenues for road repair. Customers became increasingly resentful of paying tolls as a result.

The North Devon railway line started with a takeover bid from the London and South Western Railway, hoping to spread its standard gauge railway into the southwest. Originally formed as the Taw Vale Railway and Dock Company, the North Devon Railway completed the line from Crediton to Barnstaple in 1854, connecting with trains from Exeter. The North Devon was broad gauge from 1854, mixed gauge to Bideford and Crediton from 1862 until 1876, until it was phased out in 1892. In 1865 the North Devon Railway amalgamated with the London and South Western Railway, which had reached Exeter Queen Street Station in 1860.

Eggesford Station on the Tarka Line in the Taw valley between Exeter and Barnstaple in 2022. The station today serves the communities of Eggesford, Chulmleigh, Chawleigh, and surrounding villages. Part of the building is now in private hands. It would once have housed the station keeper and his family.

(Photo by Jonathan Crofts)

EGGESFORD STATION, N. DEVON

An early postcard
of Eggesford Station

(By kind permission
of Ed Howell)

The Earls of Portsmouth were of course keen on what the railway offered to the inhabitants of Eggesford House. When the line was first built in 1854, the survey carried it across his Lordship's estate, and he insisted on the right to stop trains at the convenience of himself or his guests. Eggesford Station opened in that same year, together with a small goods yard. It was agreed that all passenger trains were to stop on signal, which might be requested by any person wanting to travel.

Not everyone was in favour of the Hon. Newton Fellowes and the new line though, particularly where the local pastime of hunting was involved. On 31 January 1852, prior to his accession as 4th Earl, *The Western Times* reported a lively exchange between his Lordship and a local yeoman:

'The 'Squire beguiled the time by roasting a worthy and wealthy yeoman of Coplestone. … we heard him [the yeoman], whilst admitting some of the benefits of the rail, expressing a regret that it would interfere with the excellent pastime of hare-hunting, which is a great solace to the yeomen of that district. The "'Squire does not care a dump for hare-hunting. He is the man for a fox", and this brought him down upon the stalwart yeoman, who had recently committed a breach of the honourable code of hunting, by digging a fox out of a drain on the 'Squire's property.

The yeoman defended himself stoutly. "They were out after a hare. The fox turned up, the dogs followed, the varmint bolted right away for the 'Squire's country, and took refuge in a drain. They had hunted an old fox before right into the same drain. One of the yeoman's tenants had lost twenty fowls, as they believed, by this very fox. Well! Were they to be done twice by the same scoundrelly varmint? No; if they were, might they never be found in the regions of bliss! They shoved a taryer into one end of the drain and placed a bag at the other – the fox walked into the bag and they walked off with the varmint. It turned out to be a terrible vixen, with her teeth worn to the very stumps by grinding down the bones of the Coplestone poultry" – for which the Eggesford foxes have a remarkably lively predilection. After bagging the varmint they turned her out the next day, and away she bolted, going right across the country, leading the Coplestone harriers a purty run of an hour and quarter, and astonishing some of the hackneys that had been more accustomed to the dodging work of hare-hunting.

The 'Squire now lectured them pretty tidily about observing the fair laws of sporting and draining their lands, and employing all the labour they could. "The best labourers were all leaving them for America, and unless the yeomen looked alive and improved their lands they would repent it." We make no apology for referring to this field preaching scene – which was held beneath the blue vault of Heaven and in the open light of day. The 'Squire was very shrewd and biting in his remarks, and the yeoman very sturdy and decided in his views of the matter. He turned on his heel and plainly told the 'Squire a bit of his mind about foxes that ate the Coplestone poultry!'

The local press presented the landowner's input into the new railway more favourably. A report in the *Exeter and Plymouth Gazette* on 7 February 1852 concluded the events of that day:

'The Hon. Newton Fellowes, who was received with a burst of cheering, said he felt honoured at the compliment paid him on the present occasion (that of selecting him to cut the first sod), and, furthermore, that this commencement he looked on as verifying the old saying, "When the work was began it was half done." He felt that he could congratulate those who were interested in the line in its being delayed; because, had it been commenced earlier, it would have caused a much larger sum in its construction, and, consequently, they would have derived a less advantage from it; but, owing to that fact, he had every reason to believe that this would be the cheapest constructed line in the Kingdom, and, at the same time, he hoped it would be beneficial to the neighbourhood.

He then alluded to the travelling by turnpike roads, and remarked that some years since, when he was desirous of getting the main road from Exeter to Barnstaple smoothed a little, and he came to Exeter to ask for assistance, he was met by Sir Thomas Acland [of the family from Killerton, Devon] with, "You are always bothering us, but you do nothing yourselves in the country."

He (the Hon. Newton Fellowes) had, however, put his shoulder to the wheel, in order that the men of North Devon might derive that advantage which was to be conferred on a neighbourhood by the construction of a railway. He had agreed to become responsible for £20,000, of which he had only been called upon for £5400; and of this one half had been repaid him in gold, and for the other half he was receiving five per cent., which was a better remuneration for investment of capital than he thought many of them were now obtaining. He doubted whether he should live to enjoy the privilege to which Mr. Sharland had alluded, but many he was then addressing, in all probability, would, and the neighbourhood generally, derive a corresponding benefit.'

Once in place, the new railway line and corresponding turnpike road shifted the focus away from the old ridgeway road, and the communities along it such as Chawleigh and Chulmleigh. It now linked Exeter Central station and Barnstaple, improving transport for commerce, the landed gentry, and those who could afford to travel.

The platform at Eggesford Station, circa Edwardian period

(Photo by kind permission of Henry Martin)

Whichever parties were originally responsible for the creation of the line, it has survived threats to its existence and continues to benefit the neighbourhood over 170 years later. On his succession to the title in 1854, the 5th Earl was well set to reap some of the rewards.

Eggesford - 2

CHAPTER 8

PATRONAGE AND POLITICS: THE FIFTH AND SIXTH EARLS

The 5th Earl: Isaac Newton Wallop (1825–91)

'A thorough country gentleman of the old school, with the full knowledge of the duties and obligations of his position, Lord Portsmouth was greatly missed. A practical farmer and breeder, a "farmer's friend" in the best sense of that sometimes abused word, his sphere of action was in the home life. In the bosom of his family, among his friends and tenants, on his hunter at the head of his hounds, he was seen in the role he probably loved best. He lived all his life among his own people at his country places, where he dispensed a magnificent hospitality. For London or public life he had no taste or liking; but he built both churches and schools, was a broad-minded man with the most genial nature, and left behind a name that is never mentioned without affection and respect.'

So was the 5th Earl of Portsmouth described in the 1908 edition of *British Sport and Sportsmen*, and his country-loving sentiments appear to have been supported by his wife the 5th Countess, originally Eveline Alicia Juliana Herbert, daughter of the 3rd Earl of Carnarvon, Henry Herbert, whose family seat was Highclere Castle in Berkshire.

Isaac Newton Wallop,
5th Earl of Portsmouth

Painting by
Sir Francis Grant

(Photo by Jonathan
Crofts, by kind
permission of
Viscount Lymington)

The 5th Earl, who succeeded to the earldom in 1854, went back to the family name of Wallop. A great huntsman, he owned racehorses, and was Master of Eggesford Hounds. Hurstbourne Park, close to Highclere Castle, became the family home initially. The Countess was known to enjoy entertaining, and there are many records of social engagements at Eggesford and in Hampshire.

Historian Eric R Delderfield adds colour to the daily life of the 5th Earl's nineteenth-century household: 'Of a house staff of twenty-two, two were kept fully occupied in trimming, lighting and attending to all the lamps in the establishment. Produce was carried to the house daily by pannier donkeys from three acres of kitchen gardens in the valley a mile away.'

Edited by John Lambert, the *Return of Owners of Land in England and Wales* (1875) listed the results of the first survey (two years earlier) of property interests across the nation since the Domesday Book. It highlights the scale of the Portsmouth land holdings, seventh largest in Devon as a whole, compared here with the other recorded landowners in Chawleigh:

		a.	r.	p.	Gross est. rental
Reed, Charles	Chawleigh	112	3	6	£100.
Reed, Edward	Chawleigh	522	-	36	£1,635. 10. -
Cawsey, M.A. (Reps of)	Chawleigh	1	-	38	£12. 15. -
Charity, Trustees of	Chawleigh	26	3	14	£74. 2. -
Portsmouth, Earl of	Eggesford	16,414	1	5	£11,399. 10. -
Reed, Richard	Chawleigh	140	1	3	£107. 5. -
Sanders, William	Chawleigh	16	3	14	£44. 4. -
Webber, John	Chawleigh	38	2	18	£123. 3. -

Family commitments extended to nephews and nieces: there is a connection with the William-Powlett family from Cadhay, the Tudor manor house near Ottery St Mary in East Devon. The William-Powletts bought Cadhay in 1935, having leased it originally. Major Barton Newton Wallop William-Powlett, who later married Emily Charlotte Tyndall Reibey, had spent his childhood in the 1880s at Eggesford House with his uncle, the Earl of Portsmouth, having been orphaned at the age of twelve.

Wider social responsibilities included support for the local community, as the *Devon Weekly Times* reported on 14 January 1870: 'The Chawleigh club and reading institute, under the patronage and warm support of the Earl and Countess of Portsmouth, is in a flourishing condition. In connection with the institute a choir has been formed, and at Christmas the singers sang several carols, etc., at Eggesford House, and various other places. Last Wednesday they, with other friends, enjoyed a successful cup and supper together at the reading room.'

Chawleigh Board School children were the recipients of the Portsmouth's largesse in February 1881, lauded by the *Devon Weekly Times*, being 'examined by the Rev. W.W. Howard, assisted by Mr. W. Turner. The children acquitted themselves well, and a bountiful tea was supplied thanks to the liberality of the Countess of Portsmouth. Her ladyship had provided a number of valuable presents for the children, who mustered 120. Mr. G. W. Challis, the master, distributed the presents.'

In February 1897 the *Chulmleigh Deanery Magazine* reports the generosity of the Earl and Countess: 'The Earl of Portsmouth has kindly sent his usual subscription of £12 to the Chawleigh and Cheldon Clothing Club which now numbers 74 depositors. The Dowager Countess of Portsmouth has also again most kindly thought of her Chawleigh old folk, and brightened many a home by her welcome presents.'

On 27 December 1889 the *Devon and Exeter Gazette* reported that 'the Countess of Portsmouth forwarded her usual Christmas presents for the aged and poor of this parish, when over 20 received valuable articles of winter clothing, tea and sugar.' And, 'On St. Thomas's Day, the Rector, the Rev. J. V. Tanner, assisted by Mr. Edmund Ford (Nethercott) attended the school and duly distributed the charities known as Aram's Gift of Money and Webber's Gift of Bread' (for the origin of these gifts, see Chapter 19).

Assuming this was repeated across the estate, it confirms that the sense of noblesse oblige (privilege entails responsibility) continued in the Portsmouths' approach to their estate workers and tenants, although political thinking of the time was already turning against people of great wealth and property, even those who felt obliged to help others less fortunate than themselves. The Great Fire of Chawleigh in 1869 (see Chapter 11) brought the 5th Earl's social responsibilities to the fore.

Despite this, the 5th Earl was perhaps best remembered for his passion for hunting, along with other local characters such as Parson John (Jack) Russell, who, according to Lapford local historian David Garton, had his 'own pack of hounds "of the purest blood and first-class character" [which] would wait patiently at the back of the nave, whilst their master preached to an almost empty church, before leaving on a day's hunt.'

Isaac Newton Wallop, 5th Earl of Portsmouth, by Frederick Sargent, pencil, 1870s

(© National Portrait Gallery, London)

Hunting today brings out mixed emotions, but in 2021 *Horse & Hound* described the contemporary Eggesford Hunt, echoing how it must have seemed in the time of the 5th Earl:

'The Eggesford is the largest hunting country in Devon, fitting snugly between Dartmoor and Exmoor in north and mid Devon. The characteristic patchwork profile encompasses up to 700 livestock farms. It is chocolate-box pretty: emerald green rolling hills, deep valleys studded with deciduous woodland harbouring streams and rivers, and hedges thick with brambles. Little has changed in centuries; only now its ubiquitous Devon banks are girdled with wire. This is an enviable old-fashioned hunting country with just the one A-road and a single railway line.'

The 5th Earl was Master of the Hunt for nearly forty years, and in 1890, just a year before his death, the Hunt became subscription based, with Major De Freville of Wembworthy as the new Master. The colourful event to mark the Earl's retirement was described by a journalist:

'With Lord Portsmouth's usual generosity, it was "open house" at Eggesford on Saturday. Breakfast was laid in the gallery, to which all comers were invited. ... His Lordship, in pink, with the Countess of Portsmouth, received a good many of the visitors in the hall. ... The first visitors to arrive were Major De Freville (in scarlet), Mrs De Freville, Miss and Master Humphrey De Freville. Others speedily followed.

After breakfast the field assembled in front of the house. On the entrance steps stood the Earl and Countess, surrounded by numerous friends ... Charlie Littleworth had brought down his 18½ couple of hounds, all looking fit for anything; a large number of farmers, mounted, made a suitable background, the whole picture being completed by a line of carriages, and on the slopes were groups of onlookers from all the country round. A moment of stillness – even the hounds obeying – and the scene was photographed by Mr. Saunders, of Winkleigh, the company present at the time numbering about 300, of whom nearly 200 were mounted.'

The warm wishes expressed and applauded by the large assembly at the time, of 'our feelings, wishes, and hopes for his lordship's future happiness and health' were dashed only eleven months later. A newspaper cutting commenting on the 5th Earl's sudden death in 1891 confirmed his love of country sports and country life, but also sang the praises of this accessible and respected man:

'By the death of the Earl of Portsmouth one of the most prominent and popular men in the West of England has been removed. Although born into high rank he was beloved by the humblest peasant as he was respected by the most exalted. Everyone who knew him, and no one was better known in the county, spoke of him in terms of the highest praise. He was the ideal of the peasantry in the neighbourhood of Eggesford. "There is not a man in the district who would not cheerfully do anything for his lordship," remarked one of the oldest inhabitants at Chulmleigh a few months ago, and I verily believe they would have done so.'

Unlike his successor the sixth Earl, who became a government minister, the journalist described him as:

'an ardent politician, but I don't think that latterly he had much love for politics. As a Liberal he never allowed his partisanship to interfere with his friendships. It was the same when he seceded from the Liberal Party on the Home Rule question. He differed from his friends, but he did not discard their friendship. The pursuits of the country gentleman suited his tastes better than the excitement any enmity engendered by the strife of political parties.

He was an accomplished sportsman, the *beau ideal* of a British fox hunter, and the full cry of the merrie Eggesford pack of hounds was to his ears the sweetest music. In his younger days he was a straight rider across country; a more genial Master of Hounds there could not be, and when advancing age obliged him to give up the hounds quite recently the unavoidable step was regretted by the whole district. ...

He associated himself heartily in many matters connected with the public life of North Devon. No man was more sincerely welcomed at an agriculturists' dinner, at the horse shows, where he frequently officiated as a judge, or the village gatherings of various kinds than the noble figure which has just passed away. The inhabitants of the northern part of the shire will be wanting in their duty if they do not raise some memorial to one of the best and kindliest of men.'

Another newspaper echoed these sentiments, reporting that the Eggesford Rector, Reverend A M Owen, referred 'in feeling and sympathetic terms to the death of Lord Portsmouth, speaking of his warm-heartedness, his consideration as a landlord, and the good name he bore in Devonshire among all classes…. The deceased enjoyed a good reputation in dealing with his tenants, and was one of the first owners of the soil in Devonshire who reduced the rents of his tenantry during the time of the great agricultural depression [1873–1896].'

The newspaper went on to report his role in public life in some detail:

'Originally a member of the old Quarter Sessions, taking an active part in the discharge of the county business, when the Local Government Act was passed which virtually annulled that body, the Earl sought the suffrages of the electors to become a member of the newly-created County Council, and was elected to a seat without opposition. When from among the body of County Councillors the first batch of Aldermen was created Lord Portsmouth was proposed, and as the result of the poll he came well out towards the top, and was declared duly elected an Alderman. Although speaking in public with some hesitancy, the noble Earl was always listened to in debate as having something to say which was worth listening to, and throughout his life he enjoyed the reputation of being a sound man of business. ... The noble Earl was a Justice of the Peace for the County, and sat in his judicial capacity at the sessions court in Southmolton.'

Another column commented, possibly with the slightly obsequious Victorian view of the aristocracy, but clearly in praise of the Earl:

'… for over thirty years [he] had taken a kind and unvarying interest in the welfare of the people of the West, and had become associated in most of the important movements of our time for the material and moral improvement of his neighbours. It is a great art to live well, and to win as Lord Portsmouth did the unbounded esteem of his fellow men, and the affection and devotion of people of all ranks with which the pursuit of business, or his genial and sympathetic spirit, brought him into contact.'

The same column gave more detail of his political life:

'He succeeded to his father, Newton Fellowes, who had heartily joined in promoting the Parliamentary Reform of 1832. Liberal by inheritance and conviction, the late Earl rendered the highest possible service to his party in Devonshire, where he was early recognised as its Leader, and led it to victory in many important contests. Our files contain countless evidences of the vigour and tact which the Earl displayed in watching over the interests of his party, one of the latest instances being the ardour with which he advocated the extension of the franchise in the rural districts. Few will have forgotten his appearance on one of the platforms in St. James' Church-field, in a great county demonstration in support of Household Suffrage [giving the vote to one householder from each household, although not yet to each adult] in the counties.

His Lordship was notable for the directness and plainness of his style. He was always found on the practical side of his subject. Whether in public social life, in private benevolence, in the sporting field, in the advocacy of Education, in the local self-government of the County, or in the discharge of his duties as a Justice of the Peace and the lord of a vast domain, he was for direct ways and practical ends, and his active life bears witness to the honest and thorough character of his daily work.'

Other newspaper accounts included his refusal of recognition for his political deeds:

'The 5th Earl was a Liberal politically, and was an Irish landowner, of the Enniscorthy estates, as well as owning lands in Devon and Hampshire. He continued his father's policy giving leasehold tenants the right to pass farms onto successors of their choice, which was made law in the 1870 Irish Land Bill. Rewarded for his support by prime minister Gladstone, who offered him the rank of marquis, and the Order of the Garter, he declined both, maintaining he did not support all of Gladstone's Irish policies, and the Garter was "beyond his merits".'

There is a moving account of his funeral:

'... the general affection and esteem in which the noble Earl was held was evinced by the attendance of a large number of people of all classes of society, literally from the peer to the present, the concourse numbering not far short of 2,000 people. ... an outer coffin ... was made from oak growing on the estate at Eggesford ... Mr. G. Vickery (Eggesford estate) and Mr. T. Hobbs (Hurstbourne) headed the procession, which was led by about 50 workmen on the estate and the following tenantry...

... during the reading of a portion of the service by the Rev. C. Stone he became very much affected, and did not resume for some seconds. Many of those in and around the church were also moved to tears as the last obsequies were being observed.

... Special train arrangements were made by Mr. White, Divisional Superintendent of the London and South Western Railway, for the convenience of passengers... At North Tawton signs of mourning were very general. A large number of inhabitants attended the funeral, and at home the shops were closed, blinds drawn, and all business suspended during the time of the funeral. About 1 o'clock the ringers gave a muffled peal on the bells of the parish church of St. Peter.'

Tragedy struck the family's residences at around this time, when the Portsmouth seat at Hurstbourne Park in Hampshire was destroyed by fire in January 1891, and it was left to the 6th Earl, Newton Wallop, and his wife Beatrice (née Pease) to rebuild it. They had been living there since their marriage in 1885, and moved into the newly rebuilt house in 1896. A legacy of financial problems now beset the family as they moved into the new century.

Son of the 5th Earl, Viscount Lymington, later known as Newton Wallop, who became 6th Earl of Portsmouth ('Statesmen. No. 436.') by Sir Leslie Ward

Chromolithograph, published in *Vanity Fair*, 13 November 1880

(© National Portrait Gallery, London)

The 6th Earl: Newton Wallop (1856–1917)

Newton was educated at Balliol College, Oxford, where he was President of the Oxford Union for a term, although it was whispered that his speeches were written by his mother. As the eldest son of the 5th Earl's twelve children, he was initially known as Viscount Lymington, and was elected as Member for Barnstaple at a by-election in February 1880, a seat he held until 1885. The Redistribution of Seats Act of that year reduced Barnstable constituencies down to one. At the 1885 general election, he stood as MP for South Molton and held the seat until he became Earl in 1891.

The 6th Earl carried on the Liberal tradition and was the most prominent politician of the Portsmouth family in national terms. In 1891 he took his seat in the Lords, acquiring an influential group of associates. Ten years later, instead of a summer in Devon, Newton joined a shooting party at Guisachan near Inverness in Scotland hosted by its then owner, the 2nd Lord Tweedmouth. Lord Tweedmouth's father, the 1st Baron, is revered as the breeder of the first golden retrievers, at the estate. Due to financial difficulties, Lord Tweedmouth sold Guisachan to Lord Portsmouth in 1905.

Newton Wallop,
6th Earl of Portsmouth,

bromide print by
Walter Stoneman, 1917

(© National Portrait
Gallery, London)

Other promising politicians attended the 1901 shooting party: a young Winston Churchill, Richard Haldane, and Sir Edward Grey. Grey's famous remark in 1914, 'The lamps are going out all over Europe, we shall not see them lit again in our life-time', presaged the events of the Great War, which not only killed millions but changed British society and the future of country estates such as Eggesford for ever.

In the 1905–08 government led by the Liberal Sir Henry Campbell-Bannerman, the 6th Earl was appointed as Under-Secretary of State for War to Richard Haldane, alongside Lord Tweedmouth as First Sea Lord and Sir Edward Grey as Foreign Secretary (a post he held through to the First World War). Their leader Campbell-Bannerman was the first politician to be officially designated as 'Prime Minister'. In these years before the First World War, the Liberal campaign was running on issues including free trade, Irish Home Rule and the improvement of social conditions. Change was in the air for landed families, and Newton went on to sell most of his estates in Ireland, shortly after starting to dismantle the Eggesford estate (see Chapter 22). His estate in Scotland, Guisachan, with its attractive Victorian house close to the mountains, continued in the family's ownership until 1935. Today it lies in ruins but is home to the Friends of Guisachan, celebrating the history of the golden retriever.

In his prime, Newton rejoiced in a flaming red beard and mane of hair to match, and became known as 'The Red Earl', cartooned by Spy for *Vanity Fair* magazine and elsewhere. Also caricatured was his predilection for motor vehicles, which at the time were still rare in rural areas. Local historian David Garton from the nearby village of Lapford has compiled a short history of Newton's exploits in his cars, extending over Devon, Hampshire and Scotland.

The Red Earl introduced his car to Eggesford and district in spring 1901, with *The Western Times* reporting: 'Lord Portsmouth, had a spin in his coach without any horses … his head was wrapped up as if he had toothache, but that was only to keep off the dust… Times change … We must change with them!'

THE EARL OF PORTSMOUTH'S NEW 6-CYLINDER NAPIER
Lord Portsmouth is a keen motorist, and often travels by car between Eggesford House in Devonshire and Hurstbourne Park in Hampshire.

Newspaper coverage of the 6th Earl's passion for motoring, *The Sheffield Independent*, 13 December 1905

Thanks to David Garton, Lapford History website (lapfordhistory.co.uk/lord-portsmouth-motoring)

By 1906, Newton was driving a six-cylinder Napier which he brought to Devon, reported by *The Western Times* as the only person to have driven a car locally, except for Albert Chevalier, a music hall star en route to perform in Barnstaple. He later acquired a Daimler (see Chapter 22).

As a politician on Hampshire County Council and in Westminster, Newton supported calls for the introduction of driving licences, speed signs in villages, and fines for driving without due care. Despite his interest in road safety, the 1903 death of a man running out ahead of his car, and his confronting a policeman who stopped him for speeding in 1905 (24mph instead of the 20mph limit), produced negative press

The 6th Earl's Napier 'fast car' in front of Eggesford House, early 1900s

(Photo by kind permission of Ed Howell)

reports. Two years later his butler died in a motoring accident on his Guisachan estate (Newton was not involved but the press picked up the story nonetheless).

Politics was not ultimately to be the high point of Newton's life, his success eventually undone by new prime minister Herbert Asquith in 1908, his one-time tutor. *The Life of Herbert Henry Asquith* (J A Spender and Cyril Asquith, Hutchinson & Co., 1938) contains an entertaining account of the later prime minister's early years with the Portsmouth family:

'...in the autumn and early winter of 1874 ... [he] was retained to coach Lord Lymington, the eldest son of the Earl of Portsmouth, who was finishing with Eton and preparing for Oxford. This involved three months' residence with the Portsmouth family, partly at Hurstbourne Park in Hampshire, and partly at Eggesford Place [House]. This last was an attractive country house in North Devon... He has testified in *Memories and Reflections* to the kindness and consideration of his hosts and to his enjoyment of an entirely new milieu. Among those whom he met there, in addition to Lord Carnarvon, were Lord Houghton and the poet, William Johnson Cory, afterwards a Hampstead neighbour and intimate companion. Lord Portsmouth was a strong, though, unlike his son, not a politically active Liberal. Asquith seems nevertheless to have attended at least one political meeting, of which he writes to his sister Eva: "I sent you the *Western Times* on Saturday with an account of my meeting at North Taunton in which the speeches are fairly well reported. The gathering took the form of a luncheon with the usual accompaniment of indigestible food and vinegary wine. Lord Houghton made a very effective speech... Lymington came out with some elaborate periods on the Press which were much applauded: his manner and delivery are extremely good and if he can compass a few ideas he ought to make a successful speaker."'

Despite his praise thirty years earlier for Lymington, later the 6th Earl, it was Asquith who excluded him from a ministerial role on becoming PM in 1908, after a disappointing performance in the House on the new Territorial and Reserve Forces Act of 1907. Portsmouth subsequently became a regular critic of the government from his seat in the House of Lords.

The Western Times (3 May 1909) reported on the Earl's passion for that military subject in a speech a

'The Red Earl', also known as 'The Demon', published in *Vanity Fair* magazine, 28 August 1907

('Men of the Day. No. 1080. "The Demon."') by Sir Leslie Ward, chromolithograph, also available in the National Portrait Gallery, London

(Photo by Jonathan Crofts)

"The Demon."

(The Earl of Portsmouth).

year later: 'We are no longer immune from the possibility of invasion ... all classes of manhood in this country should be asked, I might say compelled, to take a share of defence in the interests of the country...' This time he was talking to a receptive audience at the Lapford Rifle Club in Devon, rather than to a national assembly, however: not perhaps what he would have preferred.

He died in December 1917 at Whitchurch, Hampshire, aged 61, and was succeeded in the earldom by his younger brother, John. Newton's obituary in *The Times* on 5 December 1917 lauded his political achievements in particular, and he appeared to be ahead of his time in his attitudes regarding the House of Lords:

'As Lord Lymington he was elected Liberal member for Barnstaple in 1880, and for North Devon in 1885. In the following year he was returned for North Devon as a Liberal-Unionist, and sat for that division until he became a peer. Having rejoined the Liberal Party, he was appointed by Sir Henry Campbell-Bannerman in 1905 to be parliamentary Under-Secretary for War, and held the post until 1908. He was an Ecclesiastical Commissioner for England, Chairman of the Council of the Salmon Trout Committee, 1912, Warden of the Fishmongers' Company, and hon. treasurer of the Russia Society.

The late peer was a large landowner, his estates at one time comprising 66,000 acres. [The main part of] His Eggesford estate in North Devon, extending to 3,300 acres, was offered for sale by auction in 1914, and many parts of it were acquired by tenants, the total realized being nearly £50,000. During the House of Lords controversy he declared himself (in 1909) in favour of an independent elective second chamber and the voluntary surrender by the peers of their hereditary privileges.'

On 11 April 1918, the *North Devon Journal* reported his will, revealing his commitment to many of his staff, some of whom would have been connected with the household all their lives:

'The testator gives £5 000 and such of the household effects as shall not be made heirlooms, to his wife; £1 000 to Sir George Cave; £1 500 to E. S. Freeland; £1 000 each to his two brothers, and to his nephew Gerard; £500 each to his sisters, £2 000 a year to his brother who shall succeed to the title; £500 to his agent, Mr Tancock; £300 to his butler, Henry Peck, £300 to his late valet, William Piercey; an annuity of £60 to his housekeeper, Lucy Vickery; £200 each to his head keeper, gardener and coachman; £200 to his chauffeur.

All his real estate in England, Scotland and Ireland, and the residue of the personal property he leaves in trust for his wife during widowhood, with remainder in trust for his first or other sons, with remainder to his eldest or other daughters, and on failure of issue, with remainder to his nephews, Gerard Vernon Wallop and Oliver Malcolm Wallop, with various remainders over.'

Sadly Newton and Beatrice had no children, although their marriage was regarded as happy, and Beatrice lived on until 1935, residing at Hurstbourne Park except for her visits to Guisachan, which was finally sold off on her death. Despite Britain's patriarchal social norms in the past, the turn of the twentieth century heralded a turning point for women, and the influence of the Portsmouth Countesses could only grow.

CHAPTER 9

LITERATURE, ACTIVISM, AND CHARITY: THE COUNTESSES

The tale of John Charles, 3rd Earl of Portsmouth (see Chapter 6), has painted a picture of his mother Urania Fellowes, whose marriage to the 2nd Earl brought the Eggesford estate into the Wallop family and originated the connection with the Fellowes. Urania was unable to find a 'cure' for John Charles's mental condition and he was treated differently from how his brothers were educated and brought up.

Later marriages in the dynasty brought closer links with Devon landholding families as well as with the world of English literature and politics, and established leading female characters of the Portsmouth family in a society still largely dominated by men.

Urania Fellowes, wife of the 2nd Earl of Portsmouth

Painting by J Sanders

(Photo by Jonathan Crofts, by kind permission of Viscount Lymington)

Lady Catherine Fortescue (1786–1854), Countess to the 4th Earl

Lady Catherine Fortescue, the daughter of Hugh Fortescue (1st Earl Fortescue) of the established Devon family from Castle Hill, Filleigh, and of Hester Grenville, daughter and sister of two prime ministers, was the second wife of Newton Fellowes, who became 4th Earl of Portsmouth in 1853. Catherine suffered from deafness and had limited speech, but could lip-read and sign. She and Newton were reported to be lifelong friends, and he proposed soon after the death of his first wife, Frances Sherard (1771–1819). Their marriage was celebrated in 1820.

One descendant remembered Catherine as 'quite deaf but she was by no means dumb', since a Frenchman had taught her to 'speak and to read the motions of the throat and lips'. While she communicated with a 'curious, deep voice', her children 'spoke to her on their fingers, which her husband never learnt to do'.

They had four children, three daughters and Isaac Newton Fellowes, who was later to become 5th Earl. Her deafness 'cut her off very much' and, limited in her relationships with the rest of the family, she would often stay in Eggesford while Newton took the children to

London; nevertheless she was committed to their education and provided material for them on diverse subjects such as chemistry and the perceived duties of women. Clearly a woman of great personal warmth, Catherine's relationships with her stepson, Henry Arthur, by Newton's first marriage, and with her brother-in-law, John Charles, the 3rd Earl (see Chapter 6), were positive and affectionate. Needlework and decorating the new house occupied her, and one legacy she left for Eggesford was a new terrace garden, on which she engaged gardeners to work while Newton was out, dismissing them as soon as his carriage returned; Newton appeared to feign ignorance, perhaps through indulgence towards his wife.

Catherine was closely involved with the rebuilding of Eggesford House when she and Newton commissioned architect Thomas Lee (1794–1834) from Barnstaple. Lee was first known for his design of the Wellington Memorial in Somerset, and designed Arlington Court for the Chichester family in North Devon, his life sadly cut short by drowning off Mortehoe on the North Devon coast. He had previously worked for Catherine's father, Earl Fortescue. Lee's 1822 plans for Eggesford were 'an early example in Devon of the embattled Tudor Gothic style', according to later sales particulars from 1991, although the new house was not built until 1828.

Nineteenth-century plans still exist for a house roughly on the site of the first grand dwelling at Eggesford, the one rebuilt by the Chichesters (see Chapter 3), which may have been the initial conception, developed by Catherine, Newton and Lee. These plans were addressed to Lady Catherine Fellowes and show a neo-classical house by the River Taw, so large it encompassed the parish church, All Saints.

In 1822 the Fellowes moved into Heywood Barton, higher up the valley, to allow the rebuilding to commence. But by the time the family had overcome the challenges of the 'lunacy' trial of John Charles,

Eggesford House, heart of the original Eggesford estate, drawn by Alexander Lydon for *A Series of Picturesque Views of Seats of Noblemen and Gentlemen of Great Britain and Ireland*, 1864–1880, volume 6

(Photo by kind permission of Ed Howell)

3rd Earl, time had moved on, and they decided to build on the Heywood Barton site instead of the first Eggesford House by the church (see Chapter 3.)

Although the Lunacy Commission overshadowed his relationship with Newton (as the latter had supported him being declared a lunatic), John Charles could write to family outsider Catherine without that history directly in mind. As Elizabeth Foyster observed of John Charles in *The King of Hampshire*: 'Perhaps Portsmouth felt an affinity for this woman whose disability distanced her from society and confined her to the home.' He initially used his letters to her to address financial and related matters with his brother Newton, but over time his letters became more relaxed and affectionate, and when Newton was ill he encouraged her to 'keep up your spirits as much as possible', signing off (with his usual disregard for punctuation):

I shall be very happy to hear from you as it will give me pleasure to hear from one who loves me as yourself has always professed to do so when you used to be here which I shall never forget it.

I am my Dear Catherine

yours et al

Portsmouth

With our best Love and regards to Newton and your Family wishing him better health

Newton recovered fully, and John Charles's letters to Catherine were passed to him in case they indicated anything associated with the writer's presumed 'insanity'. His letter of 2 February 1851 was one such startling missive:

My dearest Catherine

I beg leave to inform you of our intention of being married to Miss C. Norton and niece of mine a sister of Lord Grantley she is coming down here tomorrow morning for the occasion…

… and on Tuesday next there will be a grand review to take place by all the regiments given to me by the Duke of Wellington which will be a grand thing to take place here in this park on Tuesday next of the Surrey Militia regiment of both horse and foot soldiers under command of me and the rest of the officers in Hants and Surrey… which will be a grand sight here of my own given to me by Lord Grantley… if the weather should be fine it will be a grand sight in memory of this happy day which I hope will take place tomorrow to this very nice and affectionate young Lady Miss Norton a very nice young Lady she is certainly and very agreeable one I must say she is.

This fantasy-laden correspondence would presumably have seemed entirely logical in John Charles's mind, even though English law at the time prevented a declared lunatic from taking up holy matrimony. Given his brother John Charles's history, Newton would have been aware, however, that a supposedly willing and youthful bride, combined with a convenient lack of legal knowledge in a clergyman, could once again undermine the delicate situation vis-à-vis family and inheritance. Alarm bells would have been ringing.

Following many years of travel back and forth between the Portsmouth estates, Newton was now seventy-eight, suffering from gout and still shocked at the sad death of his son and heir by his first marriage four years earlier: Henry Arthur, a bachelor, had looked after his uncle John Charles at Hurstbourne in Hampshire for years, and his body was brought to Eggesford for burial. At the funeral Newton had kept Henry Arthur's role with the family 'lunatic' quiet.

On the news of John Charles's latest wedding plans, it was therefore Isaac Newton, Newton's son with Catherine, who went to Hurstbourne to pick up the pieces.

Catherine remained the conduit for communication between the two senior brothers, even as John Charles's thoughts became increasingly disconnected: 'I am very much obliged to you for allowing your Son to come up from Eggesford on my wedding which I hope will be soon', then rambling on about his headaches and the impact of the weather on farming.

Lady Eveline Herbert, Countess of Portsmouth, wife of the 5th Earl

Painting by Henry Tanworth Wells

(Photo by Jonathan Crofts, by kind permission of Viscount Lymington)

Soon after, however, Isaac Newton and John Charles fell out over commissioning and paying for repairs to Hurstbourne and John Charles resumed his, now angry, letters directly to his brother Newton: 'I shall never part with this house and premises as long as I live… I will never let your son have it at all to come to it…'

John Charles wrote three more letters to Catherine at Eggesford, but none to Newton. On 27 June 1852 he remembered his brother's 80th birthday: 'I must most sincerely congratulate Newton on his Birthday which took place yesterday in his 80 year of his age. I hope he will continue and enjoy the day for many years to come and yourself.' He thanked Catherine for her long letter and continued about weather and farming, as usual. As Elizabeth Foyster remarked: 'This was his world now, and Catherine was the only one whom he privileged with an insight into it.'

Eveline Alicia Juliana Herbert (1834–1906), Countess to the 5th Earl

Eveline Alicia Juliana Herbert was the daughter of Henry Herbert, 3rd Earl of Carnarvon and his wife Henrietta of Highclere Castle in Berkshire. On 15 February 1855 she married Isaac Newton Wallop who became the 5th Earl of Portsmouth. She and Isaac had twelve children including another Newton, who succeeded to the title of Earl of Portsmouth on his father's death in 1891.

The Devon History Society is one of many sources for the life of Eveline, Countess of Portsmouth, who lived at Eggesford in the mid- and late nineteenth century: she was an early Devon suffrage activist, and signed a petition for the women's vote in 1892. Perhaps because more is recorded about her, and unlike Catherine she was not hindered by disability, she appears to have been the most active and prolific of the Eggesford Countesses in social, literary and political circles.

The petition she signed was presented to the Houses of Parliament by members of the women's suffrage movement. In the papers of one leader, Mrs Millicent Garrett Fawcett, Eveline's accompanying letter stated that she 'gladly signs the enclosed' (Manchester Libraries, Information and Archives).

Only twenty-two years earlier, The Married Women's Property Act of December 1870 had given married women the right to own their own property and money. And two years following the petition, in December 1894, Parliament passed The Local Government Act, enabling married and single women to vote in county and borough council elections. In 1918, the Representation of the People Act extended the national vote to women over thirty meeting certain property qualifications (as well as to all men over twenty-one). But it was not until July 1928 that The Representation of the People Act was passed, allowing everyone over the age of twenty-one to vote.

Eveline's other interests included women's education and antivivisection, but her literary associations and activities were her most common pursuit. F B Pinion's *Thomas Hardy: His Life and Friends* (Palgrave Macmillan, 1992) relates early encounters between the famous author, his wife Emma (who was another suffragiste) and the Portsmouth family:

> 'Soon after The Mayor of Casterbridge was completed Hardy and Emma were on holiday in London. One evening after visiting the Royal Academy private view, they attended a party given by Lady Carnarvon, Lady Portsmouth's sister-in-law; here Hardy met Lord Salisbury for the first time, and discussed with him the art of speech-making. At another reception there, in the middle of May, when Emma had returned home for a brief period, Hardy, who obviously felt it was to his professional advantage to be known and accepted in high society, found the atmosphere more friendly than on the previous occasion… Three of Lady Portsmouth's daughters, Lady Dorothea, Lady Margaret, and Lady Winifred Herbert who complained about the heaviness of the teapot as she did the pouring, were staying with their aunt, and regretted Emma's absence. Among those Hardy met on this occasion were Browning…'

Thomas Hardy (184C–1928), novelist and poet, friend of Lord and Lady Portsmouth and visitor to Eggesford House

Carbon print by W & D Downey, published by Cassell & Company, Ltd, 1894

(© National Portrait Gallery London)

'Dearest Emmi': Thomas Hardy's Letters to his First Wife (ed. Carl J Weber, Palgrave Macmillan, 1963) continued the story: 'Early in 1885 Lord and Lady Portsmouth invited the Hardys to Eggesford House in North Devon. They accepted the invitation and a date was fixed for the visit. When the time came, however, Mrs. Hardy found herself ill and unable to go.'

Hardy wrote to Emma from the house:

Eggesford House, Wembworthy, N. Devon.
Friday March 13, [18]85.

My dearest Em,
I arrived at Eggesford Station a little after 4, and found there L[or]d P's brougham waiting to take me up to the house, so there was no trouble at all. The scenery here is lovely and the house very handsome – not an enormous one – but telling on account of its position, which is on a hill in the park. I have had tea with Lady P and the ladies – the only members of the family at home – Lord P not having returned from hunting yet (6 p.m.). The young ladies are very attentive, and interested in what I tell them – Lady P charges them to take care of me – and goes away to her parish people etc. – altogether a delightful household. There are [other] ladies here too, visiting, but of course I have only had a glimpse [of them] as yet. They sympathise with you – and Lady P says you must come when you are well. I am now in the library writing this. I should say that a married daughter, Lady Rosamond Christie, I think she is, who is here, strikes me as a particularly sensible woman. If Lady P's orders are to be carried out my room will be like a furnace – she is so particularly anxious that I should not take cold, etc. The drawing room is lined with oak panels from a monastery. When I arrived the schoolchildren were practising singing in the hall, for Sunday in Church.

In haste (as you will believe)
Yours ever
TOM

Eggesford Station in the age of steam, as it may have appeared when Thomas Hardy arrived to visit the Portsmouth family

(Photographer unknown)

Hardy enjoyed being driven around the surrounding villages with his host and walking in the Eggesford parkland. Of the Earl, Hardy wrote: 'He is a farmer-like man with a broad Devon accent. He showed me a bridge over which bastards were thrown and drowned, even down to quite recent times.'

And of Lady Portsmouth he wrote: 'Lady P. tells me she never knew real anxiety till she had a family of daughters. She wants us to come to Devonshire and live near them. She says they would find a house for us. Can't think why we live in benighted Dorset. Emma would go willingly, as it is her native county [she was born in Plymouth]; but alas, my house at Dorchester is nearly finished.'

In October 1886 Hardy and Emma visited the Portsmouths again at Eggesford, spending time at the hunting kennels and the dogs' cemetery: 'Lord Portsmouth made his whipper-in tell Emma the story of the hunted fox that ran up the old woman's clock-case, adding corroborative words with much gravity as the story proceeded, and enjoying it more than she did, though he had heard it 100 times.'

E Sferra in *The Palgrave Encyclopedia of Victorian Women's Writing* (Palgrave Macmillan, 2021) records that Eveline was editor of *The Poetical Birthday Book; or Characters from the Poets*, published in 1877 by Hatchards, offering poetry and art. She also contributed twice to the *Woman's World* periodical while renowned poet and playwright Oscar Wilde was editor, once again supporting the women's movement as an aristocrat.

Along with Thomas Hardy and Oscar Wilde, Lady Portsmouth was known to several writers of her day, as Melinda Creech at the Armstrong Browning Library in Texas, USA, noted in 2014. Creech provides a fresh connection with the Carnarvons and their seat at Highclere Castle in Hampshire, in recent years the main location for the highly successful British TV series and films *Downton Abbey*:

'As the new season of *Downton Abbey* begins, I thought I should bring you up to date on the discoveries … from my investigation into Robert Browning's visits at Highclere Castle.

My curiosity about Browning at Downton Abbey led me to begin a correspondence with David Rymill, archivist for both the Hampshire Record Office and the Highclere Estate. Mr. Rymill's research revealed that there were three previously unrecorded Browning letters among the Earl of Portsmouth's archives, a carte de visite of Browning in an album of photographs from Highclere Castle, and four signatures of Robert Browning in the Castle's guest books.

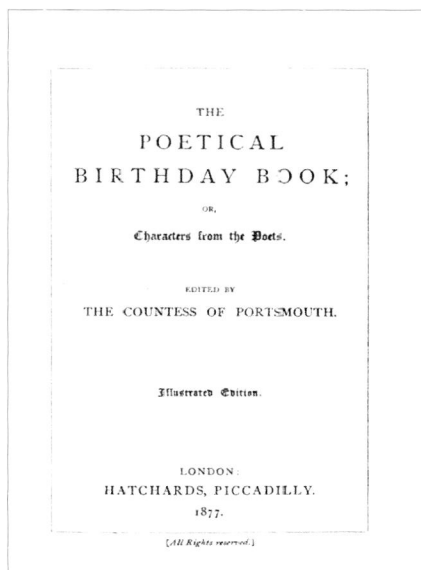

THE

POETICAL

BIRTHDAY BOOK;

OR,

Characters from the Poets.

EDITED BY

THE COUNTESS OF PORTSMOUTH.

Illustrated Edition.

LONDON:
HATCHARDS, PICCADILLY.
1877.

[All Rights reserved.]

The writings of Eveline, Countess of Portsmouth, included this *Birthday Book* published by Hatchards in 1877, and featuring selected poetry from a range of English-speaking writers

Among the three letters from Robert Browning are two letters to Lady Portsmouth, Lady Eveline Alicia Juliana Herbert, first daughter of Henry John George [Herbert], 3rd Earl of Carnarvon. … The other letter is to her daughter, Lady Catherine Henrietta Wallop, who married the Right Honorable Charles George Milnes-Gaskell.'

This spider's web of connections between Eggesford House and the Portsmouths, and Highclere and the Carnarvon family was brought up to date when Ed Howell, the latest owner at Eggesford, related the story of his grandfather: injured in the First World War, he was moved to Highclere after Lady Almina, wife of the 5th Earl of Carnarvon, established a surgical hospital there for the wounded from the trenches. Ed's grandfather met his future wife there, an Australian nurse. They were married on the ward and she nursed him back to health.

Lady Winifred Burghclere, Eveline's niece, who grew up at Highclere, published the pamphlet *Eveline, Countess of Portsmouth: a recollection* (John Murray, 1907). Lady Winifred married twice and had four lively daughters. The Carnarvon women, much like Eveline the 5th Countess of Portsmouth, were clearly redoubtable human beings.

The American (later British) novelist Henry James (1843–1916) was another literary acquaintance of the Portsmouths who visited Eggesford. He too commented on the curiosities of the family and the place, not quite as positively as Thomas Hardy:

> *I am paying a short visit at what I suppose is called here a 'great house', viz. at Lord Portsmouth's. Lady P., whom I met last summer at Wenlock Abbey, & who is an extremely nice woman, asked me a great while since to come here at this point, for a week. I accepted for three days, two of which have happily expired – for when the moment came I was very indisposed to leave London. That is the worst of invitations given you so long in advance, when the time comes you are apt to be not at all in the same humour as when they were accepted. …*
>
> *The place and country are of course very beautiful and Lady P. 'most kind'; but though there are several people in the house (local gentlefolk, of no distinctive qualities) the whole thing is dull. This is a large family, chiefly of infantine sons and daughters (there are 12) who live in some mysterious part of the house & are never seen. The one chiefly about is Lord Lymington, the eldest son, an amiable youth of 21, attended by a pleasant young Oxford man [presumably H H Asquith, the future prime minister], with whom he is 'reading'. Lord P. is simply a great hunting and racing magnate, who keeps the hounds in this part of the country, and is absent all day with them. There is nothing in the house but pictures of horses – and awfully bad ones at that.*

Henry James

by Elliott & Fry, albumen cabinet card, November 1884

Given by Elizabeth Clay (née Ponsonby), 1998 Photographs Collection

(© National Portrait Gallery, London)

The life is very simple and tranquil. Yesterday, before lunch, I walked in the garden with Lady Rosamund, who is not 'out' & doesn't dine at table, though she is a very pretty little pink and white creature of 17; & in the p.m. Lady P. showed me her boudoir which she is 'doing up', with old china &c.; & then took me to drive in her phaeton, through some lovely Devonshire lanes. In the evening we had a 'ballet'; i.e. the little girls, out of the schoolroom, came down into the gallery, with their governess, & danced cachuchas, minuets, &c. with the utmost docility and modesty, while we sat about and applauded.

Today is bad weather, & I am sitting alone in a big cold library, of totally unread books, waiting for Lord Portsmouth, who has offered to take me out & show me his stables & kennels (famous ones), to turn up. I shall try & get away tomorrow, which is a Saturday; as I don't think I could stick out a Sunday here... It may interest you [to] know, as a piece of local color that, though there are six or seven resident flunkeys here, I have been trying in vain, for the last half hour, to get the expiring fire refreshed. Two or three of them have been in to look at it – but it appears to be no-one's business to bring in coals...

I have come to my room to dress for dinner, in obedience to the bell, which is just being tolled. A footman in blue & silver has just come in to 'put out' my things – he almost poured out the quantum of water I am to wash by. The visit to the stables was deferred till after lunch, when I went the rounds with Lord P. and a couple of men who were staying here – 40 horses, mostly hunters, & a wonderful pack of foxhounds – lodged like superior mechanics.

Historian and publisher Eric R Delderfield wrote of intellectual as well as sporting connections of the Portsmouths (see Chapter 6), including those with the novelist, clergyman, social reformer and Cambridge University professor Charles Kingsley (12 June 1819–1875), whose bestseller *Westward Ho!* (1855) inspired the development of the coastal resort of that name. According to Delderfield, Kingsley shared a common birthday with Parson Jack Russell (21 December 1795–1883) and Lady Portsmouth (21 December 1834–1906). 'They used regularly to meet at Eggesford House to celebrate the occasion. Another frequent visitor was James Russell Lowell, the American poet.' Curiously, Delderfield's dates do not appear to match for Kingsley's birthday, although they are correct for both the Parson and Lady Portsmouth.

Correspondence of the Portsmouths kept at the Hampshire Archives and elsewhere reveals detail after detail of the couple's social lives, led especially by the 5th Countess, Eveline. Despite her graciousness, Henry James was not alone in being less than flattering in accounts of stays at Eggesford. Florence Glynn (a descendant of the Boscawen family in Cornwall) wrote to her husband John Henry Oglander (born John Henry Glynn, of the Cornwall Glynns) in 1884:

I got to Eggesford station (after one change at a junction) about 5.13. Lord Portsmouth's carriage and a donkey cart came down to meet me, the lodge is close to the station, so we were not long getting here and Rosamond ran to the door to meet me and seemed so glad to see me. She carried me off straight to my room and after a little talk she took me (having taken off my things) to her mother's room to tea. Lady Portsmouth greeted me most warmly. She is certainly very charming, but, oh dear, it is a funny place and a funny family. They all speak in the same rather high key as little Rosamond. I can't describe it at all. I had a very cosy tea just with Lady Portsmouth and Rosamond and afterwards Rosamond took me to a tiny sitting room which her mother had fitted up for her and we had a long talk – poor little thing, it is very sad to hear her speak so wearily and hopelessly at times and sorry now and then, and then she is so bright. She seems now to have a terrible horror of her husband – it appears his temper is something too terrible. I hope to have a talk with Lady Portsmouth. I wonder if I shall. I want you to tell me if that friend of Mr Powell's knew Mr Christie well and ever heard him swear? Will you answer this? ...

Lord Portsmouth is the funniest old thing. He was very anxious at dinner (which same was very badly cooked. Emily would have sent it up much better! Perhaps it was a chance, some was good.) He was in pain with a foot, which his hunter trod on today, so he went to bed early. Two of the party played the violin beautifully – accompanied by the Tutor. My room is so pretty and quaint. One of those old fashioned flowery papers, all the furniture black carved oak including the four post bed and hung with yellow damask. ... We went to Eggesford church – so cold – very small with some curious monuments, mostly Donnegal and some Portsmouth and Fellowes. We sat in a high square pew (left in spite of restoration) capable of holding at least 24 people, a stove outside it, steaming away, Lord Portsmouth much distressed because I did not sit by it, but it was enough to blow one's head off, and kept popping...

Rosamond Alicia, one of the Portsmouths' twelve children, referred to as 'a pretty little pink thing' by Henry James, had married Augustus Langham Christie of Tapeley Park, Instow, Devon, and had one child with him (John Christie, born 1882 at Eggesford). Augustus sadly suffered from some nervous condition which became more pronounced. It was clearly not a happy marriage, as Rosemary Lauder recounts in *Devon Families*:

'Augustus's eccentricities were becoming rather more serious, and eventually she banished him to the other Christie estate at Saunton. When Augustus died in 1930, in an act of revenge on his wife, he willed Tapeley to some distant cousin in Canada. Lady Rosamund fought the will in the law courts, eventually proving that he was of unsound mind when the will was made. She finally won shortly before her own death in 1936.'

Perhaps the Portsmouths' history of the 3rd Earl and his 'lunacy' trial was in her mind as she headed to the courts.

Lady Rosamund exerted much influence on Tapeley, working with the architect John Belcher to transform the house and gardens, exploiting many opportunities to create style and interest, while saving money, in one case using rejected gravestones for a long flight of steps, originally intended for World War One cemeteries. She also created one of the finest private collections of William Morris furniture in the country, befriending Morris and other Arts and Crafts protagonists such as Edward Burne-Jones at Tapeley, where they were known to discuss subjects such as socialism as well as art (Morris was a committed socialist activist by the 1880s, although Burne-Jones preferred an escape from the harsh realities of life through the vivid realms of fantasy and legend).

Her son John inherited the other family estate, Glyndebourne in Sussex, and married the Canadian soprano Audrey Mildmay, later founding Glyndebourne Opera Festival, and being made a Companion of Honour as a result. Although blind in one eye, he fought as a Captain on the Western Front in World War One and was awarded the Military Cross.He bequeathed Tapeley to his daughter Rosamund Christie (1933–1988), who left it in turn to her nephew Hector Christie (born 1963), the incumbent today.

Eveline, the 5th Countess, displayed her plucky nature when, along with her brother, Auberon Edward William Molyneux Herbert (1838–1906), they helped rescue the crew from a shipwreck off Westward Ho! on the North Devon coast. Dated 13 September 1869, a letter in French, in beautiful script, from the Imperial Austrian Ambassador thanked the Countess of Portsmouth for her efforts. Lady Portsmouth was later to respond, also in French.

My lady

I have the honour to enclose hereby a letter by which the warmest thanks of Her Majesty the Empress Queen are conveyed to you for your great kind help and benevolence in assisting the Austrian sailors rescued from the barque [a type of sailing vessel] *"Pare" on the 28th of December last near Bideford. Not knowing where to address a similar letter destined to Mr. Auberon W.*

In letters to *The Daily Telegraph* just after the shipwreck, Eveline and her brother wrote of their support and sadness at the death during the rescue:

Having been eye-witnesses of the conduct of the Coastguardsman Johns, who met death while discharging his duty – generously interpreting that duty to include every exertion and every risk which had for its object the saving of life – we venture to join in the appeal which Lieut-Colonel Hutchinson has made for the widow and children, in the hour of that bitterness which must remain as the household portion of some hearts, whenever the story of self-sacrifice is told.

Your obedient servants
Eveline Portsmouth
Auberon Herbert
Eggesford, North Devon, Dec. 30.

Auberon was to add that 'he interpreted his duty as every exertion & risk to save life'. Lady Portsmouth caught cold after the event. Writing in a letter on 30 December 1868, she reported:

Aubrey [her brother] *is here for the night none the worse for our great adventures on Monday though it has really thrown no small amount of thought & work into our hands.*

Lady Eveline Herbert, later to be Countess of the 5th Earl of Portsmouth

Painting by Sir Francis Grant

(Photo by Jonathan Crofts, by kind permission of Viscount Lymington)

Awarded the Austrian Order of the Iron Crown, third class, for his part in the rescue, the Countess's brother, Auberon Herbert, was perhaps one of the guiding influences on Eveline in her approach to life and people, as she was also to him. Auberon was described by *The Dictionary of National Biography* (1912) as a 'political philosopher and author, who had been first a soldier, then lectured in history and

101

The Hon. Auberon Edward William Molyneux Herbert, Eveline's brother, who assisted in rescuing survivors from the shipwreck of the *Pare* off the North Devon coast

(© National Portrait Gallery, London)

jurisprudence at St John's College, Oxford. He was an active politician for a period, visited various wars in his lifetime such as the Prusso–Danish war, helping to rescue the wounded and being made a knight of the Order of the Dannebrog in recognition; the American civil war; the Franco–German war, where he was one of the first to enter Paris after the capitulation, and nearly shot as a spy on his way in.'

Later in life he took up farming. 'Herbert, a man of singular charm, always scrupulously anxious to distinguish the system he attacked from the men who upheld or lived under it, was penetrated by the belief that the law of equal freedom is the supreme moral law. A keen sportsman and a fine rider in his youth, he gave up sport in later life on account of his objection to taking life, and for the same reason became a vegetarian.'

According to the current Countess of Carnarvon in her book *Lady Almina and the real Downton Abbey* (Hodder & Stoughton, 2011), as an Arabist he was very friendly with T E Lawrence ('Lawrence of Arabia'), and as 'a maverick MP, championed small nations, especially Albania, wrote poetry and gathered devoted friends from all over the world, thanks to his remarkable charm'. He is buried at Brushford Church on the edge of Exmoor, some twenty miles from Eggesford.

Eveline's doughty activities in Chawleigh and other villages are described elsewhere, but amongst all her visits, charitable fund-raising and private donations, she was also reputed to have ventured in person to the home of the 'North Devon Savages', a 'tribe of wild gypsies' living in Nymet Rowland, just down the road from Eggesford. The story began in *The Times* of 17 November 1869 with a report entitled 'Heathenism in Devonshire', concerning two men convicted for trespass while out poaching for game. The piece offers an unfavourable description of a farming family living in rough circumstances in and around a dilapidated farmhouse:

'To the clergyman of the parish and the neighbourhood they behave in a most shameful manner. They sing obscene songs when the reverend gentleman passes, they perform the most disgusting and nameless acts when he is in the company of ladies and those who are noxious to them they pelt with stones and mud as they go by their wretched domicile. Depredations in the neighbourhood are frequent. Gates and gate-posts and other objects of utility often disappear and threats of violence are common. We may add that members of the family have several times been convicted of offences. And yet these people continue their savage habits to the annoyance and disgust of the neighbours, treating the remonstrances of the clergyman with mockery, ribaldry and obscenity and setting the rules of civilised life at defiance.'

The story was picked up by countless publications, even reaching *The New York Times*, with its heady whiff of the fearless aristocrat attending the most feral of domestic setups.

The true story of the North Devon Savages by Peter Christie *(Transactions of the Devonshire Association*, vol. 124, 1992), refutes some of the press coverage of the Cheritons, the family in question, and 'explores the truth behind their reputation and suggests that their notoriety, though based to some extent on fact, was deliberately exaggerated by local landed interests in order to force them off their land'. This appears to be a reference to local farmers rather than the Portsmouth family. Eveline clearly survived her visit.

Following the death of her husband in 1891, Eveline eventually retired to Townsend Farm in Over Wallop, Hampshire.

On 6 October 1906, *The Western Times* reported her funeral in Hampshire and the separate memorial service at Eggesford:

THE COTTAGE OF THE "SAVAGES"

The drawing of the savages' cottage comes from Sabine Baring-Gould's *An Old English Home and Its Dependencies* (1898). Illustrated by Bond, Frederick Bligh.

The image shows a naked figure by the door, one of many criticisms levelled against the so-called 'savages'. (Thanks to the Devon History Society)

'Trains from London and the Western and South Western Counties, brought numerous mourners, and the whole countryside turned out to do honour to a lady whose personal high character, charming personality, and charitable life, made her an object of universal esteem and affection. The coffin had been brought from the deceased lady's residence, Townsend-Over-Wallop, to the magnificent family mansion at Hurstbourne, and there assembled a numerous and distinguished company yesterday afternoon for the final offices. Four magnificent horses drew the open funeral car, the beautiful coffin and the roof of the vehicle being covered with masses of lovely flowers. The lengthy string of carriages was inadequate to take all those who attended the procession, which was led by a large number of farmers and tenantry, and followed by hundreds of county gentlemen and representatives of Societies in which the deceased Countess was interested. These followed on foot for nearly three miles through the beautiful park and the village of Hurstbourne…

Simultaneously with the funeral of the Dowager Countess of Portsmouth, at Hurstbourne, a memorial service was held in Eggesford Church, which is situate on the Eggesford Estate, yesterday afternoon. It was simple, but impressively rendered, and notwithstanding the inclement weather, was attended by a considerable number of residents in the neighbourhood, by whom the deceased lady was much beloved. The Countess of Leitrim, who is for the present occupying Eggesford House, was among the congregation…'

Eveline's family connections in Devon persist to this day. Henry Mowbray Parker, current owner of Downes House on the outskirts of Crediton, is Eveline's great-great-grandson. He is also the great-great-nephew of General Sir Redvers Buller, VC, GCB, GCMG, Commander in Chief in the Second Boer War, 1899–1902, and renowned for the relief of Ladysmith and as the saviour of Natal (from the British perspective). Buller is commemorated in the impressive Church of the Holy Cross in Crediton, as well as with a fine equestrian statue in Exeter. Henry and Susan Parker continue renovations of Downes House, built in 1692, which now features a family museum and is occasionally open to the public.

In her lifetime, Eveline was inspired on the death of a beloved hound in 1878 to write:

A lineage high and noble blood
And manners not to be withstood,
And parent of a race as good,
Gentle sharp and true.
For keen resolve and courage
Stout, and knowing well her way about,
And daring all the pack to flout
None ever equalled Fu.
And though she saw her decade round,
Out-lived many, a tough old hound,
By age at least she's gone to ground
And Death has claimed his due.

Perhaps the same could have been written about Eveline herself.

Beatrice Mary Pease (1866–1935), Countess to the 6th Earl

The 6th Countess, Beatrice Mary Pease, was the only child of Edward Pease (1834–1880) of Darlington. The Peases were a successful Quaker family of industrialists and philanthropists, who supported anti-slavery and peace campaigns and created the first public railway in the world to use steam locomotives, the Stockton & Darlington. Beatrice's grandfather, Joseph Pease (1799–1872), was the largest colliery owner in South Durham, the first Quaker Member of Parliament, and President of the Peace Society, as well as a fervent champion of animal rights.

When her father died, Beatrice was given a home by her uncle, Sir Joseph Whitwell Pease (1828–1903) until she married Viscount Lymington in 1885. After her marriage, she won a lawsuit against her uncle claiming that his bank had mismanaged her inheritance. Obliged to pay the penalty of £500,000, he was forced to sell the bank to Barclays.

Beatrice became Countess of Portsmouth in 1891, on the death of the 5th Earl, her father-in-law. As well as writing copious diaries and correspondence, she was instrumental in documenting the Wallop family history, making notes on photographs and elsewhere, and acquired a library of rare books and early printed matter. She and the 6th Earl had no children of their own.

Like the 5th Countess, Beatrice too had a wide acquaintance, including politicians, diplomats and artists. Much engaged with charitable work, especially the Red Cross before and during the First World War, amongst other activities she helped to arrange accommodation for wounded Belgian soldiers. She also took just as great an interest in her estate workers and their families as Eveline.

The loss of the main family home, Hurstbourne Park in Hampshire, in a fire in early 1891, was a shock but she and the 6th Earl commissioned a new house, being closely involved with the rebuilding alongside the architects. They moved in on 14 September 1896, and it became their main residence rather than Eggesford.

Beatrice, Countess of Portsmouth, wife of the 6th Earl

Painting by Douglas Chandor, 1923

(Photo by Jonathan Crofts, by kind permission of Viscount Lymington)

The Dundee Evening Telegraph on 14 December 1935 reported her death after being 'ill for months', the Earl having died in 1917: 'The Countess took a great interest in local organisations, and was closely associated with temperance work in Hampshire, being at one time president of the Hants. and Isle of Wight Band of Hope Union. She had been a J.P. since 1927 and was a past president of the Young Women's Christian Association.'

The Countesses' focus had finally shifted from their Devon properties to Hampshire, but estate villages with long histories like Chawleigh would go on to flourish as politics and ownership gradually evolved and tenant farmers and others 'took the reins' with their lands and animals.

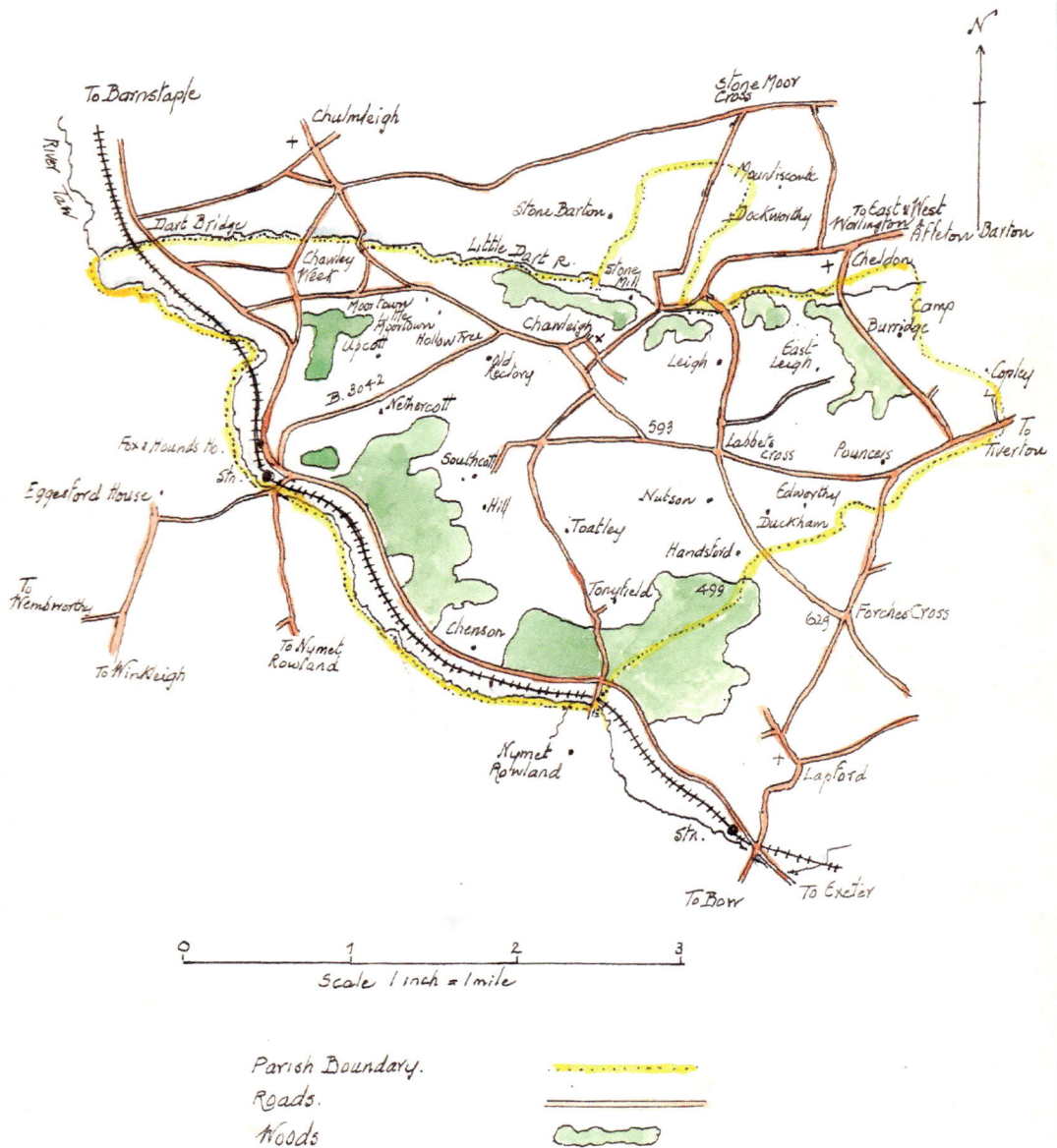

Map of Chawleigh Parish, c.1963, drawn by Algernon Pepperell / F W Hillman, *Chawleigh Notes*
The northern boundary mainly followed the Little Dart River, with the Taw in the southwest representing much of the southern boundary. Note the position of the Old Rectory on the west side of central Chawleigh, today's Ashley Court, home of the Amber Foundation. Cheldon, to the north-east, sits outside the parish boundary.

CHAPTER 10

CHAWLEIGH: A BOROUGH AND A VILLAGE

Iron Age to Saxon Chawleigh

Chawleigh's origins date back to ancient times, as evidenced by the Iron Age (800 BC to 43 AD) fort at West Burridge, above Cheldon Bridge on the Little Dart River. Burridge Camp was listed as a Scheduled Monument by Historic England in 1958, a site of national archaeological significance. It is classed as a slight univallate hillfort, rare across Britain but more widely represented in Devon. Dating from the transition between the Late Bronze Age and the Early Iron Age (eighth to fifth centuries BC), it would likely have been in use for some 150–200 years. Enclosures were bounded by an inner bank (the rampart), surrounded by a flat ledge (the berm) dropping down into a ditch, the whole thing encircled by a second outer rampart. Typically two entrances gave access across a causeway into the inner enclosure. These earthworks are thought to have been used to contain stock, as 'redistribution centres', to shield a small permanent settlement or provide refuge to an attached community when under attack.

Set high over the valley of the Little Dart River, much of Burridge Camp survives, and it 'contains archaeological and environmental information relating to the settlement and exploitation of this area during the Iron Age.' Oval in shape, it is just over 90m (300ft) long and nearly 80m (260ft) wide. Material from digging the ditch was used to construct the single rampart, its curving stone banks flanking the original entrance to the south-east, and offering access to the farmland beyond. Opposite in another break in the structure, a simple bank over the ditch leads to the farmland beyond, showing another way out and in. A triangular earthwork runs from this feature across two neighbouring fields, while a little further round, a possible remnant of the original outer rampart runs parallel with the remaining rampart and ditch. Other parts of the fort have eroded into the hillside or lie partly overlaid by later tracks or field boundaries. A section of the outer ditch was trodden over long centuries by travellers and beasts so that it now appears as a hollow way, its origins long obscured.

1920s Ordnance Survey map showing the site of the Camp, an Iron Age hillfort, above Burridge.

Stone Barton castle appears to the north of Chawleigh, and Affeton Barton (where the Castle gatehouse still stands) not far from West Worlington.

(Reproduced with the permission of the National Library of Scotland.)

The first farms were probably established in the Early Medieval period by the Saxons between 650 and 750 AD – bringing new agricultural techniques, these people had migrated from areas now in modern Germany, and were responsible for clearing many of Devon's 'leighs' in the woodlands as pasture for their animals. It was in this period that an English Church emerged, although as the other name for this period, the Dark Ages, suggests, relatively little is known about early religious sites in places like Chawleigh. The National Library of Wales, however, holds a map copy of 'a prehistoric trackway and sanctuary near Chawleigh'.

Many of the present-day farms, most of them shown in the map drawn in 1963, can be recognised from the Devonshire Lay Subsidy of 1332 (Taxation of Land Owners) for the Hundred of Northtauton (today's North Tawton), which recorded non-ecclesiastical land holdings. A Hundred was a subdivision of a shire or county, larger than a single parish. Some of the local farming families go back at least six hundred years, and a few farms may go back to Saxon times.

Occupier	Farm Name	Tax (shillings and pence)
John de Braderigge		2s
Hamelin Bysshop		8d
Walter Cok		12d
Hugh de Courteney		5s
Fohn [John?] de Fythecotte		2s
Robert Page		8d
Richard de Snowdon		8d
John de Borridge	Burridge?	2s
Richard de Rurridge	Burridge?	8d
Juliana de Wyke	Chawleigh Week	2s
Stephen de Wyke	Chawleigh Week	12d
Robert de Wyke	Chawleigh Week?	12d
Thomas Cheigny	Chenson	2s
William de Yadeworth	Edworthy	12d
William Vytecotte	Fiddlecott	8d
Henry atte Ford	Ford	2s
William ate Hulk	Hill	2s 6d
William de Leghe	Leigh	2s
Adam de Leghe	Leigh	18d
Simon de Nithercote	Nethercott	8d
Sarra de Notyngeston	Nutson	12d
Roger de Totelegh	Toatley	8d
William de Totelegh	Toatley	12d
Walter de Uppecotte	Upcott	8d
Henry atte Wode	Woodhouse	18d

Local farms listed in the 1332 Devonshire Lay Subsidy for the Hundred of Northtauton (North Tawton)

Toatley Farm, Chawleigh, c.1900

(By kind permission of Yvonne Gerry)

Not all of the existing farms were listed or existed in the fourteenth century; some may once have been part of a larger farmstead. Even so, many farm names have survived as farm or family names today.

One ancient feature on the perimeter of Chawleigh would have been familiar to these farming families and their ancestors, and it remains in use to this day. Up on the ridgeway just outside the village and with sightlines to other high points in every direction, is the site of the Chawleigh Beacon. Built across Devon and the rest of the country on sites with long-distance visibility, fire beacons were the system of early warning signals used at least since late Roman times and reintroduced against the threat of the Spanish Armada in the sixteenth century.

The history and significance has been recorded by the *devonheritage.org* website:

'Fire Beacons were an ancient form of early warning signals. They were set up on hill tops so that they connected to form a continuous link across the countryside – the lighting of one was the signal to light the next and so on and this proved to be a very rapid means of passing on news about the approach of enemy invaders – in times of national danger, look-outs were posted to watch for adjacent fires and it is said that news of the arrival of the Spanish Armada in the English Channel in 1588 was signalled from Plymouth to York within 12 hours. By this means, the entire County of Devon could be alerted in less than an hour.

The system required that every beacon should be constantly attended. Sometimes the beacons consisted of iron baskets on timber supports – others were lower stone hearths with a platform below to create a draught. In either case, dry kindling had to be provided by the parish together with a plentiful supply of dry fuel plus the manpower to keep the fire alight for a prolonged period. The system had its drawbacks but proved how effective it could be in 2002 when a chain of beacons were lit to celebrate Queen Elizabeth II's Golden Jubilee.

Chawleigh Fire Beacon connected:
To the east with Stretch Down and Stoodleigh
To the south with Beacon Cross and Crediton
To the south-west with Cawsand Beacon
To the north-west with Beaford Moor
To the north to Beacon Moor, Chulmleigh, to Codden and Barrow Hill.

Chawleigh Beacon is 593 feet above sea level and the OS map reference for finding it is SS 718117. Various sources suggest that a look-out clearing was made at Tottley/Toteleigh/Toatley approximately a mile away.'

R R Sellman's *Illustrations of Devon History* (1962) describes the Armada Beacons Network of Intervisibility:

'The network prepared against the Armada shows the system fully developed with watching points on the coast linked by lines of sight across lower ground to the inland hills. Each spot was chosen not only for local warning, but as a part of a chain, connected with those of neighbouring counties. The actual beacons were sometimes iron fire baskets on timber supports, and sometimes low circular stone erections providing a platform with underneath draught. With prompt work, the whole county could be alerted in half an hour.

… In operation the system required every beacon to be constantly attended and watch kept on all neighbouring sites from which warning might come. Material was necessary to get the fire going promptly even in wet weather; but heavy mists on high ground would have made things distinctly difficult. One drawback was the danger of false alarm, and the lack of means to cancel one. An overanxious coast-watcher mistaking friendly for enemy ships, or a heath fire mistaken for a beacon, might set the whole County in an uproar which would take days to settle.'

The Chawleigh Beacon was last lit for the late Queen Elizabeth's Platinum Jubilee in June 2022. Elizabeth II was to die a few months later, after a lifetime of public ceremony, including celebrating Eggesford Forest as the first plantation of the Forestry Commission (see Chapter 4). Her sense of commitment and public duty was intermingled with a complex family life, much in common with the Portsmouths and so many other dynasties in Devon, noble and otherwise.

Medieval Chawleigh (1066–1485)

Calveleia in 1086, as cited in the Domesday Book; Cheluelega in 1227; Chauveleg in 1228; Chauvelegh in 1254; Chaveleg in 1275; Chalvelegh in 1285 and 1291–1292; Chalfelee in 1286 – the name Chawleigh has had many forms since the Norman language introduced via the Conquest of 1066 gradually merged with older Anglo-Saxon forms and morphed into the language we know as English today. It can be loosely translated as 'calves clearing', and at least five other variants have been noted over the course of history (Calvelis, Chademelegh, Challeigh, Chalvelly, Chawley). Chawleigh Week, on the Chulmleigh side of the main Chawleigh village, was recorded as 'Wyk' in 1242 and Challeigh-weeke in 1612; its possible meaning was 'the dairy farm of Chawleigh'.

Westcote's *A View of Devonshire in MDCXXX With a Pedigree of Most of its Gentry* (1845, original manuscript 1624–1636) describes Chawleigh and its environs: 'And Chawley or Chalveley, Baldwin the Baron of

Okehampton had it, and Courtenay, Bilchester and Langford; now Stukeley: where we perceive by the ruins, that a castle was there sometime seated, but by whom or in what age we find nothing.' This is believed to refer to the Stone Barton castle, rather than Affeton Castle to the east, a current home of the Stukeley or Stucley family; masonry stones were still visible in Westcote's time.

In the *North Devon* volume (1952) of his celebrated *The Buildings of England*, Nikolaus Pevsner refers to 'STONE BARTON, 1¼m. North. Scanty ruins of the C13 castle of Isabella de Fortibus, Countess of Devon' as part of Chawleigh, although it is today within the parish of Chulmleigh. Isabella's lands passed to the Crown after her death, and following disputes over succession of the title, the heir of the Courtenay family was eventually created "Earl of Devonshire".'

As with Burridge Camp, Historic England now classifies the castle north of Stone Barton as a Scheduled Monument, this site listed in 1963. Much of it survives, a relic of military activity in North Devon at the time of the Normans. The castle is a ringwork, a class of fortification dating to the medieval period, roughly covering the late Anglo-Saxon period anywhere up to the late twelfth century, with only two hundred such structures recorded across the UK. As with the earlier hilltop forts, ringworks represented a small area surrounded by a large ditch and bank, for ease of defence against marauders. Fewer than sixty of them feature an adjoining bailey, which was a mound within a smaller enclosure that could be defended with fewer men.

Generally constructed as strongholds for military operations, a number of ringworks defended settlements centred around a manor or aristocratic residence. A timber palisade running along the top of the bank would have offered a measure of security to those living and fighting on the inside, even more so at the few sites where this took the form of a stone wall.

Built on top of a hill straddling the river valleys to the north and south, Stone Barton castle would have commanded fine views of approaching danger. The roughly circular area at the heart of it measures nearly 40m (just under 125ft) from north to south and almost 35m (115ft) across, set within large banks. Bumps in the terrain suggest that walls, no doubt built from the stony soil dug out of the ditch, have collapsed in over the centuries. A long bank runs east–west across the enclosure from the outer rampart.

To the north, where the perimeter of the enclosure remains highest, a large curving bank slopes down and away towards the south-east. Within and beyond the enclosure, some of it partly extending beneath the modern-day fields, lie a low mound and scatters of material and other indications of D-shaped, circular and rectangular structures, signs of buildings presumably, long since vanished. To the south of the enclosure are two banks cut off at the far end by a field boundary.

The Reverend T W Whale analysed the *Exeter Domesday in Hundreds* in 1903, and, like Westcote, listed Chawleigh and Eggesford under Baldwin the Sheriff, holding Chawleigh as land directly from the Crown, and the immediate lord over the 'peasants' after the Norman Conquest, who paid tax to him as tenant-in-chief. Chawleigh originally belonged to the Hundred of North Tawton (and later the Hundred of North Tawton and Winkleigh).

Domesday Book data, from William I's survey of his kingdom in 1086, has since been made publicly available online by Hull University (thanks to Professor John Palmer, George Slater and *opendomesday.org*). Chawleigh was then known as Calveleia:

'Households
Households: 30 villagers. 6 smallholders. 12 slaves. 3 other population.

Land and resources
Ploughland: 30 ploughlands. 6 lord's plough teams. 10 men's plough teams.
Other resources: 1.0 lord's lands. Meadow 10 acres. Pasture 1 * 0.5 leagues. Woodland 20 acres.

Livestock
Livestock in 1086: 20 cattle. 10 pigs. 200 sheep.

Valuation
Annual value to lord: 12 pounds in 1086; 10 pounds when acquired by the 1086 owner.

Owners
Tenant-in-chief in 1086: Baldwin the sheriff.
Lord in 1086: Baldwin the sheriff.
Lord in 1066: Siward of Hemington.'

There are some indicators of other early owners or tenants of land in the Chawleigh area post the Domesday survey. Reverend O J Reichel, in his *Devonshire Association* paper (circa 1807) 'The Hundred of North Tawton', references the Hundred Rolls of 1274 and many of its settlements and occupiers: 'Before Bartholomew le Young (le Juvene) and his fellows: Laurence Axe [perhaps = Hals], Randolph de Byr [Beer, Northtawton], Alured de Porta, William le Spek [of Brushford], Richard de Bengin, John de Estleg [in Coldridge], Walter de Wasseburne [of Hermanest], Reginald de Bera [Cherry–beare], Philip de Wyke [Chawley Wick], Robert de Bradenimet, Richard le Peffur [Pafford], William de Chenestune [Chenson, Chawley], say upon oath: John de Walletorta holds the Hundred of Northtauet, of the Honour of Plimpton, by descent and heirship, and it is worth 2 marks yearly.'

'Chawley Wick' refers to what is now Chawleigh Week, just outside the main part of the village (see above). Similarly, the names of Mary Week and James Week have survived to the present day, close to Chawleigh Week. 'Cherry–beare' is the ancient manor of Cherubeer, Dolton.

In addition Reichel lists 'Knights' Fees and Estates liable to Tenths and Fifteenths in North Tawton Hundred': 'Wyk (Chawley Week), ¼ fee, held by William de Bray of the honour of Okhamton [Okehampton]… Hardwinsleigh [Hardingsleigh], Chenson, and Chawleigh Week are sub-manors of post-Domesday creation…'

In feudal England at the time, a knight's fee was a measure of land regarded as large enough to support the knight, his family and servants, including providing for horses and armour to carry out his feudal duties to his overlord in battle. Hardings Leigh remains a working farm on the edge of Chawleigh.'

Feudal Aids 1284–1431 (published by HMSO in 1899) indicated that in 1284–86 Hugh de Courtenay, ancestor of the current Earl of Devon, held the manor of Chawleigh – then known as Chalvelegh – together with Dughelton (Dowland), part of the Honour of Okehampton. An Honour was effectively a group of estates with a castle at their heart, this one at Okehampton. By 1316 Eggesford (Egeneysford) was included in the list of holdings.

By 1346 Roger de Wrey was holding a ¼ Knight's Fee in Chawleigh Week, formerly held by Walter de Wrey. In 1428 this was split between John Wrey and John Robyn.

The Wrey family later held an estate at Tawstock near Barnstaple. In the sixteenth century one son of the family married a Dynham heiress, the family who founded Hartland Abbey, which is now in the possession of the Stucley family (see Chapters 3 and 17), who also own Affeton Castle near Chawleigh.

The Reverend W Wykes-Finch, a Wrey / Wykes descendant, who bought his old family house at North Wyke in South Tawton near Dartmoor in 1895, presents a series of connections between properties of the Wyk / Wik / Wyke / Wykes / Wrey / Wray family in his book *The Ancient Family of Wyke of North Wyke, Co. Devon* (first published in his 1903 paper for the *Transactions of the Devonshire Association*). He postulated that Chawleigh was originally on the route for red deer 'rambling' between Dartmoor and Exmoor, and part owned by a family with direct royal connections:

'The lands held by William de Wigornia, that is, de Wik' … were extensive, and though scattered over a considerable area, practically lay in one particular tract of the county: that along which the red deer would travel on their way between the two royal forests of Dartmoor and Exmoor, and which was of high importance to the great families of the county when the pleasures and excitements of the chase were the exclusive privilege of its territorial lords. For, among other lands, the said William held the manor of Wray in Moreton [originally named Moreton Hampstead] under the King, and Wyke in Chawleigh, under the Baron of Okehampton.

… a road [probably the old pack-saddle road] runs in an almost straight line through the district, extending from Moreton to Chawleigh, and that in its course it passes either through, or by, the parishes of Chagford, Drewsteignton, Throwleigh, South Tawton, Spreyton, Sampford Courtenay, North Tawton, Nymet Tracy or Bow, Honeychurch, Broadwoodkelly, Bondleigh, and Winkleigh …

… on both sides of the road … there are many homesteads called Wyke, not one of which is mentioned in *Domesday*, nor earlier than the reign of King John. They are all within the tract of the county described, over the greater part of which there can be no doubt the red deer rambled at their free will. The River Taw waters a considerable part of this their tramping ground, and as it travels on its way to the sea, it is fed by streamlets passing through many a thicket where they would find abundance of shade and food and water … After disafforestation, however, in 1204, a great change necessarily came over this part of Devon, and large tracts of waste lands would be brought into cultivation and enclosed. …

Now, on either side of the road I have indicated, the Wyke homestead … prevails… It appears in Chagford, in North Tawton, in Winkleigh, in Chawleigh, and several times in the large parish of South Tawton, all of which were, I believe, held by William de Wyk. …

Now, who were the overlords of almost the entire tract covered by the parishes from Moreton to Chawleigh inclusive at that period? They were the near blood-relations of the said William de Wyk, for they were the King, the Earls of Devon, Cornwall, and Gloucester; the Barons of Okehampton and Flamsted [de Tony]; the Lords Valletort, Brewer, and Botreaux. …

… many of these lands, and others at their disposal, were given to the said William after the expulsion, in 1204, of his family from all their Norman and French estates; and that where these lands had no name, he followed a not uncommon custom of the day of calling them "Wyk", after his own, and where they had, sometimes by adding it as a prefix or affix. Hence the frequency of the Wyke homesteads throughout the said tract.

… The old mansion of North Wyke lies about midway between Moreton and Chawleigh. … in the early days of the family in Devon, the Wyke lands lay scattered both north and south of their chief residence; on the south, through South Tawton and Chagford to Moreton, and on the north to Chawleigh through North Tawton and Winkleigh …'

The Reverend W Wykes-Finch also offers an explanation for the origins of the Chawleigh farm of Tonyfield:

'The said William [known also as "de Wray" and "de Chevereston," because he held those manors] … held South Teign, if not under the King or the Earl of Cornwall, his cousin, then under another cousin, Ralph de Tony, Baron of Flamstead, under whom he also held North Wyke, Ash, and the other Wyke homesteads in South Tawton early in the thirteenth century. Wyke in Chawleigh he held under his nephew or cousin, Robert Courtenay, Baron of Okehampton Castle, but he probably held other lands there under Ralph de Tony, for the name of "Tonifield" still lives in the parish. Anyhow, the lands he held under the great de Tony family were many. This is readily explained by the fact that he was Ralph de Tony's cousin… We know that William held largely under de Tony early in the thirteenth century.'

Wykes-Finch concluded that William de Wyk and his son Roger obtained lands via William's marriage with Roger's mother, of the de Tony line, who was connected with the royal family through her kinswoman, mistress of Henry II. Father and son continued the custom of affixing their family name to existing place names, or applying it where none yet existed.

'Wyke, in Chawleigh, one of the fees of the aforesaid Roger, was held in 1400 by Joel Wyke, who was certainly either his son or grandson, inasmuch as Roger held it in 1346. The said "Joel and his wife Nichola" had the grant of an "oratory 12th June, 1400, to celebrate divine service in the chapel of St. James within their mansion of Flambard's Wyke in Chawleigh. William, son of Roger, succeeded to the chief estates, lived at North Wyke, and is the first of his family in the Wyke pedigree of the Heralds' Visitations, the earliest of which for Devon is dated 1531. … And Pole states that this was so with the Wyke family, and that, henceforth, too, they were no more called "Wray". They were, therefore, no longer of Wyke, or of Wray, but "Wyke" only, as a surname.'

The de Tony family was the Norman House of Tosny, also named Toeni, who were part of the court of William I (the Conqueror) and believed to have been standard bearers at the Battle of Hastings in 1066. Although there is supposition as well as fact in his beliefs, Reverend Wykes-Finch describes them as 'near-of-kin to the ducal [William, Duke of Normandy's] family'. It certainly seems possible that today's Tonyfield Farm in Chawleigh belonged to the family with royal connections (as so many farmsteads were named after their owners).

Later research by Pepperell and Hillman in their *Chawleigh Notes*, compiled in the 1970s, established the pedigree of the Chawleigh branch of the Wrey / Wyke family down to the seventeenth century, linking one family line by marriage into the prominent Courtenay and Chichester families.

Other research as part of the *Transactions of the Devonshire Association*, vol. 30, describes the ownership of the neighbouring settlement of 'Chedeldon (Cheldon) and Indriscot in the North Tawton Hundred held by John Keleway for 5/6 fee of the Honor of Gloucester' (circa 1302) and earlier (circa 1243) with different spellings of the names: 'William Cailleway holds in Chedeldon and in Yedescott 5/6 fee of the Honor of Gloucester'. 1276 it is noted that 'John de Bacckewill holds Chedlon for ¼ K./fee of the Earl of Gloucester, and the Earl of the King.'

Given intermarriage between the old established Devon families, this spider's web of local historical connections spans the centuries: the Keleway / Kellaway family, with branches prominent in Devon history, also held Stafford Barton in Dolton, which was later the home of Charles F C Luxmoore (1872–1933), who purchased the Eggesford House site in 1923 (see Chapter 24), heart of the Eggesford estate, and relocated part of its fabric to his Dolton home.

Tudor to Georgian Chawleigh (1485–1837)

The concept of a 'village borough' is believed to originate from the twelfth century, meaning a town, village or hamlet where tenanted properties were 'held in free burgage' (rent paid as money, with little or no expectation of the agricultural services otherwise required of most rural tenants). Not typically urban in nature, a borough generally had a market and a court held separately from its local manor.

The earliest record of Chawleigh being established as a 'village borough' by the lord of the manor is in 1422, and there is documentation from circa 1340 listing it as one. However it was one of the thirty-five or so Devon 'boroughs' which did not succeed in this aspirational development. The expected growth in tolls and burgage rents, on top of agricultural rents, failed to materialise from the weekly market, an annual fair, and passing road traffic, and the village never actually became a town.

Relating to this period, Forges Field, on the parish boundary, is noted (by H P R Finberg in *The Place-names of Devon*, 1952–3) in 1416 as 'Le Forchys', where the gallows formerly stood (furca and fossa comes from the Latin for gallows and pit – men would be hanged on the gallows, and women drowned in the pit). Forches Cross is the name today of the junction to Morchard Bishop on the road south from Chawleigh towards Lapford.

The 1811 version of Tristram Risdon's *The Chorographical Description or Survey of the County of Devon* (completed circa 1632) laments the felling of trees in the village of Chawleigh; the village is still partly known for its timber today:

> 'CHAWLEIGH, or Chavelege, was the lands, anciently, of the barons of Oakhampton, afterwards, earls of Devon. The barons held three hides of land in this tything, in the reign of William Rufus. This manor is now become the inheritance of Edward, lord Chichester, baron of Belfast, and viscount Carickfergus. … In this parish hath been a castle, whose ruins only shew its circuit, in a wood, lately apparelled with tall timber trees, now felled, whereof the place may complain, as did New Forest thus wasted:

Of thousands of fair trees, remains not one
For the eagle to beak or set his foot upon.'

Risdon's *Survey* suggests that Chawleigh was inherited from the barons of Okehampton by the Courtenays, Earls of Devon, before being granted (manor and borough) to Sir Humphrey Stafford in 1464, during the tumultuous period of the Wars of the Roses. Sir Humphrey (who became Lord Stafford of Southwick) was created 1st Earl of Devon in 1469 (in the second creation of the title). Thomas Courtenay had been attainted (had to forfeit lands and rights) in 1461, and so was deprived of the earldom of Devon, having supported the Lancastrian side during the Wars of the Roses. He was eventually beheaded.

Stafford was Earl of Devon for three months, executed by a mob after a rebellion which he had been sent to quell in the north. There was no issue from his marriage to Isabel and the title became temporarily extinct, but was restored for John, Thomas Courtenay's brother, in 1470, together with ancestral lands.

John Courtenay, also a Lancastrian, was also attainted, and killed in the Battle of Tewkesbury in 1471 by the forces of Edward IV. He died with no heir, and the earldom of Devon was not recreated until 1485.

Sir William Pole of Colyton, East Devon, a historian whose work *Collections Towards a Description of the County of Devon* was published in 1791 (he died in 1635), describes Chawleigh as the seat of Radford, where 'Patron of the Church at Chawleigh is… Stewkley, Esq. Value £25.13.2d.' – a reference to the Stewkley, Stucley or Stukeley family who today reside at Affeton Castle, near neighbouring West Worlington, as well as their larger seat at Hartland Abbey.

This fits with the account in *Affeton Castle: a lost Devon village* by John Stucley (1967), which explains that:

> 'By 1610 the estate had expanded to include the manor of Cheldon and West Thelbridge and half the manor of Chawleigh which, with other parcels of land at Knightstone in the south and Romansleigh in the north, represented a holding of about 12,000 acres around Affeton alone, although much of it was and remains poor agricultural land…

> … From 1610 onwards the Affeton estate dwindled away rapidly. Sir Lewis Stucley, who succeeded in that year, had had East Cheldon settled on him several years previously and had also been given all the standing timber in Burridge Wood in Chawleigh together with "divers great sums of money" by his father. Sir Lewis was far from content to live a bucolic life in East Cheldon awaiting his father's death and preferred the excitements to be found at Court in London.

> He was one of the many courtiers who were knighted by James I at Whitehall in 1603 on the King's arrival in England. By the time Sir Lewis died (in disgrace for his part in the arrest and execution of Sir Walter Raleigh) there was little left of his inheritance. His son John, obliged to mortgage Affeton to the Chichester family for £1,000, left only Affeton, West Worlington, Cobley and Burridge Wood in Chawleigh. Some 8,000 acres had been disposed of.'

Chenson (formerly known as Cheinstone, just off the modern-day A377 route in the Taw valley, south of Chawleigh village), which had been held by the Radford family for decades, passed eventually to the Hon. Newton Fellowes Wallop, the 4th Earl of Portsmouth (see Chapter 6): Ambrose Radford (died 1703) was the last of the family to hold Chenson.

Volume 6 in Daniel and Samuel Lysons' *Magna Britannica*, published in 1822, covered the county of Devonshire and described the two communities of Chenson and Chawleigh, and their ownership by Newton Fellowes Wallop:

'CHAWLEIGH, in the hundred of North Tawton and in the deanery of Chulmleigh, lies about two miles from Chulmleigh. There are cattle-fairs at Chawleigh on the 6th of May and the 11th of December. Risdon says that Chawleigh was inherited from the barons of Oakhampton by the Courtenays, Earls of Devon. It was afterwards in the Irish branch of the Chichesters, and has passed with Eggesford to the Hon. Newton Fellowes, who is the present proprietor, and patron of the rectory. Mr. Fellowes possesses also Cheinstone, in this parish, for many descents the property and residence of the Radfords, for some of whom there are memorials in the parish church. There was formerly a chapel at Chienstone.'

The Lysons also describe the neighbouring parish of Cheldon, north-east of Chawleigh above the Little Dart River, en route to Affeton Castle and the Worlingtons:

'CHELDON, in the hundred of Witheredge, and in the deanery of South Molton, lies about four miles from Chulmleigh. The manor belonged, for several descents, to the family of Kaleway. Sir William Kaleway sold it to the Stucleys before 1600: it was afterwards in the Chichesters. About the year 1718 Cheldon was purchased of Arthur St. Leger, Viscount Doneraile, (who had inherited from Arthur Chichester, Earl of Donegal,) by William Fellowes, Esq., and is now the property of the Hon. Newton Fellowes.

East Cheldon was held under the Kaleways by the family of De Cheldon for several descents; it was afterwards a seat of the Southcombes. In the reign of James I [1603–1625] it belonged to the family of Chase: it is now, by a late purchase, the property of the Hon. Newton Fellowes, who is patron of the rectory.'

The church at Cheldon is dedicated to The Blessed Virgin Mary, its story also covered in Beatrix Cresswell's book of 1919, *Notes on Devon's Churches*. The advowson belonged for generations, as described by the Lysons, to the Kelway / Kaleway / Kelloway family, and Roger de Kaylloweie was made Rector on 11 July 1313, with no patron's name mentioned.

A 1919 report by the Exeter Architectural Society mentions a former 'Chapel at Chrienstone (Chenston) [Chenson]. St. Mary's [in Cheldon] and St. Giles' Chapels [the latter in Chenson] were licensed on August 25th, 1400. St James' also the same year. Stafford's Register, Vol. 1.' The Reverend H J Hodgson added: 'Apparently, no trace remains now of any of these Chapels.' Speculation suggests any vestiges of this early chapel of St James are under the foundations of the current St James' Church, although it may also have been part of an earlier mansion elsewhere.

Eighteenth- and nineteenth-century patrons for Cheldon are recorded: from 1737 Coulson Fellowes, followed by Hon. A. Fellowes (possibly Henry Arthur), Hon. Newton Fellowes, and finally 'Lord Portsmouth' (by this time Isaac Newton Fellowes, 5th Earl) from 1877.

Cresswell also notes that the stands in the Cheldon church are believed to have come from Eggesford House when it was rebuilt in the 1820s. 'The Revd. C.R. Stone formerly Rector of the parish observes: "I always heard that the metal screens came out of some old country mansion, Lord Portsmouth had a fancy for oddities, but his taste was not churchy.'" They are believed to have been made circa 1700–20 by the eminent metalworker Jean Tijou, a French Huguenot refugee, who also created the magnificent gates and railings at Hampton Court Palace, Kensington Palace and St Paul's Cathedral in London, with numerous other pieces at stately homes and grand locations across England.

St Mary's Church in Cheldon was restored by Isaac Newton Fellowes, the 5th Earl of Portsmouth in 1873 at a cost of £500, in his role as lord of the manor and sole landowner in that parish as well. Cheldon was abolished as a parish in its own right, and merged with Chulmleigh, in 1986.

Chawleigh – the Early Victorian period (1837–1868)

Chawleigh was and is a sprawling parish stretching between the rivers Taw and the Little Dart. Primarily a farming community, it was for centuries largely self-sufficient in terms of the trades and services available locally. New working practices and ideas crowding in with the Industrial Revolution from the second half of the eighteenth century turned old norms on their head, and nowhere more so than in smaller, more remote settlements such as Chawleigh, Cheldon and Chenson.

Ordnance Survey map of Chawleigh, Surveyed 1886 to 1887, Published 1888.

(Reproduced with the permission of the National Library of Scotland)

The arrival in this period of records such as White's *Devonshire Directory* (1850) provides fuller information about the contemporary status of the village and the buildings at its heart:

'CHAWLEIGH, a parish and village on the south side of the Little Dart valley, 2 miles S.E. of Chulmleigh, contains 850 inhabitants, and 5478 acres of land; and has two cattle fairs, on May 6 and the Tuesday before the last Thursday in October.

L.W. Buck, Henry Reed, Cpr. Northcote, and the Rev. J. Russell have estates here, but about three-fourths of the parish belong to the Hon. Newton Fellowes, who is also lord of the manor, and patron of the rectory, valued in K.B. at £25. 14s. 2d., and in 1831 at £501, and now in the incumbency of the Rev. P.F. Clay, M.A., who has an ancient residence and 95 acres of glebe. The tithes were commuted in 1849 for £470. 5s. 10d. per annum. The *Church* (St. James) has an embattled tower, six bells and a handsomely carved screen. The Independents and Bible Christians have chapels here. The parish has 24A. of land, ten houses, and several gardens let for about £90, which is mostly applied in the service of the church.

The *Free School* and master's house are vested with the trustees of the parish lands; and here is another school supported by the rector. The poor parishioners have about £6 yearly from various bequests.'

The Directory revealed the key occupations and trades in a mid-nineteenth-century community of this scale: in addition to nineteen farmers it lists Richard Gough as schoolmaster; Samuel Alford as schoolmaster and shopkeeper; William Anstey, Samuel Hooper, Giles Webber as shopkeepers; George Dilling and William Webber as smiths; J Middleton as saddler and grocer; J Saunders as shoemaker; Thomas Edworthy as wheelwright; Richard Edworthy as wheelwright and victualler (licensee) at The Royal Oak; Thomas Reed as victualler at the London Inn (now The Earl of Portsmouth); Thomas Luxton as victualler at the Schoolmaster Arms (later the Schoolmaster Inn, see Chapter 14) – plus of course Reverend Clay as rector. There are separate entries for Cheldon.

Billing's Directory and Gazetteer of the County of Devon (1857) adds some additional description, citing a Chawleigh population in 1851 of 833 inhabitants but only 29 voters (universal suffrage for men over twenty-one not being introduced until 1918, and for women in 1928).

Apart from the Portsmouths owning some 'three fourths of the parish', Billings also cites estates belonging to 'L.W. Buck Esq., Messrs. H. Reed, Williams, C. Northcote and a few others'. There is a little more detail than White's about people, with farmers naturally predominating: Stephen and Richard Cann are farmers, maltsters and brewers (at Nutson); William Adams Kemp (at Great Burridge), Thomas Kemp (at Leaches), Henry Lewis (at Sowden's Burridge – Sowden's Leigh near Burridge), Robert Middleton (at Fiddlecott), Henry Phillips (at Mildon's Leigh), all as farmers; with Robert Phillips milling and farming at Stone Mill, and John Rattenbury milling and farming at Week Mill. Edward Reed was farming at West Leigh and Henry Reed at Upcott and Nethercott; his namesake farmer was busy at Toatworthy and also served as churchwarden; two Richard Reeds farmed at Handsford and Ponsford; Anthony Saunders at Tonesfield [Tonyfield]; Jeffrey Saunders at Chawleigh Week and Thomas Saunders at Mary Week; William Saunders as farmer and maltster at Chawleigh Barton and Chenstone; Edward Snell at Little Moortown and William Snell at East Ford; Richard Stone at Duckham and Edworthy farms; Samuel Trick at Homeland; John Vickery at East Hill.

Occupations in the parish were becoming more diverse as rural society steadily evolved. Mrs Rebecca Gough worked alongside her husband at the National School; William Challice as tailor and shopkeeper; James and John Goss are listed as thatchers; James Baker as carpenter and James Harris and John Sanders as shoemakers; Edward Holmes as the station master at Eggesford Station; John Hookway as the Relieving Officer and Registrar of Births and Deaths for the Crediton Union (at Moortown); Rebecca Hooper as shopkeeper; William Josland (senior) as shoemaker and parish clerk; Thomas Lake and Thomas Sage as masons; John Ley as shoemaker and baker; Thomas Luxton again as victualler and farmer (with Schoolmaster's this time listed as an Inn); Simon Newcomb as butcher; Richard Passmore as Nurseryman; Thomas Reed still the victualler at the London Inn; Richard Tancock as carpenter and shopkeeper; William Webber as tailor and shopkeeper, and his namesake a cooper, with a third William a blacksmith and ironmonger.

Prior to the UK's welfare state and benefits system of today, it was then the job of the local Relieving Officer to identify those in need and to help them with whatever funds or means were available, including entry to a workhouse. The 1834 Poor Law Amendment Act had introduced a National Welfare System (of poor relief), creating new administrative areas across England and Wales called Poor Law Unions. Each Union operated a workhouse, run by an elected Board of Guardians who employed the Relieving Officer, amongst others. Apart from receiving food and clothing, children in the workhouse were educated, and adults expected to work.

The Crediton Poor Law Union embraced 29 parishes, including Chawleigh and Eggesford. As far back as 1777, a parliamentary report had catalogued workhouses in Chawleigh (housing 24 people), Chulmleigh (36), Crediton (90), with a total of 95 workhouses spread over Devon.

Nine years later the *Post Office Directory* of 1866 shows farming still as the principal occupation, adding John Adams and Richard Elston as farmers; William Cole and John Harris at Burridge; William Davy as miller and farmer; William Drake at East Leigh; William Kemp now at Leaches; John Saunders at The Barton; William Saunders as farmer and maltster at Nutsons; William Saunders junior at Chenson; Peter Tucker at West Hill; William Western at Hardings (Leigh).

Other trades reveal Edward Snell no longer listed as farmer, but as a carpenter; Edward Holmes (formerly station master) now at the Fox and Hounds Hotel in Eggesford; Mrs Mary Newcombe as butcher; James Nott as shoemaker; Henry and George Tancock as carpenters; John Webber at the London Inn as well as active as a butcher and farmer; John Whitfield as baker.

There was clearly mobility in trades and other occupations as the community strove to make a living. Life was not easy, and a few short years later, disaster struck the village with some eighty inhabitants finding themselves homeless and their possessions gone.

CHAPTER 11

A 19TH-CENTURY DISASTER: THE GREAT FIRE OF 1869

On Friday 27 August 1869, *The Exeter and Plymouth Gazette* recorded the devastating fire which started in the building next to Leaches Farm (now Leaches House). The neighbouring property was occupied by the unfortunate Tancocks and their carpentry business. Leaches Farm and its highly flammable thatched roof was spared as the wind was blowing in the opposite direction:

'DESTRUCTIVE FIRE AT CHAWLEIGH

WEDNESDAY 25TH AUGUST 1869

THE GREATER PART OF THE VILLAGE BURNT DOWN

On Wednesday last, a most destructive fire broke out in the village of Chawleigh, burning freely for about seven hours, in which time the whole of the centre of the place was destroyed, with the exception of two blocks of houses on opposite sides of the road, which were saved mainly owing to the exertion of the inhabitants and others. The greater part of the houses burnt were in the occupation of tradesmen and farmers, and almost all the furniture was destroyed. The fire was first observed in a piggery at the back of the houses occupied by Messrs Tancock, smiths [they were in fact carpenters]. It quickly spread to the shop and dwelling house and the fire engine was sent for from Chulmleigh, but it was almost useless. Some water, however, was obtained from wells, and some was fetched in carts from the Little Dart, almost a mile distant.

The Reverend Pelham Fellows Clay, the vicar of the parish, and the Reverend George Cuddington Bethune, Rector of Chulmleigh, and the whole of the inhabitants of the village were indefatigable in their exertions, but, without water, their labours were of little avail. In all, 21 houses were burnt, representing 21 families averaging 4 in a family who were rendered homeless, and were obliged to camp for the night in the fields, in the midst of the small portion of furniture that was saved.

The first buildings which the fire reached after Messrs Tancocks' was a malt-house adjoining, which was used as a storehouse, in the occupation of Mr. Dinning, smith. The malt-house was quickly in flames, and the wind being fresh at the time, the flames spread across the road, and ignited the thatch of the London Inn, a public house, in the occupation of Mr. Webber who is also a butcher. From the London Inn, the fire seized on a block of adjacent cottages, in the occupation of Mrs. Knott, Robert Burridge, John and George Webber and Betsy Stuart; the whole of the tenements were destroyed. The flames then crossed the main road and caught the houses on the opposite side, and at the same time ignited a bakehouse in the occupation of Mr. Whitfield.

Through the exertions of Mr. Holmes, of the Fox and Hounds Inn, Eggesford, and Mr. Edworthy and others, who entered Mr. Whitfield's house and continued throwing water on the roof, that, as well as several other cottages adjoining, were saved. This block of houses had slated roofs, but those on the opposite side of the road were thatched, and the wind carrying the flames across the road, the whole of the houses opposite were quickly on fire. A barn adjoining Mr. Whitfield's house containing corn, which had only been placed there on the previous day was also burnt. The corn in the barn belonged to Mr. Joslin.'

The thatched cottages on the other side of the street were burnt to the ground, as were also the outhouses and a rick of hay at the back. While these houses were on fire, the wind shifted and blew the flames back in a slanting direction, and the result was that several cottages above Mr. Whitfield's and the houses adjoining were also burnt. The Chulmleigh Town engine arrived on the spot between three and four o'clock. At that time, the whole of the centre of the village was in a blaze, with the exception of the houses occupied by Messrs. Webber, Dilling and Smith, and Mr. Whitfield, Baker, and the immediate adjoining houses, and the efforts of the firemen were directed to saving these houses, which they succeeded in doing.

Messrs. G & H Tancock	Philip Dart, mason	Robert Burridge
Mrs. Knott, widow	Grace Olding	Grace Webber
Mr. Dilling	Mr. Joslin junior	Betsy Stuart
Mr. Webber "London Inn"	Caroline Joslin	T. Moger
Mr. Joslin, grocer	John Ware	Edward Hayman
Mr. Chalice, grocer	John Ley	
Mr. Webber, sexton	Mrs. Cosway	

The list of those who were burnt out, or had their houses damaged is as follows:

Mr. Webber, smith	Mr. Dilling, smith	Mr. Whitfield, baker'

In this period, a tenement referred not to a slum infested by multiple desperate families feeding gin to quieten their babies, as satirised by William Hogarth, but rather to a home with a tenant, often with messuage: outhouses and a plot of land to sustain the family.

An account in *The Architect: A Weekly Illustrated Journal of Art, Civil Engineering and Building* (Vol. II, July–December, 1869) was indignant about how the fire was not brought under control earlier, apportioning blame to the local water company:

'The quiet village of Chawleigh, situate next to Eggesford Station, on the North Devon Line, was almost destroyed by fire a few days ago. Twenty-one dwellings with other buildings were consumed, out of about ninety houses in all, sheltering some 80 persons, mostly of the labouring classes.

One account says that about seventy-five houses were in flames; if so, far more than twenty-one must have been destroyed. There was what sailors call a chopping wind; it veered round several times during the conflagration, so that the houses on either side of the street were alternately ignited.

The fire commenced at 2 pm, but not until 4 pm did an engine from the neighbouring town of Chulmleigh make its appearance – and then there was no water! What say the Sun and Royal

Farmer's Insurance Offices to this neglect? The explanation lies here. In various parts of the provinces, the local companies only allow their water to run into the house cisterns during, say, one hour in the morning, and perhaps one in the evening; not the slightest provision is made against accidental fire, except at these certain times; and yet engines are constructed to pump away, householders are advised to flush away, and insurance companies to advertise for policy-holders.

Is not such conduct little better than insane? Two hours are taken to bring an engine a few miles, and then it is discovered that the great need is water!

Why did not the local company at once turn on its mains? Why did Chulmleigh not hasten faster to the rescue?

Only on the supposition that all the inhabitants of this part are builders in want of contracts can we understand the simultaneous sight of a burning village, empty water pipes and no engines.'

The *devonheritage.org* website some 150 years later offers more detail about those involved:

'Richard Edworthy kept the Royal Oak further up the street, and lived in an adjoining house from which he ran a wheelwright's business. According to the press report in the Exeter and Plymouth Gazette, "the house was ignited several times but was put out". His neighbour across the street, Samuel Mair, wasn't so lucky but the destruction of his house marked the end of the fire on that side of the street.

All the property on both sides of the street between the Royal Oak and the Earl of Portsmouth Inn had eventually to be rebuilt … the Devon Weekly Times describing the event some days later, called the village "a scene of desolation".

Chawleigh and most of the land surrounding it formed part of the vast estate of the Earl of Portsmouth who lived just close by at Eggesford House. There was a tiny local Fire Brigade consisting of estate workers under the direction [of] a Mr. Lovell, and they did what little they could to help. The ruin may have been complete but at least there was no loss of life.

It was Lord Portsmouth who organised the gradual reconstruction of the street we see today. He ordered the use of traditional materials so that now, a century and a half later, signs of the damage have virtually disappeared.'

Ironically the *Devon Weekly Times* reported a contemporaneous fire, presumably also whipped up by the strong gusts that day:

'Three large ricks of wheat, the produce of 10 acres, estimated at 30 bushels per acre, and a rick of vetches containing about 40 bushels, the property of Mr. Robert Middleton of Fiddlecott Farm, were destroyed by fire on Wednesday last, by the carelessness of one of the labourers lighting his pipe and throwing down the burning match by the side of the ricks.'

The cause of the disastrous Tancock's piggery fire does not appear in the record. Whatever its origins, the close-knit farming community with the support of their 'squire' stepped up to help its own people.

THE FIRE

Messrs Tancock's premises. This is where the fire started

Glebe Cottage

↑ To Tiverton

Mr & Mrs R. Gove

Leathes

Mr Gove's walled garden

Mr Lake

← Lane

Forge

← To Stone Mill

Forge House

Wembley House

Inn

Old Bakery

Shop

Mr Player Thorns

Mrs Stuart Thorns

Mr C Way

Mr Andrews

Mr C Way's walled garden →

Barn

Public Footpath

Lane

Mr Woodman

Mr C P Webber

Mr B Webber

Easter Cottage

Palm Cottage

Mrs Trethewan

Gardens

Mrs Gove

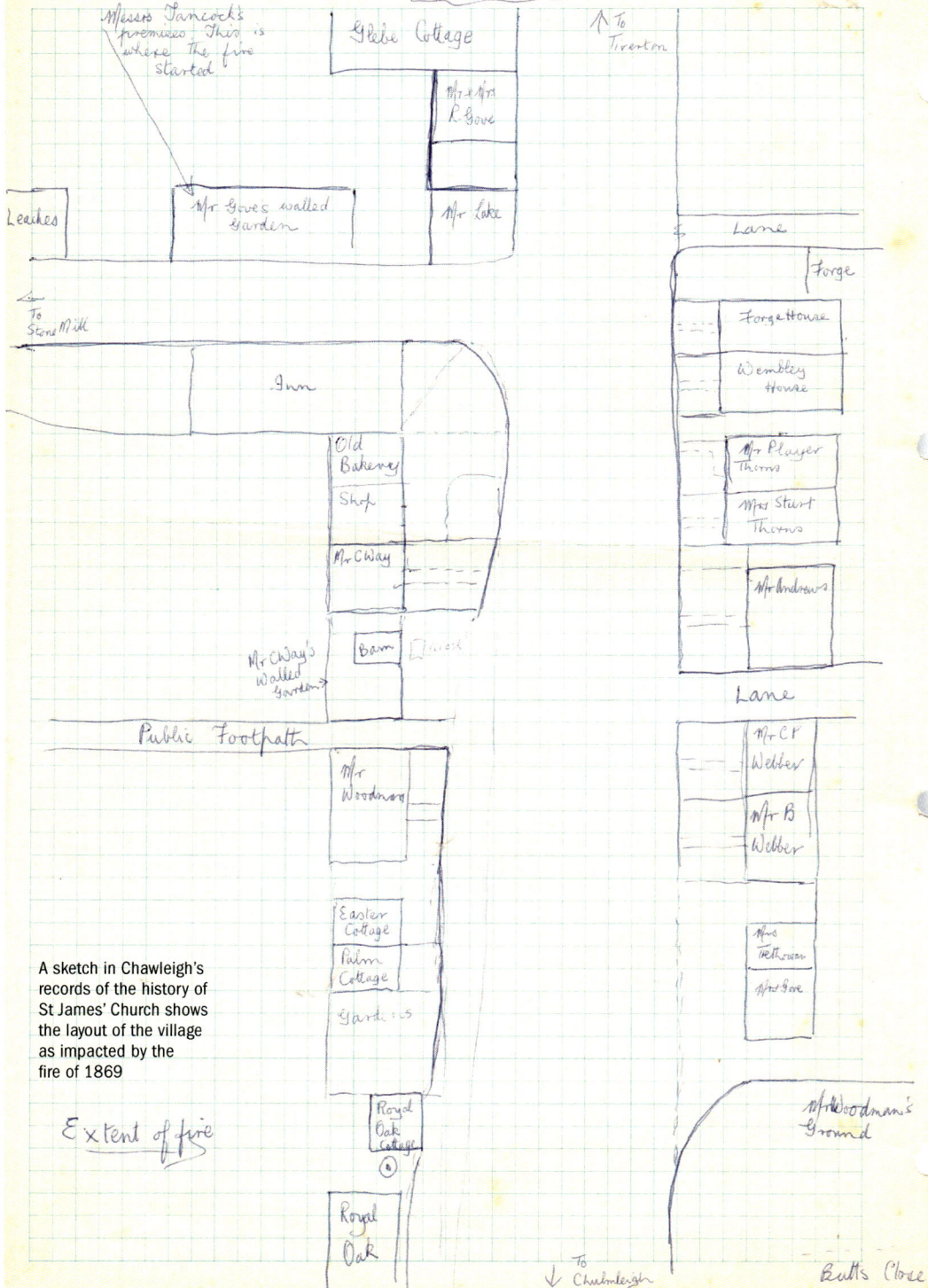

A sketch in Chawleigh's records of the history of St James' Church shows the layout of the village as impacted by the fire of 1869

Extent of fire

Royal Oak Cottage

Mr Woodman's Ground

Royal Oak

↓ To Chulmleigh

Butts Close

CHAPTER 12

THE 'DEATH CLUB' – FOR MEN ONLY

The women of Chawleigh had to wait until 1934 to form their own exclusive club with their branch of the Women's Institute (see Chapter 23). Following the calamitous Great Fire, while the women of the community would have worked tirelessly in support, the men of the community drew together to help those in dire need with their male-only society which survives to this day.

The 1851 census had shown a village population of almost 850 people, of whom some 80 were made homeless by the fire. Fortunately perhaps, the Chawleigh Friendly Society had been formed a few weeks before the disaster on 10 July 1869 with the aim: 'For supporting the sick and burying the dead'. In Chawleigh, their efforts were quickly redoubled in helping to support the newly destitute.

Henry Martin, brought up at Leaches Farm (now Leaches House) and today a parish councillor for Chawleigh, gives an account of the Society's history and its impact on the village. He references the four days of the calendar's quarters traditionally used for charging rent in England: Lady Day (25 March), Midsummer Day (24 June), Michaelmas (29 September), and Christmas Day (25 December):

'Chawleigh Friendly Society was established … by 13 Chawleigh men with the first subscriptions being paid on the midsummer quarter day 1869… The Friendly Society is a men's society that all working men under the age of 45 can join. … On Chawleigh Fair day a Roll Call and the Annual Club Walk takes place followed by a church service and members' lunch. In the afternoon there are:– children's fancy dress and sports, car boot sale and stalls, barbeque and refreshments.

The membership increased rapidly by Midsummer 1870 to be 32 members, 52 members by Midsummer 1871. This was undoubtedly spurred on by the effects felt after the "Great Fire of Chawleigh" which occurred on Wednesday the 25th August 1869. It started in the piggery of Messrs Tancock situated next to Leaches Farm and then spread rapidly towards the Square, crossing the road to destroy the London Inn… From there spreading to the adjacent cottages and crossing the road, to destroy the whole of the centre of Chawleigh and … 21 households.

The 1st Article states – That this Society shall never be removed out of the village of Chawleigh; and so long as 3 members continue to support this Society it shall not be dissolved. The Society room being situated above the Skittle Alley of the Royal Oak, there was an outside set of stairs to it. …

On the Anniversary Day (6th May) all members residing within a 5-mile radius of the parish of Chawleigh shall attend in the Society room precisely by 10.30 in the forenoon, when the roll call shall take place. From there the members shall walk in a regular and decent manner to the parish church and back for the Annual dinner.

In 1934 the Annual day was held on the 4th June "in the usual way with Roll call at 11am." Miss Edworthy of the Royal Oak provided a hot dinner with plum pudding at 2 shillings and 6 pence.

Fines were applicable under several of the rules, and these were rigorously levied. Each year a committee was formed to organise the fair day. Tokens were at one time sold to each member to be redeemed at the Royal Oak. These tokens had a face value of 6d (6 old pennies = half a shilling before decimalisation, face value now of 2 and a half New Pence).

For the 100th Anniversary it was decided to have a Fair Queen, also a banner with the year of formation on it and a Carnival Float "Now and Then" which was entered into local Carnivals at Chulmleigh and High Bickington.

The Annual luncheon was held every year in the Club room at the Royal Oak right up until the committee meeting in 1975 learnt that "the room at the Royal may not be available"! During this meeting there was uproar as you can imagine. It was decided to ask Mrs A. Pike to arrange the luncheon in the Jubilee Hall on the 9th June.

In the 1920s the swing boats were positioned between the Royal Oak and Royal Oak cottage (before the Royal Oak cottage was extended). The races were held along the road with stalls by the side of the road outside the Royal Oak.

The Chawleigh Fair sports were held in several different fields over the years, including down Blackwalls Lane, Butts Close field, Tower View field on Coronation Day 1953, Broadclose field (behind Sunnyside cottages) and the Fair field (opposite the Garage) for many years, until it moved in 1993 to Porters Park where it is still held.'

A Chawleigh Fair float, c.1925

(Photo by kind permission of Yvonne Gerry)

Porters Park was given to Chawleigh Parish Council in 1991 by the Porter family of The Old Hall to provide recreational facilities for Chawleigh inhabitants. The Parish Council bought the old school playground and small play area when the Primary School closed.

The Friendly Society has been closely linked with Chawleigh Fair since its formation, but on 25 April 1890 considerable dissent was reported by the *Devon and Exeter Gazette* about which Band should be selected to play:

> 'The selection of the band formed the subject of considerable discussion, and notwithstanding a resolution proposed by the Chairman and the advice of the club in favour of the Chawleigh band, the matter was ordered to stand over for a week and tenders from other bands were solicited. It is hoped that the differences that existed at the last meeting will have blown over before the next.'

However, the same newspaper reported on 2 August 1890:

> 'The Clerk (Mr. Thomas Sage) stated that he had connected with four different bands in the neighbourhood, but that only one application had been received and whose tender greatly exceeds that of the town band. Mr. Lawrence suggested that no band be engaged, but the proposal was immediately ruled out of order – subsequently Messrs. Lawrence and Smith left the meeting. The Chairman proposed that the tender of the Chawleigh Band be accepted. Mr. Lewis Webber seconded, and the motion was carried.'

The Western Times of 13 May 1898 suggested that disputes of this sort had eventually been settled, recording:

> 'Chawleigh Fair was held Friday last weekend [and] was well attended. The proceedings commenced with the Chulmleigh Brass Band led by Mr. Fred. Lovell. The usual assembly of members proceeded to the church where the Rev. J. Vowler Tanner officiated, assisted by the Rev. John Morgan (Rector of Cheldon) who preached. The procession reformed and paraded through the village to the Royal Oak Hotel where an excellent dinner was provided by host and hostess Edworthy.'

The Society has survived other differences of opinion over the years, and continues to the present day, still entirely male. These local friendly societies formed in every village or town to help workers such as farm labourers and tenant farmers address their fears for their families in the case of sickness, death or similar misfortune – and so the term 'death club' emerged. Members paid a few shillings a year to avoid broken homes, poverty and other misery. Some death clubs aimed to provide a small pension in old age.

J M Slader reported in *The Western Morning News* on 3 June 1963: 'Only in one parish in Devon does a death club survive. At Chawleigh, a community as remote from civilisation as one can find today, it carries on despite the Welfare State… The subscription today is one guinea a year (originally it was ten shillings) which entitles members to 14 shillings a week sick pay. On death the next of kin receive £10 funeral benefit. Still a prosperous society, it has over £400 invested.'

The impact of the Great Fire of 1869 was felt for decades: in 1884 the proceeds of the tea and collections on the day of the Chawleigh Harvest Festival were noted by the *Devon Weekly Times* of 12 September to 'be distributed to the poor people who suffered at the last disastrous fire in the village.'

The Harvest Festival started with a 'special service at four o'clock in the afternoon' which was 'tastefully decorated by Mrs. Tanner (of the Rectory), Mrs. Baker (The Barton), Miss L. Webber (The Portsmouth Hotel) and several other kind helpers… After the service about 200 of the adults marched to the Rectory grounds when a public tea was provided. The tables were presided over by Mrs. Tanner, Mrs. Benson, Mrs. Challis, Mrs. Phillips, Mrs. Ford, Mrs. Partridge and Mrs. Saunders. Mr. W. Challis (Leaches), Mr. E. Ford (Nethercott) also assisted.' As usual, the farming families were much in evidence.

That year's Festival had its other more sombre moments: 'the address was given on "Temperance and Moderation", by the Rev. J. Vowler Tanner, and the Rev. G. Welsh Owen'. However, as Harvest Festivals were generally followed by an evening of drinking and dancing, how temperate and moderate the gathering would have remained in the later hours is uncertain.

Fires were relatively frequent in the Victorian period. A fire in two unoccupied cottages was reported at Little Moortown Farm in Chawleigh on 25 November 1881 by the *Devon Weekly Times*: 'The flames were not extinguished before the interiors of the buildings were destroyed. The fire is supposed to be the act of an incendiary.' The reasons behind the arson were unknown.

On 27 December 1901, the *Devon Weekly Times* was sadly to report another, smaller, Christmas Day fire, this time at 'East Leigh Farmhouse, the residence of Mr. and Mrs. Isaac Phillips' which was 'burnt to the ground'. Another thatch fire, and another Earl of Portsmouth property, although the tenant this time was lucky to be 'insured in the Sun Office':

> 'The fire is supposed to have originated in the ash-house at the back of the house, the heat from which must have ignited the thatch, and it being a large old-fashioned farmhouse the fire must have soon spread over the whole roof. Only a few articles were saved, and many are the expressions of sympathy for Mr. and Mrs. Phillips, who had only just settled in, having been married only in September last. The whole of their valuable presents were lost, and also all their wearing apparel.'

Road accidents too were relatively common: Thursday 24 March 1870 saw Mr. Robert Middleton, junior, 'returning on horseback in company with his father from a sale at Merton', come into a 'violent collision with a trap driven by Mr. W. Anstey, a young man residing at Merton Mill. Middleton broke and otherwise injured his right leg… he now lies in a critical state.' He was of the same Middletons at Fiddlecott Farm who were to suffer the accidental blaze of their hay ricks on the same day as the Great Fire of Chawleigh nearly thirty years later.

And on Thursday 6 January 1870 a local farmer from Chawleigh Week Mills, Mr Davey, was killed on the North Devon railway while on his way home from feeding his sheep, as the *Devon Weekly Times* rather graphically reported:

> 'He was first noticed after the accident by the packers on the line. He had a very severe cut on the hinder part of his neck, but his head was not severed from his body. One of his legs was cut off, with the exception of some skin, and one of his ankles severely injured. … No account can be given of how he met with the accident, but that it occurred from the railway carriages passing when he was on the act of crossing the line. No one witnessed it.'

A distressing and lonely end.

Just as disturbing was the industrial accident that befell a young girl at another farm near Chawleigh (*Devon and Exeter Gazette*, 1 February 1895):

'A girl named Polly Fewlings, aged 13, servant at Handsford Farm, has just met with a severe accident. Mr. Cook and his staff were threshing corn in the barn and the girl was driving the three horses to keep the machinery in motion. While doing so she unfortunately got one hand and arm entangled between the cog wheels, and they were severely crushed. Dr. Tucker was quickly in attendance but it is feared she will be deprived of the future use of the hand.'

The weather was also the cause of much hardship in the later nineteenth century. Four days of The Great Blizzard heavily affected southern England and parts of Wales. *The Devon Weekly Times* of 21 January 1881 described the impact on the county:

'The storm commenced on Tuesday 18 January and continued for some days, the great fall of snow being accompanied by severe gales, and was considered the worst storm since 1866. In Barnstaple streets the snow was several feet deep, many shops did not open, and the majority of those that did closed again. Railways were blocked and engines embedded in drifts. Hatherleigh was cut off and mailbags eventually arrived on horseback.

Many deaths were reported from exposure to frost. In Exeter 30 degrees of frost was recorded. Near Barnstaple Cross toll-gate roads were completely blocked with snow, and Mr Pollard, the toll keeper, reported that there was 12 feet of snow round his house and he had to be dug out.'

The cold weather continued into the next month: 'On Tuesday 25 February, 23 degrees of frost was recorded during the night, and hundreds of persons were skating on the Exe.' In March 1891 another Great Blizzard was recorded, for some the worst winter storm of their lifetimes.

But the Chawleigh community struggled on, families and neighbours pulling together to survive the weather and, where they could, whatever else life threw at them.

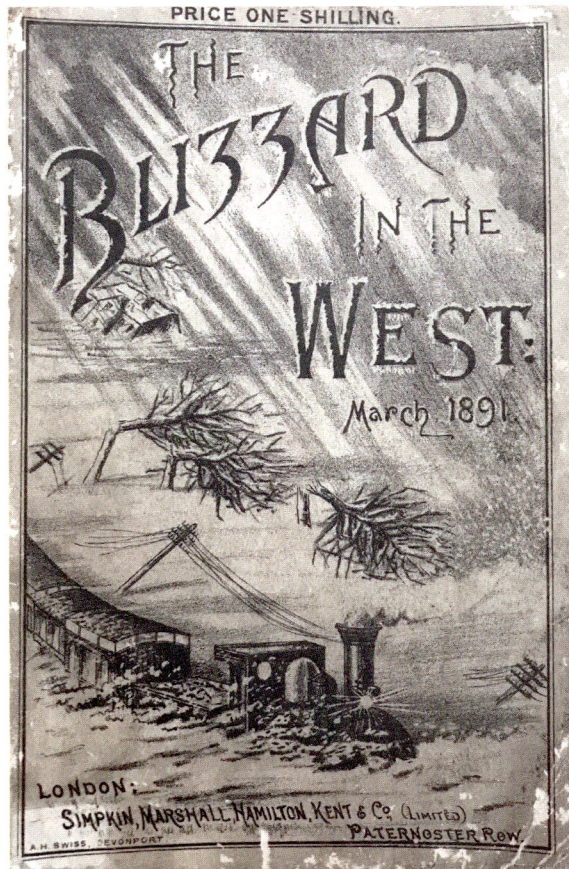

The *Great Blizzard* of 1891 was so significant that books were written about it at the time, citing 'the gravest atmospheric disturbance of the century – in that part of the world, at all events – would come to spread terror and destruction throughout town and country'

CHAPTER 13

CHAWLEIGH AFTER THE GREAT FIRE

Chawleigh – the Late Victorian period (1870–1901)

Life had to return to a new normal after the Great Fire, especially for those still with homes and incomes. The Earl of Portsmouth assisted with rebuilding the part of the village destroyed in the conflagration.

The Post Office Directory of 1873 records the Reverend Pelham Fellowes Clay, MA, still with the 'Living' (a Rectory value of £470 plus 95 acres of glebe, the latter being land used to support the parish priest). The curate in charge was the Reverend John Vowler Tanner, residing at Eggesford, supported by the parish clerk William Josland, listed in *Billing's Directory and Gazetteer of the County of Devon* of 1857 as working as a village shoemaker.

New names and occupations include Richard Bird and William Shipman as shopkeepers; William Chalis (spelling incorrect) now farming at Leaches; John Ley having turned his hand to farming rather than shoemaking; William Elworthy having taken over at Duckham Farm; William Kemp having moved from Leaches Farm to Mildons Leigh, along with Richard Partridge; Henry Phillips at East Leigh; James Peters as a farmer; and Thomas Reed (not the former victualler at the London Inn, who had died in 1859) now farming at Toatworthy.

Thomas Sage added the new profession of shopkeeper to his trade as a mason; Mrs Ann Saunders emerged as farmer and maltster at Nutsons; and a new Snell, Thomas, was now installed as farmer at West Hill. The Great Fire of 1869 (see Chapter 11) took place before this new edition of the *Post Office Directory*, so some changes may have resulted from the damage and upheaval it caused.

The 1878–79 edition of *White's History, Gazetteer & Directory of Devonshire* provides more colour about Victorian-era Chawleigh, as being:

'… in the Crediton union and county court district, South Molton petty sessional division, Chulmleigh polling district of North Devon, Tawton Hundred, Barnstaple archdeaconry and Chulmleigh rural deanery. The parish had 759 inhabitants (382 males and 377 females) in 1871, comprised in 156 families, living in 150 houses on 5020 acres of land. The Earl of Portsmouth is Lord of the Manor and the owner of about three fourths of the soil, the other landowners are Sir George Stucley, Sir F. Williams, and Messrs. R. Reed, T. Reed and R. May. Chawleigh has two cattle fairs, on May 6 and the Tuesday before the last Thursday in October. Eggesford market is held on the second Wednesday in each month near the Fox and Hounds Hotel, in this parish, and is an important cattle and general market'.

White's also describes the church, and then the educational and charitable work associated with it:

'The glebe is 95 acres, and there is a dilapidated rectory-house. The tithes are commuted at £470.5.10d a year. The Independents and Bible Christians have chapels here. The School Board for the united district of Chawleigh and Cheldon was formed on Feb. 19, 1873, and consists of the Earl of Portsmouth (chairman), the Rev J. Vowler Tanner, B.A. (vice), and Messrs. R. Reed, Henry Reed and W. Short. Mr J. Hannaford is their clerk, and resides at Chumleigh. The Board Schools are the property of the feofees of the "Church Property", who let the schools and the master's house to the School Board for a nominal rent, reserving the right to use the school-room for the Church Sunday school. Twenty-four acres of land and houses, let for about £90 a year are vested in twelve trustees for the repair and uses of the church; and the dividends of £300, left by the late Dr. May of Exeter, and invested in the 3 per cent Consols [government bonds issued by the Bank of England], are divided among the poor of the parish yearly on Dec. 4 at the discretion of the minister, churchwardens and overseers. The poor parishioners also have £3 yearly from the various bequests.'

There is a final note about rural 1870s postal services: 'Post from Chulmleigh which is the nearest Money Order Office. There is a wall Letter Box cleared at 6.20 p.m. weekdays only.'

Staff at the Portsmouth sawmills, c.1920s-30s (By kind permission of Daphne Cockram)

New names appearing in this 1878–79 edition of *White's* include John Bartlett, station master at Eggesford; John Bradford, boot and shoemaker; William Clarke, agent to Ward, Cann & Co. at James Week (manure, oilcake and general merchants, later also coal merchants); Philip and William Dart, masons; Richard Grinney,

farmer; William Josland, appearing as parish clerk at The Rectory; James Kennedy, farmer at Ford; a second John Sage, mason; two female members of the Saunders family appearing in their own right – Mrs Maria at Nutson and Mrs Mary at Week; and William Simmons as a shopkeeper.

Kelly's Directory of 1883, a few years down the line, introduces William Cheriton and John Sing, farmers at Moortown and Poundsford respectively; John Lethern, a baker; and a reference to George Vickery, clerk of works to the Earl of Portsmouth, based at the Saw Mills. The Devon Buildings Group's newsletter of October 1988 describes George Vickery as a significant architect who 'was to finish his career as resident architect of the Earl of Portsmouth's Eggesford estate. Vickery died in 1904 and his obituary in *The North Devon Journal*, written by the ubiquitous Harry Hems, describes him as "one of the cleverest craftsmen Barnstaple ever produced. It was this same George Vickery who was the general contractor for [Robert] Fulford's restoration of Colaton Raleigh church. Not only the contractor, in fact, but also the executant craftsman for the decorative scheme…"'

Richard Josland is also listed in 1883 as not just tailor and grocer but also 'post office'. It was typical for rural post offices to be incorporated into the village shop at this time, much as the arrangement today in Chawleigh.

By 1889, *Kelly's Directory* suggests a community evolving into a gradually wealthier and more diverse grouping, with trades such as tailor becoming more widespread, so finding sufficient custom (Isaac Bater and James Gardner); Miss Fanny Saunders as dressmaker; James Dilling no longer just a blacksmith but also a rate collector; Lewis Petherick as another blacksmith; Edward Lawrence as another shoemaker, and so on.

Amongst the farmers, Charles Tucker is now running the farm at Leaches; with Robert Pickard at Chenson; Richard Parkhouse is farming at Ford and also active as a 'cattle dealer'; and two farmers are cited also as 'landowners': Thomas Reed at Toatworthy and Isaac Saunders at Tonefield (Tonyfield).

White's Directory for 1890 lists the population in 1881 as numbering 871, and offers further insight into everyday affairs: Richard Josland's post office handles letters 'received 7 a.m. and dep. 6.20 p.m.', and he is also parish clerk, this now seemingly a family tradition. James Dilling becomes 'farmer & agr. implement maker and asst. overseer'. Mrs Elizabeth Holmes is now shown at the Fox & Hounds Hotel; Walter Keenor as another mason; Henry Page as a clerk; Miss Bessie Petherick as another dressmaker; and John Rippon now installed at East Hill Farm.

Miss Lucy Snell, from the long-standing Chawleigh family, is shown as mistress of the Infant Board School; Miss Sarah Ware has set herself up as a dressmaker; and John Webber has become sexton, toiling in the churchyard. Edwin Podger is serving as the village Police Constable, presumably resident in the police house, which still carries the Portsmouth crest today. There was a police officer stationed in the village until the 1950s.

Kelly's Directory for 1893 shows a population in 1891 of 613, fewer than previously, although this appears to exclude Cheldon which was listed separately. The Mixed Board School with capacity for 120 children had an average attendance of 36 boys, 40 girls and 27 infants. Of the 27 farmers shown, only one is a woman, Mrs Mary Elworthy at Duckham.

Kelly's for 1897 records Mrs Barclay-Sharpe as a 'resident' alongside the Reverend John Vowler Tanner, the only two non-commercial listings – presumably financially independent and / or retired. Albert and Bartholomew Cook emerge as farmers at Fiddlecott and Stone Mill respectively, and John Down at Handsford. Frederick Hill is a new shopkeeper, and John Nicholls has set up as a wheelwright. John Shopland is farming at Ford but also serving as farm bailiff to the Earl of Portsmouth.

In an interview with Mr Turner by Miss F W Hillman in the mid-1960s, he recalled that Stone Mill was in use until Mr Webber had it, 'doing a little "grease grinding" for local farmers'. It originally had a wooden wheel, before the millwrights Garnish & Lemon of Barnstaple fitted a new one some seventy years later. One story went that a gentleman named George Way, "slightly fuddled by cider", was going to help with haymaking but fell off the plank over the millstream, becoming rather damp before trying to help Mr Stentiford, the miller and farmer at the time. Other memories included poaching being popular in the millstream, trout being caught with a hair noose on a long stick. A quarry over the road from the mill was owned by the Portsmouth estate, along with the mill itself.

The *Kelly's Directory* for 1902 now lists four 'residents' for Chawleigh: Mrs Kane, Alfred Luxton, Robert Pickard, and as before, the Reverend Tanner. Amongst the 'commercial' listings, William Tucker has taken over at Leaches Farm, Charles having moved to Southcott. Emmanuel Tonkin is a new thatcher, William Ware a butcher and at the Portsmouth Hotel, with George Way (presumably he who was fuddled by cider) farming at Butts Close.

PC 321 Robert Edward Rundle, father of former Chief Supt. Brian Rundle, who was born in the bedroom over the police sign (right) at the police house in 1937.

PC Rundle is standing over a Chawleigh village well, c.1935-45.

The police house had no electricity or inside lavatory, and is believed to have been the only house in the village at the time to have running water, supplied by a handpump over the sink.

The police house is another Chawleigh property with the Portsmouth P and crest displayed at the front (not visible here).

Photo from the Rundle Collection, Devon Heritage Centre, South West Heritage Trust

Chawleigh Quarry in the early 20th century – health and safety was viewed somewhat differently at the time

(Photo by kind permission of Daphne Cockram)

Political events were celebrated in this remote farming village, as the *Devon and Exeter Gazette* reported on 25 January 1889, often accompanied by church bells and a brass band: 'The result of the poll for the County Council Electoral Division was received here at noon with much enthusiasm. Throughout the afternoon the church bells were rung by Messrs Dilling, Edworthy, Tucker, Lawrence, Cass, Smith, Dilling junior, and others. The brass band paraded the streets in the evening.'

Another event for celebration was the 'Relief of Mafeking', an event in the Boer War (also known as the South African War) when Robert Baden-Powell became something of a national hero for leading the defence of Mafeking over some 217 days, to be eventually relieved by British, Australian, Rhodesian and Canadian forces (supported by 'Black South African drivers'). *The Devon & Exeter Gazette* recounted that on Friday 18 May 1900, Chawleigh too joined in the British Empire-wide rejoicing:

'The relief of Mafeking was received here with the greatest enthusiasm and although no public festivities were held in honour of the event, still the knowledge that Colonel Baden Powell and his brave little army were at last freed from their perilous position was a source of gratitude. Flags and bunting were displayed at the post office and other prominent places in the village and merry peals rung out on the church bells.'

The *Gazette* also reported a range of local events showing a community conscious of its immediate agricultural needs as well as broader international developments, such as on 22 June 1900:

> 'Mr Thomas Baker (The Barton) presided over the Technical Education Committee meeting held in the schoolroom for the purpose of deciding what subjects will be taught during the ensuing year. There were also present: Messrs Charles Tucker (Southcott), Edwin Webber (Moortown), J. Reed, Partridge (Leigh), Samuel Snell (Pouncers), and John Baple (Secretary). It was decided to apply to the Crediton District Committee for assistance to hold classes in ploughing, horticulture and fruit culture.'

An annual ploughing match and competitions were fixed for November 1900. George Lambert (later 1st Viscount Lambert), intermittently the local MP between 1891 and 1945 (and the fifth longest-serving MP of the twentieth century), agreed to officiate at that evening's dinner.

Chawleigh streets remained unpaved into the 1920s, and transport was still dominated by horse-drawn power

(by kind permission of Henry Martin)

The Village, Chawleigh

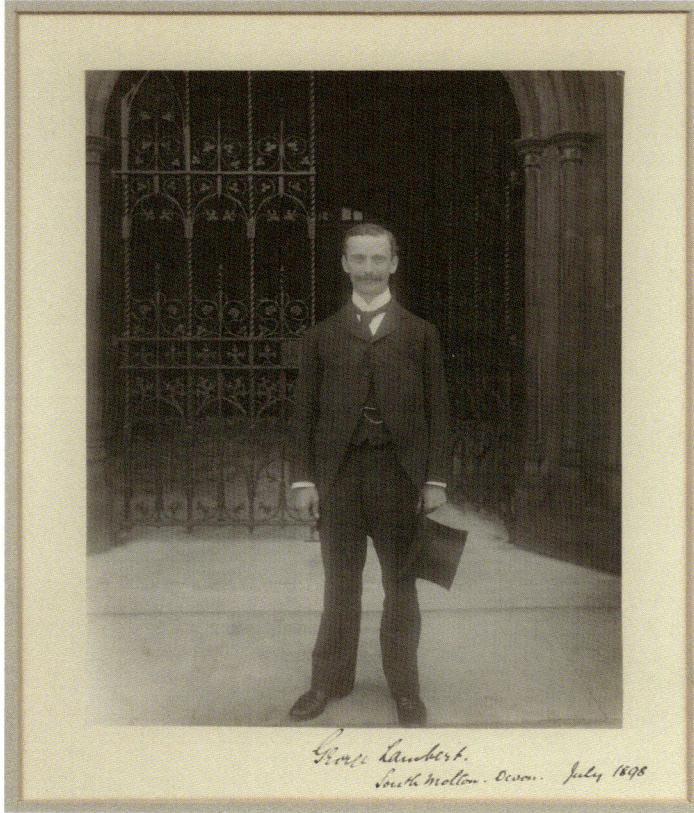

Lambert was a farmer from the village of Spreyton in Mid Devon. He became a county councillor and county alderman, and was selected as Liberal Party candidate for the South Molton constituency, which included Chawleigh, for the 1891 by-election campaign. The seat had been Liberal under Viscount Lymington, son of the Earl of Portsmouth. The 5th Earl, who died in 1891, was well respected in Devon, even though his son Lymington (later the 6th Earl) did not seem to elicit the same response locally. The political tide was turning against large landowners, and parliamentary elections reflected this.

Chawleigh – the Edwardian period (1901–1914)

The turn of the century brought a more rapid change in politics and social divisions and of course a new monarch, Edward VII. Chawleigh would not have been immune to these developments, and the prominence of The Old Hall in the village meant it continued to house more well-known figures with interesting if convoluted stories of their own.

In 1906 Kelly's lists three 'residents', including Miss Leach at The Cottage and the Reverend Frederick Sumner, MA, at The Rectory (now the home of the Amber Foundation). Frank Moulton-Barrett, MA, also a Reverend, lived at The Old Rectory (today's Old Hall): born in 1865 at Combe Head, a manor house in Bampton, Devon, he had been educated at Marlborough and Magdalen College, Oxford, and served as a curate in Harpenden (Hertfordshire). He died in 1920 at Bewley Down in East Devon, and was buried in Wambrook, Somerset. He served for a time as vice-president of Lapford Shooting Club.

Through his father Henry Moulton-Barrett, Frank Moulton-Barrett was connected to the famous poets Robert Browning and Elizabeth Barrett Browning. According to the Brownings Correspondence website (*browningscorrespondence.com*), Elizabeth Barrett Browning (née Moulton-Barrett), wife of Robert (see Chapter 9), left her Diary to her sister Arabella, who in turn passed the first part of it to Browning himself. The text was later to be inherited by their son Robert Barrett Browning.. The second part of the Diary was inherited from Arabella by her brother George, and in turn by another brother, Henry, Frank's father.

When Henry died in 1896, Frank inherited this part of his aunt's Diary, and finally left it to his own brother, Lt.-Col. Harry Peyton Moulton-Barrett. This Harry was in 1924 given charge of the first part of the Diary and other papers by the family, so reuniting the two parts. From Chawleigh to the United States, the Diary now sits in the Henry W and Albert A Berg Collection in the New York Public Library.

With an example of a more developed financial system spreading across Great Britain, 1906 listings also reveal bankers in the parish for the first time: Fox, Fowler & Co. Ltd, originally named Fox Bros. According to the Lloyds Banking Group Archives, Thomas Fox, a prominent Quaker and serge-maker in Somerset, founded the bank in 1787 in Wellington, Somerset, starting off as a woollen merchants offering banking services, and issuing banknotes (continuing this until 1921). It took over the business of the failed West of England & South Wales District Bank in 1878, and was renamed Fox, Fowler & Co., becoming prominent in private banking in the West Country.

> 'Following the outbreak of the First World War in 1914 the bank's senior partner, John Fox, feared that there would be a run on the bank. He travelled to London to bring back necessary funds to cope with the prospect of mass withdrawals, returning to the West Country with £100,000 in gold and coin. He packed the money in three wooden boxes which he took with him and stored in his railway compartment on the journey back. Fortunately, the bank survived the war unscathed.'

With fifty-six branches, the firm was eventually amalgamated into Lloyds in 1921, John Fox becoming a director of Lloyds. Whether any of that '£100,000 in gold and coin' reached Chawleigh remains to be discovered.

New names in the parish of 1906 included Frederick Gibbings as a tailor, Ernest Gough as a carpenter, William Littlewood at the Fox & Hounds Hotel, William P Marshall as a coal merchant, John Pike now farming at Pouncers, John Underhill at Fiddlecott. William John Snell has become not only parish council Clerk and Overseer, but also Collector of Income and Land Tax.

By 1910 the Reverend Francis Hudson is installed at The Rectory, and Thomas White at the 'Constabulary Station'. George Leaker is firing up his ovens as a baker, and Thomas Tucker has taken over farming at Leaches. Henry Wright is identified as gamekeeper to the Earl of Portsmouth.

Chawleigh – The First World War

Chawleigh suffered heavily in the First World War, as did most communities across England and the other British nations. Commemorating the Fallen of this so-called Great War, the *devonheritage.org* website has listed twelve losses from the Roll of Honour, hand-painted on a sheet of parchment and mounted within a wooden frame in St James' Church. Twelve names, the youngest aged sixteen, from a population of around six hundred, including three from the Webber family, which had been established in the village for decades.

Below the Roll of Honour for the First World War, on the inside wall of the church, framed in wood and mounted in marble, another plaque commemorates Private

---

CAPTAIN HENRY PRICE ROWE
Captain Henry Price Rowe of the 3rd/1st Wessex Div. Signal Coy. Son of William Ellis and Mary Price Rowe and husband of Josephine Rowe. Born in Hampstead in the September Quarter of 1889. Died 6 November 1918 aged 29. Buried in the churchyard of St. Mary's, Brixham.

PTE. SAMUEL BATER
Private Samuel Bater of the 8th Battalion, the Devonshire Regiment. Son of Samuel and Diana Bater of Chulmleigh and brother of Mrs. Margaret Ann Sanders of the 'Barnstaple Inn' Chulmleigh. Born in 1900 in Chittlehamholt. Died 6 September 1916 aged 16. Awarded the Military Medal.

PTE. WILLIAM FULFORD
Believed to be **Private William Fulford** of the 8th Battalion, the Devonshire Regiment who was born in Birmingham in 1888 and killed in action on 26 October 1917.

PTE. WILLIAM HARRIS
Private William Harris of the Royal Marine Light Infantry, *HMS Formidable*. Son of John Harris who lived in Chawleigh before moving to London. Born in Chawleigh in 1889. Died 1st January 1915 aged 26.

CORPORAL ERNEST RIPPIN
Corporal Ernest Rippin of the 16th (Devon Yeomanry) Battalion, the Devonshire Regiment. Son of George and Matilda Rippin of Hill Town, Chawleigh. Born in Colebrook in the June Quarter of 1887. Died 19 January 1917 aged 29.

(Additional research by Alan Regin MBE suggests that Ernest, one of eight children, was a bellringer and 'one of the best shots' at Chawleigh rifle club. He died of pneumonia in hospital in Egypt, and is commemorated at Ismailia War Memorial Cemetery there. Both Rolls of Honour describe this man as being in the R.N.D.H – the Royal North Devon Hussars, who became the Royal North Devon Yeomanry in 1908 and fought in the Great War as the 16th Battalion of the Devonshire Regiment.)

PTE. FRANK SMALLMAN
Information updated by a family member in 2013:

Private Frank Smallman of the 1st/6th Battalion, the Devonshire Regiment. Son of Mrs. Catherine Smallman (widow). Born in Dublin in 1897. Died 8 June 1916 aged 19.

Ronald Pinn of the 5th Battalion, Dorset Regiment, killed in action 4 October 1944, who was the only Second World War loss of life from Chawleigh: he died aged twenty-six at the Battle of Arnhem. He and his wife Bessie (née Shapland) both came from Chawleigh.

The sadness and destruction of this 'Great War' of 1914-18 would have been marked in the local hostelries, communal venues for commiseration, commemoration but also celebration when this war and later conflicts ended, bringing soldiers, sailors and airmen (and by now, women in auxiliary roles too) home to their families. A few faces missing in the revelry, however.

PTE. ERNEST TONKINS

Private Ernest George Tonkins of the 8th Battalion, the Somerset Light Infantry. Son of Charles and Jane Tonkins. Born in Chawleigh in the March Quarter of 1897. Died 12 July 1917 aged 20.

CORPORAL WALTER TREMAIN

Corporal Walter George Tremain of the 95th Brigade, the Royal Field Artillery. Son of Elias and Augusta Tremain of Bare Hill [Barehill Moor], Chawleigh. Born in Chawleigh in the December Quarter of 1894. Died 15 September 1916 aged 21.

PTE. JOHN WARREN

Private John Warren of the 8th Battalion, the Devonshire Regiment. Son of George and Emma Warren of Hardings Leigh Cottage, Chawleigh. Born in Chawleigh in 1893. Died 2 July 1916 aged 23.

(Additional research suggests John worked as horse man for farmer Ernest Petherick at Handsford in Chawleigh; he was wounded on 1 July, the start of the Battle of the Somme, and died a day later.)

PTE. GEORGE WEBBER

Private Henry George Webber of the 9th Battalion, the Devonshire Regiment. Son of William and Emily Webber of Chawleigh. Born in Chawleigh in 1875. Died 1 July 1916 aged 41.

PTE. SAMUEL WEBBER

Private Samuel Webber of the 1st Battalion, the Devonshire Regiment. Son of the late John and Ann Webber of Chawleigh and brother of Miss Ann Webber, 6 Hellingbourne Rd., Herne Hill, London. Born in Chawleigh in 1881. Died 19 June 1916 aged 34.

CORPORAL WILLIAM JAMES WEBBER

Corporal William James Webber of the 1st/6th Battalion, the Devonshire Regiment. Son of James and Fanny Webber of East Street, Chulmleigh and husband of Emma J. Webber of 2, Fore St., Chulmleigh. Born in Chawleigh in 1885. Died 8 March 1916 aged 31.

CHAPTER 14

HOSPITALITY: INNS AND PUBS

The Fox and Hounds, still known as a country hotel, was a significant part of the Eggesford community in the time of the Earls of Portsmouth, and closely associated with hunting and fishing (on the River Taw).

An advert in the *Billing's Directory and Gazetteer of the County of Devon* of 1857 names John Edwards as the proprietor of the establishment with all its amenities:

> *Family, Commercial and Railway Hotel*
> *and Posting House*
> *near the Eggesford Station.*
> *Well-aired Beds. Good Stabling and Coach-Houses.*
> *Porter, Burton and Pale Ales.*
> *Superior Wines and Spirits, Cigars, etc.*

See Chapter 3 for more of the history of the site, linked with the railway station and goods yard, the sawmills, and the cattle market.

Away from the Taw valley, the London Inn in Chawleigh had its origins in the seventeenth century and was so named (like other pubs in the area) because it was built on the main Exeter to Ilfracombe road, providing connections through to London in the other direction. The establishment was a coaching inn, usually inhabited by the blacksmith and his family who looked after the post horses and travellers as well as serving the local population.

The 1908 sale catalogue description ran: '0a. 1r. 10p. [measured in acres, roods and perches] in the occupation of Mr. W Ware. The Hotel contains 2 Sitting Rooms, Tap Room, Kitchen, Larder and Dairy, Cellar, 6 Bedrooms and E.C. upstairs. The Outbuildings comprise Stabling for 7 Horses, Trap House, large Open Shed and usual Offices. There is also a large Garden. Lease granted for a term of 70 years from Michaelmas, 1870. Annual Ground Rent payable to the Earl of Portsmouth £2. 10s. 0d.'

The name of the pub was changed to The Earl of Portsmouth in recognition of the 5th Earl of Portsmouth, Isaac Newton Wallop, who helped to finance its rebuilding (and many of the other twenty properties affected) after the Great Fire of 1869. It later became The Portsmouth Hotel but was eventually changed back to The Earl of Portsmouth, the name under which it still operates. Having survived the next 150 years, sadly it closed for two to three years around the time of the Covid-19 pandemic of 2020–2022, but has subsequently reopened.

Chapter 10 names some of the 'victuallers' (persons licensed to sell alcoholic liquor) from 1850 onwards. The Edworthy family were the incumbents at The Royal Oak Inn (the other establishment affected by the Great Fire) for many years, often with dual occupations as these buildings served as coaching inns as much as purveyors of food and drink: Richard Edworthy was wheelwright as well as victualler at The Royal Oak in 1850, for example. Women were permitted to hold these roles too, in what was otherwise still a largely male-dominated society: Mrs Eliza Edworthy, daughter of Richard, is listed as the victualler of The Royal Oak in *White's Directory* of 1878.

Isaac Newton Wallop, 5th Earl of Portsmouth, 1861, benefactor to his tenants after the Great Fire of Chawleigh in 1869

Original engraving by Maxim Gauci, published by A H Baily & Co

(Photo by Jonathan Crofts)

The Portsmouth Hotel and The Royal Oak Inn were put up for sale by the Portsmouth estate in 1908, along with land and buildings from a range of neighbouring villages (see Chapter 22). The Royal Oak had an 'Area 17 poles … occupied by Mr. F. Edworthy [whose family by this stage had been at the inn for at least 60 years] … Kitchen, Drinking Room, Parlour, Bar, Cellar, Dairy, Brewhouse, Skittle Alley, Bedrooms and Long Room used for public dinners. The Outbuildings comprise:– 5-Stall Stable with Loft over, Piggery Yard and usual Offices; also Blacksmith's Shop. The whole is covered with slate and tile. Lease granted for a term of 70 years from Michaelmas, 1872. Annual Apportioned Ground Rent payable to the Earl of Portsmouth £1 14s. 0d'.

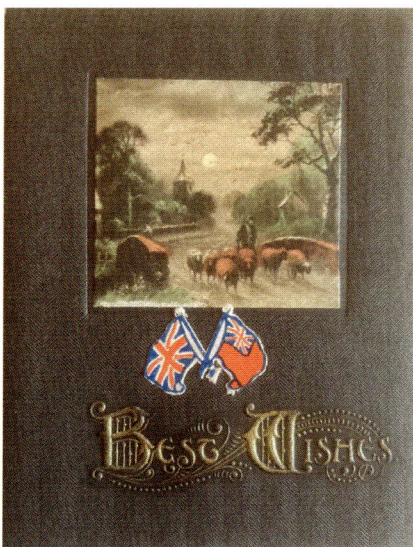

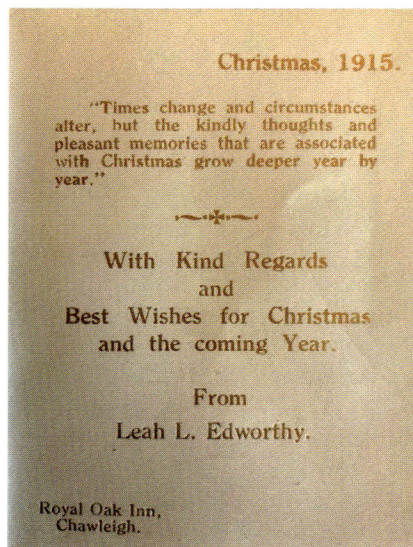

A First World War Christmas greeting from the Edworthy family at The Royal Oak Inn

(Photo by Jonathan Crofts, by kind permission of Jim Stevens)

(Above)

In 2024 The Royal Oak hosts an impressive hat business as well as a part-time pub

(Photo by Jonathan Crofts)

(Right)

A room of the 16th-century Royal Oak on the main B3042 road in Chawleigh, now a retail showroom for the Gamble & Gunn hat business.

(Photo © Gamble & Gunn)

Today, The Royal Oak serves as a part-time pub but also as the home of an extensive hat business, Gamble & Gunn, selling 'current stock alongside our collection of vintage hats, accessories and curios': everything from boaters and top hats to panamas and pork pie hats for every occasion and gender.

Down in Chenson, in the Eggesford area of the Taw valley, another hospitality venue had emerged, in addition to the Fox & Hounds. An advertisement in *Trewman's Exeter Flying Post* on 9 February 1837 confirmed new ownership of the Schoolmaster Inn:

SCHOOLMASTER INN AND POSTING HOUSE

On the Exeter and Barnstaple New Road.

James Williams respectfully announces to the Nobility, Gentry, Commercial Gentleman and his friends in general that he has taken the above Inn and commences business at Lady Day.

J.W. begs to assure those Ladies and Gentlemen who may favour him with their patronage, that they will find every comfort provided for them.

The house is situated on the banks of the River Taw and in view of the old and beautiful woods of the Eggesford Valley.

Excellent stabling, good Post Horses, and careful drivers; a neat Post Chaise, Fly etc.

In the 1970s, Mr Victor Watts of the Old Tollgate Cottage, Chenson, confirmed that the inn had belonged to the Earl of Portsmouth and the coach houses had later become cottages, with filled-in loft doors visible on their walls. On the front exterior, the head of the arched entrance to the cellar had also been filled in. The Earl decided to demolish the inn building in the 1860s once trade declined after the railway was constructed. Stone from it was used to build the Park Cottages near Eggesford Station, which were known as 'Wash-Houses' as they provided accommodation to the laundresses from Eggesford House, the Devon seat of the Earl.

The inn was listed in *White's Directory* of 1854 (against 'Thomas Luxton, Victualler and Farmer') and in *Belling's Directory of the County of Devon* in 1857, but does not appear later, suggesting it closed around the late 1850s.

The Schoolmaster Inn also appears in the memoir of Reverend John 'Jack' Russell (1795–1883), who developed the Jack Russell terrier and was vicar of St James' Church, Swimbridge, near Barnstaple:

'… rode back to Iddesleigh, took out the hounds, found a fox in Dowland, and killed him close to the Schoolmaster Inn in Chawleigh parish, twelve miles as the crow flies. I then turned my horse's head for Tordown, and was sitting down to dinner at my own table, and all the hounds home, at six o'clock, the distance being fully twenty miles from the said Schoolmaster Inn to this house.'

The coach house buildings became 1, 2 and 3 Chenson Farm Cottages. The stable building of the inn on the other side of the road was used as a Mission Hall (possibly for the Methodists) and then became a barn.

There was a fourth inn, in Chawleigh village, The New Inn, which is now split into separate residential properties, and is believed to date back to the sixteenth century: another former coaching inn with forge and barn.

With multiple establishments in the village offering a fine tankard of ale or cider at the end of a hard working day, opposition was to be expected from ecclesiastical bodies looking rather to the saving of souls, especially perhaps the two chapels of the emerging Wesleyan and Methodist denominations. Alcohol-based entertainment has often run counter to the 'purer' pursuits of faith and worship, although the latter have played a significant part in family and community life for centuries – and for many, still do.

A 1970s sketch showing the layout of the earlier Schoolmaster Inn in Chenson, drawn by Algernon Pepperell and F W Hillman, *Chawleigh Notes*, c.1970

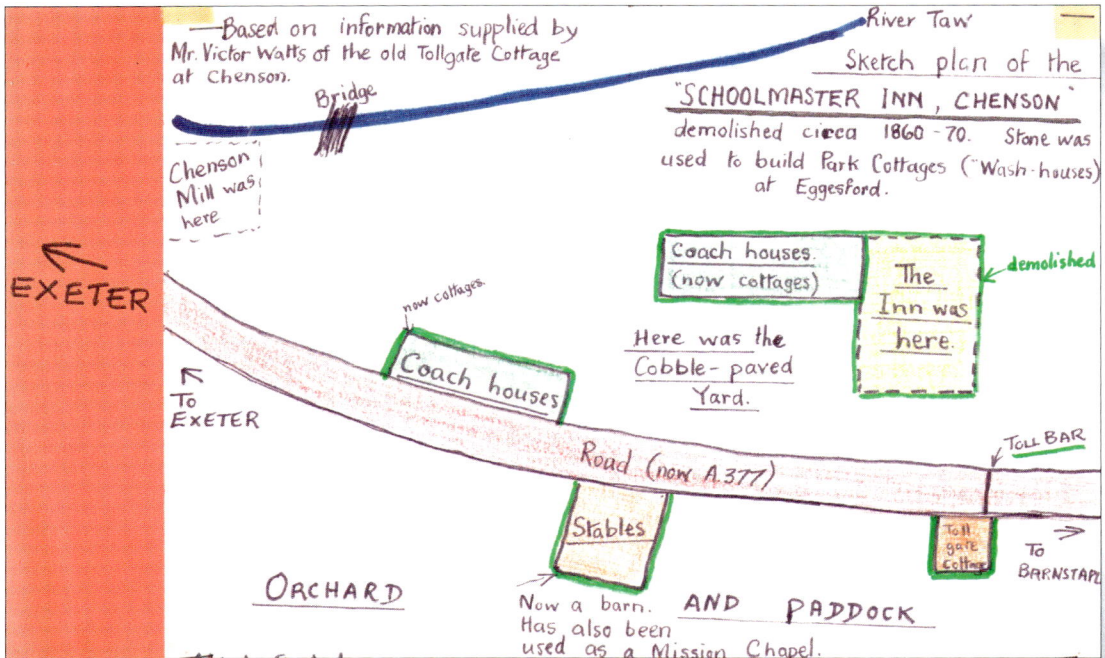

Based on information supplied by Mr. Victor Watts of the old Tollgate Cottage at Chenson.

Bridge

River Taw

Sketch plan of the "SCHOOLMASTER INN, CHENSON" demolished circa 1860-70. Stone was used to build Park Cottages ("Wash-houses) at Eggesford.

Chenson Mill was here

EXETER

To EXETER

now cottages

Coach houses

Coach houses. (now cottages)

The Inn was here.

demolished

Here was the Cobble-paved Yard.

Road (now A377)

Toll BAR

Stables

Now a barn. Has also been used as a Mission Chapel.

ORCHARD

AND PADDOCK

Toll gate Cottage

To BARNSTAPLE

145

CHAPTER 15

CHAWLEIGH: CHURCH AND RECTORS

St James' Church

John Betjeman, Poet Laureate 1972–84, had a passion for 'church-crawling' (a more high-minded alternative to the traditional pub-crawl), of which he wrote: '…it leads you to the remotest and quietest country; it introduces you to the history of England in stone and wood and glass, which is always truer than what you read in books.'

St James' Church in Chawleigh is no exception, and like so many rural churches, a sense of history pervades its structure, having witnessed countless hatchings, matchings and despatchings, and survived centuries of national and local events, good and bad.

The church has recorded some of its own history and collected documents from its more recent past. It was Grade I listed in 1965, as of exceptional architectural and historic interest – among only 2.5% of all listings in the country – and the full listing can be found on the Historic England website.

The earliest reference to a Rector at the church dedicated to St James the Greater (patron saint of Spain and buried in the cathedral at Santiago de Compostela in northern Spain) is 1277, although the exact period of the building's construction is not known. Equally uncertain is whether there was a place of worship here before the Domesday Book of 1086; there was a diocese and bishop based in nearby Crediton until 1050 (when they moved to Exeter), but in religious matters Chawleigh may have been more closely linked with the North Tawton Hundred in which it was situated.

Beatrix Cresswell (1862–1940), Devon antiquary and topographer, documented early records of a chapel in Chawleigh as far back as the start of the fifteenth century: '1400. June 12. Joel Wyke and Nichola his wife, granted licence for the chapel of St. James in their mansion of Flamberty's Wyke in Chawleigh, for divine service to be held there on the feast of St. James.'

The Feast of St James was celebrated on 25 July; England was Roman Catholic at the time. The location of Flamberty's Wyke is uncertain, although Wyke probably relates to Chawleigh Week, just outside the main part of the village today. The Devonshire Association suggests that 'In 1428… a John Wrey was successor of Joel Wyke of Chawleigh Wick, in succession to a William Wrey… then the William Wrey who took the name of Wyke was son of Roger Wrey of Chawley Wick…' and also confirms 'Nichola, wife of Joel of Chawleigh Wyke 1400' (For more information on the Wrey / Wyke family, see Chapter 10.)

The church was rebuilt in the fifteenth century, according to the Perpendicular period of architecture, with the vestry added in the twentieth century (1929) at the east end of the south aisle. The walls are local sandstone with granite surrounds except for replacements in Bath stone on the north side. Granite also formed the pillars in the arcade dividing the nave and the south aisle.

CHAWLEIGH CHURCH.

Sketched and Drawn on Stone by W. Spreat.
Printed by C. Hullmandel.

Over the nave and south aisle the wagon-shaped ceilings are divided into panels with moulded ribs. Wagon roofs were typical of churches in southwest England, and the chancel roof is similar although less elaborate. Around the edge of the ceilings runs a carved and painted cornice. The chancel roof benefits from richly decorated ribs, bosses and wall plate with pierced cresting, all executed in plaster work, probably from the nineteenth-century restoration by the then Lord Portsmouth.

Outdoors, the fifteenth-century porch has decorated battlements with distinctive carvings, and a slate sundial fixed to the wall at the east end of the south aisle probably dates to the eighteenth century, most churches of the time being fitted with a south-facing dial.

St James Church, Chawleigh, 1842, lithograph by William Spreat

(Photo by Jonathan Crofts)

147

Perhaps most notable are the beautiful fifteenth-century rood screen across the nave and the aisle, and a parclose screen of the same period dividing the aisle from the chancel. The screen has elaborate tracery, vaulting and cornice cresting in the traditional Bradninch style as described by the historian W G Hoskins, Bradninch Church in Devon being notable for its rood screen design and decoration. Originally the screen would have had a loft (or platform) approximately 150cm (almost 5ft) wide, bordered by a span of panelling set with carved wooden effigies. A sizeable Rood (a figure of Christ on the Cross) would have faced the nave in the centre, flanked on either side by St John and St Mary, for the congregation to venerate during the lengthy sermons.

A stone staircase led up to the loft enabling decoration with flowers, foliage and lit candles on Holy Festival days, and during Lent the Rood was veiled. Sadly, overly enthusiastic restoration (possibly that of 1910, overseen by the churchwardens E Webber and J Saunders, feoffees – trustees – of the Chawleigh Church Lands Charity under the Reverend Francis Hudson) has scrubbed away all colour and the gilding which originally decorated the screen; something like the original effect can still be admired in the church at nearby Morchard Bishop. The Gothic Perpendicular fan vaulting is ribbed with applied bosses (carved knobs) at the intersections. Several of the bosses are carved in the shape of a Tudor five-petalled dog rose – the emblem of Henry VII who came to the throne in 1485. He was succeeded by his son Henry VIII in 1509, who in the same year married his first wife Katherine of Aragon. A boss on the vault of the screen by the pulpit bears a rose with a pomegranate (Katherine's emblem) at its heart.

The screen happily survived orders during Elizabeth I's reign to remove all rood lofts and examples of idolatry (anything considered to glorify false idols, such as objects or images representing deities or lesser holy figures), and associated with the Catholic faith that her father had stamped out in his quest for a male heir.

In their book *Roodscreens and Roodlofts* (Pitman, 1909), F Bligh Bond and the Reverend Dom Bede Camm emphasised the quality of the screen at St James':

> 'A fine screen with tracery of the Bradninch type spans the nave and south aisle. It has cornices almost identical with those at Kentisbere and other screens in the south-east district, but inferior in execution. The vaulting is good, the treatment of the spandrel-fillings being especially worthy of notice. There is a very good tall cresting fixed over the cornice of the screen, which has evidently come from another position, and belonged to a former roodloft gallery. A small portion of a somewhat similar cresting remains at Heavitree. That on the restored roodloft at Kenton follows the same design.'

The restoration of the church by the fifth Earl of Portsmouth in 1874, together with the Rector (his cousin, the Reverend Pelham Fellowes Clay) and the feoffees of the day, cost £1400 and replaced the seats and gallery of the west end with pitch pine pews. Prior to the Reformation (1530s onwards), fixed pews were becoming more common, but congregations generally stood or knelt, or perhaps brought their own seat with them; those less able may have found a stone ledge to rest on. The church would have appeared largely empty to modern eyes.

The piscine (basin), set in the outside of the Radford Chapel, was the traditional place for washing the chalice (communion cup) and the paten (plate) after mass. This chapel now houses the organ. The chalice and paten, of late Georgian style, are dated 1832. The flagon is dated 1845, and the alms dish

The beautiful fifteenth-century rood screen across the nave and the aisle of St James' Church, Chawleigh.

A parclose screen of the same period divides the aisle and the chancel.

(Photo by Jonathan Crofts)

has the same marks. None of the plate has any local inscription. There are royal arms of George III, and an ancient chest remains at the eastern end of the church. The registers covering births, marriages and deaths commence in 1544, not long after this was introduced across the land by Sir Thomas Cromwell, who had recognised the value of keeping community records.

The font dates from 1830, and the altar rail is Victorian (an oak rail on iron standards replacing earlier dark Jacobean rails). The handsome pulpit is dedicated to the memory of the Reverend John Vowler Tanner, Rector 1879–1903, and the lectern to his wife, Mrs Eliza Tanner, dated 1909. The organ was given in memory of Mr Isaac Philips of East Leigh in 1927.

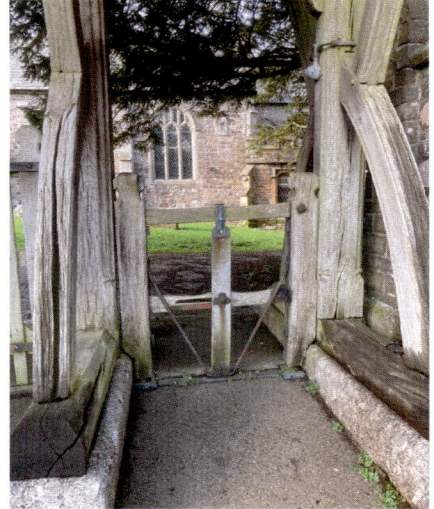

Unique in Devon, the lych gate is listed separately from the church as Grade II by Historic England (then English Heritage) since 1986. Made of oak by a local craftsman, its mechanism is ingenious although sometimes challenging to open, and the space to pass through is not wide. It was documented in 1850 as costing £50 at the time, over £5,500 in today's money.

A letter amongst the church records from Marion Flinn details some of the history of the gate:

> 'Richard Gough who made the Lych gate was born in Chawleigh … and learnt his trade as a wheelwright and carpenter. His Father was the Headmaster of the Chawleigh School, and a staunch Congregationalist. His tombstone stands at the entrance to the Jubilee Hall (the old Congregational Chapel). Richard Gough married and went to live in Chulmleigh, and carried on his trade there. His workshop was at the back of the old Police Station, down on the Green. The architect of the Eggesford estate designed the Lych gate. Richard Gough knew the oak trees that he wanted and chose them for their bent branches. They were oak trees on Colleton Manor (not Eggesford) and when he went to fetch them the owners had put the price up, which upset Richard. The Lych gate was made in Richard's workshop at Chulmleigh, his principal tool being a handsaw, and he also had a mortising machine in his workshop. Richard Gough will have walked from Chulmleigh to Chawleigh and back to carry out the work, and the parts of the Lych gate will have been conveyed in a hand cart or horse and cart and fixed together on site...'

The tower was built in three stages with corner buttresses and square louvred windows on each side. At the top are a battlemented parapet with stump pinnacles, a copper weather vane in the shape of a cockerel, and a flagstaff. The clock was

The unusual lych gate at St James' Church, Chawleigh is on the right-hand side of the main churchyard gates

(Photos by Jonathan Crofts)

added in 1874, and regilded in 1897 for Queen Victoria's Diamond Jubilee, at a cost of £4.10s. The projection in the north wall indicates the position of the flight of steps which once gave access to the rood loft.

The exterior of the church is noted in the Deanery for its beautiful paths surrounding the churchyard, amidst a gracious avenue of trees. Leading up to the private gate to The Barton (and its now converted barns), the view across the gentle slopes is perhaps at its finest around Easter, when daffodils cover the entire expanse, shortly to be followed by bluebells and other wildflowers. Bisecting the area is a grassy gully caused by damp erosion and the collapse of ground dug over too many times. A large rookery provides the soundtrack today, and perhaps it always did.

There were seventeenth- and eighteenth-century declarations by churchwardens and clergy recording the status and personal misdemeanours of parish members. Anglican law demanded that churchwardens and sidesmen (broadly meaning their assistants) were obliged to make 'presentments' regarding anyone who contravened ecclesiastical law at least once a year, such as at Easter and Michaelmas, as well as on the 'visitation' of a bishop, archbishop or deacon, who would then set out the 'articles of enquiry' requiring responses, known as 'declarations'. Voluntary presentments were possible at any time if a cleric needed otherwise to bring a matter to light. The clergy also had to make personal affirmations of faith known as 'declarations' on being ordained, and each time they moved to a new parish or see.

In his books on Devon parishes, C A T Fursdon noted the Chawleigh presentment of 3 December 1662 by John Northcott, churchwarden:

'To the first titul concerning the Church and Chappels, with the ornaments and furniture there unto belonginge; I answer and say that all things therein required and fitt, Except the booke of homilyes and the booke of Canons, and the printed table of degrees, all which wee could not git for money, but they shall be forthwith provided assoone as wee can git them for money.

To the second titul, concerning the Churchyard, the houses, glibes, and tithes belonging to the Church, I answer and say that I know nothing in the same to be presented, Except the terrier of al the glibe lands, the which we shall be redy to provyd against the next visitation.

To the third titul, concerning ministers, I answer and say that our minister doth distribut much amongst the poore. I know nothing in the same commanded that is in any way omitted, nayther is ther any thing in the same forbidden, that is in any way suffered by our minister to be done.

To the foworth titul, concerning the parishners, I present Thomas Yolland for not coming to Church and not submitting to the government that now is established. Allso there is one George Heywood who has tow childe unbaptised, but hee hath promysed to bring them in to the minister to have it done. Allso there are some children will bee made redy for confirmation against Easter. Allso I have had reported that there is a will and testament of one George Reed that… unproved, I did quistin… denyed.

I lived 4 yeares in the parish and know no new seates bulded since my time.

To the fift titul concerning parish clarks and sextons; I answer and say that I know nothing in the same to be presented.

To the sixth titul, concerning hospetals, schools, schoolmasters, physitians, chirugeons and midwives, I present Elizabeth —udall who takes upon her the excercies of a midwife.

To the 7th titul, concerning Churchwardens and sidemen, I answer that I know nothing therin to be presented, it is omnybeny ['omnibenevolent', generally used with reference to God as being all-loving and all-good; John Northcott here is using it in the context of all being well with him and his assistants].

John Northcott, warden
The incumbent is Mr. John Shugbeare.
The patron is my Lord Chichester.
The reputed value is 80 £ yearely.'

Clearly the seventeenth-century Chawleigh population was carefully monitored on behalf of the religious authorities, Thomas Yolland and George Heywood being noted for their perceived transgressions.

Some 160 years later, the Reverend Pelham Fellowes Clay, nephew of Lord Portsmouth (the 4th Earl), was similarly expected to reply to a set of queries before 'visitation' by Bishop Carey of the Diocese of Exeter in 1821. Clay's responses concerning Chawleigh included:

'"176" Families in your Parish.

"No papists – About nine or ten reputed Methodists".

"Yes" – Divine Service is performed twice every Lord's Day, "At 11 in the morning, and 3 in the afternoon".

"A charity school, and two private schools".

Sacrament of the Lord's Supper is administered "Eight times a year. The average number of Communicants is thirty-five".

"No" Alms-houses, Hospital or other Charitable Endowment… any Parochial Library

"No" Chapel within your Parish.'

A century later in 1923, the Reverend H J Hodgson compiled a set of notes on the church for the Deanery:

'Rev. J. Vowler Tanner was curate of Chawleigh and Eggesford, and resided at the rectory house at Eggesford. Later he became Rector of Chawleigh and built the present house [which is now home to the Amber Foundation]. The parish clerk of Chawleigh (W. Josland) lived at the dilapidated old rectory house, now restored, and known as the "Old Hall".'

Although critical of much of the built environment of the Church, Hodgson enthuses about the churchyard:

Interior of
St James' Church,
Chawleigh, looking
towards the chancel

(Photo by
Jonathan Crofts)

'The Churchyard is large and the most beautiful in the Deanery, with many handsome ornamented shrubs, judiciously planted, not in formal rows. The greensward is an undulating ground and a charming ravine divides the yard into two portions. …

Doubtless, in the careless and irreverent period of the 18th century – and later – sheep were allowed to graze in the churchyards and then gates were a necessity.'

He was also effusive about '… the chief glory of the church – the grand ROOD SCREEN – which extends right across the building, a distance of 36 feet. There are many references to it by various visitors, most of whom regard it as a beautiful piece of work.

Like most of our Deanery churches, Chawleigh once possessed a GALLERY, or rather, in the words of Mr Davidson, "raised seats at the west end of the church for the singers, where the clerk leads". …

There is a poor house and schoolroom…formerly called the CHURCH HOUSE… it is now divided into three dwellings, the largest used as a schoolroom and dwelling for the schoolmaster, the second by Mary Ann Reed, and the third as a vegetable store.' (See Chapter 18 for more on the Church House.)

Bells and bellringers

As with so many English churches, the bells at St James' have their own history, still ringing out their rounds and changes today. A 1553 Inventory of Church Goods lists "Challeigh iiii belles in the towre their" (four bells in the tower). In 1720 the four were recast into five by Evan Evans of Chepstow (who together with his son William had set up a foundry in Braunton in 1713). The late Geoffrey Cruwys discovered from his parish accounts at Cruwys Morchard in 2012 that their new bells had been brought over from Chulmleigh in 1722, rather than Braunton as had been thought. Possibly Chawleigh's bells were also cast in Chulmleigh, where the Evanses may have taken over the foundry of John Stadler for local work – they also cast a new ring of bells for Chulmleigh in this period. Stadler is known to have cast nine bells, the last dated 1714, so may have retired and sold up. William Evans cast a sixth bell for Chawleigh in 1754.

Thanks to the benevolence of the 5th Earl and Countess of Portsmouth, the tenor and the fifth bell were recast in 1874 by Mears & Stainbrook of London after damage was identified ten years earlier. In 1912 the feoffees and public subscription funded the remaining four being recast by Warner's of Cripplegate in London, their new iron frame on a steel base being eventually replaced with galvanised steel in 1998.

In Victorian times there was an annual dinner and reunion of ringers young and old in the parish, significant enough for a write-up in the local *Gazette*. Invitations were customary to other interested parties including the Rector, churchwardens, farmers, James Dilling from the ironworks, and more. 'Mr. George Challis and the Ringers' Committee made the arrangements.'

On 31 May 1912, the latest set of bells were welcomed with fresh celebrations: 'The reopening … and dedication of new chimes presented by Mr. Isaac Philips [the farmer at Eastleigh], and the annual ringing festival for the parishes of the Deanery of Chulmleigh, attracted a much larger gathering than for many years. The six bells have been recast at a cost of £220 of which £155 was provided by the feoffees.'

The bells now hanging all bear inscriptions, some of these having been replaced over time, with 'EE' corresponding to Evan Evans, and 'WE' to his son, William Evans:

1. Treble Prosperity to my Benefactors W (bell) E2754

2. When you ring me I'll sweetly sing EE (bell) WE 1720

3. God preserve all our benefactors EE (bell) WE 1720

4. God preserve the Church and King EE (bell) WE 1720

5. Mears & Stainbrook Founders London 1874
   (formerly 'Peace and Good Neighbourhood EE9 (bell) WE 1720')

6. Tenor Mears & Stainbrook Founders London 1874
   The gift of the Isaac Newton 5th Earl of Portsmouth and Eveline Alicia his wife

(Formerly "William Fellowes, Esq. 'A good benefactor' EE9 (bell) WE 1720")

One past glory dates from 29 April 1929 when Chawleigh won 'the Heanton Shield at Swimbridge bellringing contest, [and] rang an almost perfect peal, losing only 10 marks'. An enthusiastic team of bellringers still come together at St James' today.

No longer however able to call on local landowners or patron to raise vital funds, the church must instead rely on the diocese and the goodwill of the local community and charity trustees. In the early 2020s sufficient funds were raised to enable a series of renovations and improvements to the church, carried out in 2023–2024. Nevertheless, while some believe the future of the Church of England more broadly is under threat as congregations dwindle, across Devon and elsewhere, for now St James' remains at the heart of much of village life.

St James' bellringers, c.1930s

(Photo by kind permission of Daphne Cockram)

The Rectors

The Calendar of Patent Rolls of 1297 recorded the 'Parsons' of Chalvele [Chawleigh], Lappeford [Lapford], Ragensford [Rackensford] and Ekenefford [Eggesford] as Godfrey de Renham, Robert de Umfravill, Michael de la Stane, and William – the Norman names still very current at this time.

Other early references to the rectors of Chawleigh, taken from the Bishop Edmund Lacy's Register (1420–55), record the death of Sir Matthew Wonston in 1450 (with Chawleigh under the name of Chalveleghe at that time), followed by the resignation of Sir Geoffrey Motte in 1451, and the institution of Sir Laurence Raleighe, chaplain, on 31 August of the same year. The Earl of Devon, Sir Thomas Courtenay, was then Patron. In 1453 Raleighe exchanged benefices with Master Robert Geffrey.

C A T Fursdon's histories of Devon parishes highlight the long-standing links between the Eggesford and Chawleigh parishes and churches, not only because of geographic proximity, but because rectors originally depended on their parishioners for their income through the tithes they paid. Eggesford on its own, with a smaller population, would not have provided much of a 'living' for a rector, so the living of Chawleigh was often awarded alongside. Rectors were referenced with their 'patron', and in the thirteenth century this included Sir John de Reigny; by the fifteenth century, the widow of his descendant, also known as John, became patron in his absence:

'John Westcott, succeeded 27 May 1489. Patron, Ibota, relict of John Reigny.'

As Nicholas Orme points out in *The Church in Devon* 560–1560 (Impress Books, 2013), the succession of Mary Tudor to the throne after the death of Edward VI in 1553 meant a return to Catholicism, if only for some five years. A series of new laws to encourage this turnabout included depriving clergy of their benefices if they had married: for the first time since the Reformation there were penalties for doing something that was legal when it was done. Along with others, Anthony Hunt, Rector of Chawleigh (1542–54), was allowed to be reemployed if he renounced his marriage and could find a patron to present him again, and he moved to Knowstone and Molland as a result. It is not clear whether his poor wife had died or consented to the annulment.

The Civil War period (1642–51) in England is noted for its impact on Devon and villages like Chawleigh. Nearly four hundred years later, it is possible to walk into a pub in neighbouring Chulmleigh where the locals will make wry comments on the differences between the two communities: Chulmleigh was reputedly Parliamentarian (Roundhead) – and Chawleigh Royalist (Cavalier). North Devon as a whole was Parliamentarian, the population having suffered from heavy taxation to fund Charles I's wars. In the upland pastures of Mid Devon, sheep were a common sight and the impact on shipping had also affected the wool trade badly. The population of Chulmleigh welcomed and supported the Parliamentarian army under General Fairfax.

Dr John Walker in his *Sufferings of the Clergy in Devon and Cornwall during the Grand Rebellion* (circa 1714) references the Rector of Chawleigh, John Shugborough (also recorded as Shuckbury and Shugbeare) as being one who 'was ill-used though never sequestred'. Many loyalist ministers suffered harshly and were ejected under the Commonwealth, as the 1653–58 rule by Oliver Cromwell was known.

Fursdon notes some later rectors too:

'**Abraham Branscombe.** Exeter College, Oxon. 13 Oct. 1710. Adm. 12 Feb. 1722 on resignation of Roger Rosier. Patron, William Fellowes, Esq. This rector resigned for Chawleigh and was buried in a tomb within its churchyard, 17 May 1743.

George Paddon. Adm. on Branscombe ceasing 30 Oct. 1742. Patron, Coulscn Fellows, of Eggesford, Esq. He resigned for Chawleigh, and was buried in its churchyard near his predecessor Branscombe, 7th May 1781.

John Churchill. Corpus Christi Coll. Oxon. Succeeded 14 May 1783 on death of Lewis Greenslade. Patron, Henry Arthur Fellows, Esq. He was also preferred to Chawleigh on the death of the Rev. George Paddon, but was buried at Eggesford 26th Mar. 1818.

Lloyd Williams. Ad. 6 May 1818 on death of John Churchill. Patron, Hon. Newton Fellows, 2nd son of John 2nd Earl of Portsmouth by Lady Maria da. [daughter] of Coulson Fellows, Esq. He was also Rector of Chawleigh. He died in Exeter 1819. Buried at Whitchurch, Hants. where he has formerly resided.

Pelham Fellows Clay. Adm. to the living and to Chawleigh also 18 Jan. 1821 on resignation of Richard Brain and on presentation of his uncle the Hon. Newton Fellows.'

The Reverend Pelham Fellowes Clay was a longstanding Rector of Chawleigh from 1821 to 1879, with the same dates at Eggesford. He was born in 1796 at Eggesford, and educated at Sidney Sussex College, Cambridge. John Lambert's *Return of Owners of Land* cites the Reverend P F Clay in 1873 as owning 263 acres of land in the Bideford area. Whether this was inherited land or purchased, clearly his many years of service to the church had allowed him to prosper.

Rectors drew their income from tithes, a form of taxation on their spiritual flock which had originally demanded one tenth of each household's farming produce to support the local church and clergy. Lay owners who acquired church lands during the Reformation of the 1500s were then also entitled to receive these dues.

In the early 1800s, industrialisation, religious dissent and poor harvests resulting in agricultural depression made tithes paid in kind unpopular, and the 1836 Tithe Commutation Act legislated for tithe rent charges, payment in money, instead. The Tithe Survey, carried out by travelling assistant tithe commissioners, identified land with tithes paid in kind, valuations, ownership, and liabilities for payment. Where possible a tithe agreement was then made, or a tithe award if the terms were disputed. This tithe apportionment became a legal document, with a map, signed by the Tithe Commissioners.

In Eggesford and Chawleigh one result of the tithe reassessment was a dispute between the landowner (Newton Fellowes, 4th Earl of Portsmouth); the rector (the Reverend Pelham Fellowes Clay, nephew of the aforesaid Earl); and occupiers of the land, namely farmers such as William Saunders, Thomas Kemp and John Ford. The aristocratic family was in dispute with itself.

An *Appendix To The Reports of the Select Committee of the House of Commons on Public Petitions (Session 1846)* describes:

'The humble petition of the Honourable Newton Fellowes of Eggesford in the county of Devon,

Sheweth,

That your petitioner is a landowner to a considerable extent in the parishes of Eggesford and Chawleigh in the county of Devon, and patron of both the livings, and your Petitioner presented the present rector to them as early as his age would permit, and who was held them to the present time, viz. between twenty and thirty years.

That in the years 1838 in 1839, at the earliest period after the passing of the Act, meetings were holden in the said parishes by assistant tithe commissioners for the purpose of commuting the tithes under the Act of Parliament for the commutation of tithes in England and Wales.

That at such meetings a claim of exemption from tithes was set up by your Petitioner in respect of the Barton of Eggesford, and of the coppice lands in the parish of Chawleigh, which claims had existed uninterrupted for a very long period of years, and beyond the memory of man. That at the spring assizes for the said county of Devon, in the year 1840, your Petitioner tried an action upon a feigned issue against the rector of the said parishes; in which action your Petitioner sought to establish his claim to an exemption from tithes in respect of the said Barton of Eggesford, as he was advised he might do under the statute 2nd and 3rd Will. V c.100, commonly called Lord Tenterden's Act.

That the said action was tried by a special jury who found that the said Barton of Eggesford had been held exempt from the payment of tithes for 63 years, including two full incumbencies and three years of a third incumbency.

That the sufficiency of that finding having been questioned, the point was soon afterwards argued in the Court of Queen's Bench; when the judges were equally divided.

That the question still remains undecided; that the tithes of the said parishes are taken in kind to a very great extent, and your Petitioner has not grown any corn on his farms in those parishes for many years.

That your petitioner has in the two parishes very large young plantations in which larch and fir trees are introduced; and inconsequence of the tithes no thinnings or improvements in them can take place, to the non-employment of the labourer and the loss to the owner.

That all the other districts in the neighbourhood enjoy the benefits of the Tithes Commutation Act, and that the two parishes aforesaid are the only instances to the contrary.

That the delay in setting these tithes questions perpetuates the existence of the tithe commission, at a great expense to the country, and puts a stop to all improvements in agriculture.

Your Petitioner therefore humbly prays for such relief in the premises as to your honourable House may seem fit.

N. Fellowes

Eggesford, 6th August, 1846'

The detail of the Petition is thorough but is firmly rebutted by the occupiers of the land in question:

'The humble petition of the Occupiers and Owners of Land in the parishes of Eggesford and Chawleigh in the county of Devon

Sheweth

That your Petitioners are occupiers or owners and occupiers of certain lands in the parishes of Eggesford and Chawleigh in the county of Devon which were among the first parishes who called in the aid of the tithe commissioners, to commute the tithes and affix the rent-charges in lieu thereof.

That the Rev. Pelham Fellowes Clay, the Rector, attacked the exemptions from the payment of tithes of the Honourable Newton Fellowes; and during the delay arising from that cause your Petitioners have been subject almost ever since to the payment of tithes in kind.

That your Petitioners are debarred by that system from making the most of the lands, or of adopting the best new and improved modes of agriculture.

That most of the labourers of the parish of Eggesford dare not cultivate potatoes in their gardens or in the fields in this parish, lest the tithe should be taken from them in kind, as the rector would not agree to compound with them.

William Saunders

Thomas Kemp

John Ford

&c. &c. &c.'

These petitions suggest that both agriculture and labourers were suffering. The financial and day-to-day reality for nineteenth-century farmers and labourers in Chawleigh and Eggesford – and for all those who relied on the fruits of their labour – was clearly not easy.

CHAPTER 16

CHAWLEIGH: CHURCH LIFE AND THE CHAPELS

Traditional Church and Social Life: Harvest and Celebrations

Farming and religion were intertwined since ancient times, given the vagaries of the weather, pestilence and external factors – often all a farmer could do was pray and hope for divine intervention, and give thanks in times of abundance. There is an account in the *Chulmleigh Deanery Magazine* of August 1896 highlighting the impact of farming on children of the Chawleigh community:

'On the morning of Friday, July 17th, the children of Chawleigh Sunday School for once felt no anxiety as to the weather for their Annual Summer Treat, some perhaps would have been glad to have felt a shower of rain, but among all the merry voices we heard no such wish expressed – the day was indeed a typical one for an outdoor tea – the trees afforded ample shade for those who preferred it to the more open and sunny lawn. The Rectory party were well supported in entertaining their guests by many kind and willing helpers – it was half-past nine before the party numbering over 130 broke up. Harvest work prevented many from accepting the invitation to be present.'

Harvest Festival a few weeks later was a great success, the timing explaining the absence of so many children from their Summer Treat:

'Rarely, if ever, has our Harvest Festival been celebrated so early in the year as on this occasion … this year on [August] the 21st… Seldom, too, has the harvest gone off so lightly and with so little trouble. At 3 o'clock p.m. the Church, which had been brightly and very tastefully decorated with corn, flowers, and fruit, was well filled; the service was a bright and cheery one. The Rev. J.H. Thompson, Rector of Romansleigh, preached an impressive and very appropriate sermon. After the service, tea was provided on the Rectory grounds by Mr. Ford, when about 250 sat down. Unfortunately, just as tea was over, a somewhat smart shower of rain fell: much as we all had been longing for rain, few of us wished to see it just then. However, the shower soon passed away, and dancing was commenced and continued for some hours in lovely moonlight, the Chulmleigh Brass Band affording excellent music. The offertory, amounting to £2. 5s. 6d. was devoted to the North Devon Infirmary.'

In June 1897 Queen Victoria's Diamond Jubilee was celebrated 'at both the morning and afternoon services in the Parish Church: at both, the hymn "O King of Kings" specially written for the occasion by the Bishop of Wakefield, was sung to the tuneful music of Sir. A. Sullivan, and at the close of each service the National Anthem, with a special verse, was sung and heartily taken up by the full congregation.'

125 years later the village celebrated the Platinum Jubilee of Queen Elizabeth II – Victoria's longevity as Queen later outdone by that of her great-great-granddaughter Elizabeth.

In 1897, £4.10s. was voted 'towards regilding the two faces of the Clock Tower out of about £19 collected to commemorate the Queen's sixty years reign. The remainder was spent in giving a free tea to the

Parishioners on Wednesday, June 23rd, and providing music and entertainments for the occasion, when each child was presented with a Jubilee Cup.'

A later edition of the *Chulmleigh Deanery Magazine* added more about the festivities:

'On Wednesday, June 23rd, the Jubilee festivities were celebrated here with every demonstration of loyalty by the inhabitants of this Parish and Cheldon. The early morning was ushered in by cheerful peals from the Church bells. In the afternoon a general holiday was observed. The School children were the first to arrive numbering 120… Each child was presented with a Jubilee cup, and then a move was made for an adjoining field kindly lent by Mr. Tucker of Leaches [Farm], where Tea Tables had been laid. The Chulmleigh Volunteer Band was in attendance and the proceedings commenced with a hearty singing of "God Save the Queen" accompanied by the band. … After tea, sports and dancing were indulged in, and well kept up until 10 p.m. Over 460 sat down to tea…'

The tradition of maypole dancing by the Church, here in the twentieth century

(Photo by kind permission of Daphne Cockram)

That summer was also the occasion for 'members of the Choir, S.S. [Sunday School] Teachers, Bible classes, with other friends' to take part in the 'Annual excursion to the seaside… Exmouth was the place selected… Each one returned with the feeling that the day had been a successful and pleasant one.'

These occasions were the high days and holidays for the inhabitants of this farming community. Generally speaking, however, life would have been one of hard graft.

The Gazette in 1889 showed Chawleigh with a postmaster, Mr Josland, who was 'librarian and parish clerk, and was very interested in Church work'. Sadly he died on 27 August 1889. However, a report on 13 December saw the annual meeting of the Parish Library attended by about eighty people, with tables for tea, and 'A vocal and instrumental concert followed with a brief address by the Rector who spoke of the successful working of the library for the past 20 years.'

In October of that year, *The Gazette* reflected on Britain's role in the world, with an evening at the school 'in connection with the Society for the Propagation of the Gospel in Foreign Parts'. The Society was founded in 1701 as a Church of England missionary organisation, and in the eighteenth and nineteenth centuries was active in the British colonial world across the Atlantic. The Reverend and Mrs Tanner provided the inevitable tea and cake, assisted by the usual ladies at such functions – there was no mention of men being involved other than the Reverend.

The connection between St James' and the Portsmouths (Wallop) family was finally brought to a close a century later. In 1987, Quentin Wallop, the tenth Earl of Portsmouth, transferred the 'Advowson and Right of Presentation of and to the Benefice of Chawleigh with Cheldon… to the Right Reverend Hewlett by Divine Permission of the Lord Bishop of Exeter'.

Much earlier, however, the more traditional religious life and status of the village had come under threat, when the 'dissenters' emerged locally, in the early nineteenth century.

The Chapels

The Bible Christian denomination formed as a subsect of the more mainstream Wesleyan Methodist movement in 1815 under William O'Bryan, a local preacher who appointed himself an evangelist and established a preaching circuit centring on nearby Shebbear in Devon. It evolved into a separate movement and devised its own hymnbook in the 1820s.

Mrs Muriel Petherick, of Handsford Farm, Chawleigh, wrote an account of *Methodism in Chawleigh* circa 1974, which shows that the site for the original Bible Christian chapel was purchased in September 1849. It was built by Mr Thomas Sage, who lived with his wife Ann at South View just along the main street through Chawleigh. Together they were founder members and local preachers, starting a Sunday school over his carpenter's shop, and as there was originally no provision for music in the chapel, his daughter Lucy played a small organ carried up the road from their home each week.

Older members included 'Miss P. Webber, daughter of Mr. Webber, blacksmith, whose sister married a Mr. Lewis Petherick, whose family were keen workers during the life of the Chapel. Other known members were Mr. J. Down and family, Handsford; Mrs. Reed, Toatley; Mr. and Mrs. Skinner, Fiddlecott; Mr. Western, Southcott; Mr. and Mrs. B. Petherick, Chawleigh; and Mr. and Mrs. E. Petherick, Handsford.'

Exterior United Methodist Church, Chawleigh.

The Old Chapel in its time as a place of worship for the Bible Christians and Methodists. Note the war memorial outside, now resited in St James' churchyard

(By kind permission of the owners)

Lewis Petherick, blacksmith, who lived at The Forge on Chawleigh Square, was the grandfather of Fred Petherick of The Garage, Chawleigh. Lewis's son established the first petrol pump in Chawleigh, outside his house on the opposite side of the road.

The Devon Weekly Times of 6 July 1883 noted that 'Considerable alterations have been made at Chawleigh Chapel at a cost of £20': this was to the Bible Christian place of worship.

Deterioration of the building in the early twentieth century, lack of a Sunday school room, and a growing membership led the trustees to select a new location for the chapel. Mr Elias Milton of Exeter bought the site (from the then owner of Leaches Farm) and a collective effort by the Chawleigh community dug foundations, with farmers' horses and carts removing earth and bringing in stone. Holsworthy architect Mr S Parsons oversaw the building and it opened in 1922, identified as a 'Methodist Church – Siloam AD 1922' on a plaque at the front of the building. The old building further along the B3042 was sold as a residence, named Hillside.

1935 saw the installation of a new organ. Even more exciting, electric heating was added following the arrival of mains electricity to the village, in 1960. A legacy to the Chapel in 1972 and fresh donations enabled redecoration and improvements to kitchens and cloakrooms, with the old stable turned into an extra room.

163

A service on 10 May 1973 celebrated the reopening, followed by a South Molton Male Voice Choir concert in the evening.

In more recent years the Old Chapel was itself sold as a private home, described by Stags the estate agent as: 'a converted Methodist Chapel ... Planning permission was granted in 1998 for the conversion of the imposing building into a residential dwelling and it has been sympathetically converted whilst retaining period features including arched mullion windows and original vaulted roof timbers.'

Describing another group of the faithful under the Nonconformist or Independent banner, *A Short History of the Congregational Church, Chulmleigh*, compiled by the Reverend J G Cording (Minister of the Church), records their purchase of the freehold of their Chawleigh church (or chapel) in 1889, opposite the Church House, and the appointment of new trustees. (Presumably it had been a chapel since its construction circa 1840-50 – see below – but the freehold was not yet

The present Jubilee Hall in 2022, renamed as such in 1935 to mark the Silver Jubilee of King George V

(Photo by Jonathan Crofts)

owned.) In 1893 the Chawleigh chapel was reseated and repairs carried out to the fabric and the graveyard wall under the lead of the Reverend W G Andrews (minister 1887–1901). From 1901 the district was divided with Chulmleigh, Chawleigh and Bridge Reeve placed under the care of the minister at Chulmleigh.

A Grade II listing was awarded to today's Jubilee Hall in 1986, stating that the building dates to 'Circa 1840–50, converted 1935.' The listing also refers to the original symmetry of the road-facing side with its three Tudor-style arched windows, as having been disturbed by the new left-of-centre porch attached in 1935. The chapel was no longer in use and it was bought by the parish on behalf of the community and renamed in honour of the jubilee of George V, grandfather of Elizabeth II. The original doorway in the left end wall was also blocked up at this time.

In the late 1990s St James' Church held a service of thanks to the Chawleigh Methodists for the gifts from their old chapel of the wooden crucifix, altar table, hymn board, portable font and lectern, and their 1914–1918 war memorial plaque.

The stone obelisk war memorial was resited to the village churchyard, cleaned and rededicated.

Chawleigh's ancient church and newer chapels commemorate not just the Fallen in war, but others who have been significant in the religious and collective life of the village, going back at least five hundred years. Looking at their lives and families helps paint a vivid picture of the social history of the community.

The stone obelisk war memorial, resited to the churchyard

(Photo courtesy of St James' Church History)

CHAPTER 17

OLD CHAWLEIGH FAMILIES

St James' Church has profited over the centuries from benefactors offering money and time. While not every family that has donated financial or other help is commemorated in the Church, there are a number whose inscriptions will likely last as long as the building still stands, and these are described in this chapter.

One such is Richard Cann of Chenson, died 2 October 1775, whose inscription can still be seen in the church floor. The Canns were to be found in many of the local settlements, including Chulmleigh, and a Stephen Cann is noted in the history of the schoolhouse and Chawleigh Parish Lands Charity (see Chapters 18 and 19).

Other families' names will live on via gravestones and tombs out in the churchyard, or simply in the memories of their friends and descendants.

The Radford family

Beatrix F Cresswell's *Notes on Devon's Churches* (1919) recounts much of the background of the church up to that year, including some history of the Radford family who are commemorated inside; the stone memorial in the Radford Chapel is dedicated to Ambrose Radford of Chenson, 1703:

> 'A piscina remains in the church aisle, which is known as the Radford chapel, or Cheniston aisle. It is separated from the chancel by a good parclose screen of the 15th century. At this date Chenstone belonged to the Caleway (Kelway) or Kelloway family. On August 26th, 1400, Edmund and Joan Caleway had licence to celebrate divine service within the chapel of S.S. Mary and Giles in their mansion of Chensen. (Note: mansion at this date implied manor, and it does not necessarily imply a chapel in the house: it may have been on the estate.)
>
> They may also have been benefactors to their parish church, and have erected the Lady chapel at the east end of the new aisle. Some time later Chenson belonged to the Radfords, who are commemorated on floor slabs in this aisle, and by a large memorial on the wall to Ambrose Radford. An earlier mural tablet, formerly in the chancel, is now above the south door, where it is nearly illegible...
>
> On either side of the central shield are two others, which have borne Radford impaling other arms. The Radford charge is no longer distinguishable, one of the impaled coats has perished, it is just possible to tell that the other is Ermine a chevron gules, for Melhuish of Witheridge.
>
> George Radford's grandfather, another George, married the daughter of Thomas Melhuish; her mother was Appolonia, or Palmer, daughter of Robert Courtenay of Molland.'

According to St James' Church History, the memorial plaque above the main door reads:

IN MEMORIAM GEORGE RADFORD de CHENISTON
GENEROS. OVI MORTI OCCVBVIT 25 die APRILIS 1666
Et MARGARETAE VXORIS EJUS, FILIAE IOHANNIS BURY
De COLLETON, ARMIGERI, QUAE DECESSIT HANC
VITAM 29 OCTVBRIS 1657
ARTHVRVS ACLAND de WINKLEY et ROBERT
NVTCOMBE de CLAYHANGER GENEROS, et
PRIDHAM de MORCHARD EPI RECTOR, CONVGES
TRIBVS, SORORIBVS PRAEDICTI GEORGIJ
KATHARINAE, ELIZABETHAE, et DOROTHEA, AMORIS
ERGO POSVERVNT 1667

PARATI ETIAM ERGO EПOTE

MARTH 24 v 44

St James' Church History translates this memorial plaque as ('Morchard Bishop' refers to the nearby village):

IN MEMORY of GEORGE RADFORD of CHENISTON
GENTLEMAN, WHO MET HIS DEATH on 26th of APRIL 1666
AND of his WIFE MARGARET, DAUGHTER of JOHN BURY
of COLLETON KNIGHT, WHO GAVE UP LIFE ON
29th OCTOBER 1657
ARTHUR ACLAND of WINKLEY and ROBERT
NUTCOMBE of CLAYHANGER GENTLEMAN, and
PRIDHAM of MORCHARD, BISHOP, RECTOR, having married
three sisters of the said GEORGE
KATHARINE, ELIZABETH, and DOROTHY,
FOR LOVE'S SAKE ERECTED THIS MEMORIAL 1667
SO YOU ALSO MUST BE READY
MATTHEW 24 v 44

The Radford memorial in
St James' Church, Chawleigh

(Photos by Jonathan Crofts)

HERE LYETH LIKEWISE
BVRIED Y BODY OF RICHAR
RADFORD GEN SON OF Y AECA
NAMED GEORGE RADFOD WH
DYED THE 17 DAY OF IVNE
Anno Domini 1666
The Dormitorie of Thomas Radfor
y Eldest Sonne of Richard y Son
of George y Sonne of Thomas
Radford of Chenilton Gent & one
Englands holy Catholique Church
dyed y thirtieth day of August & w
Buried y fourth day of September
Ætatis Su 60

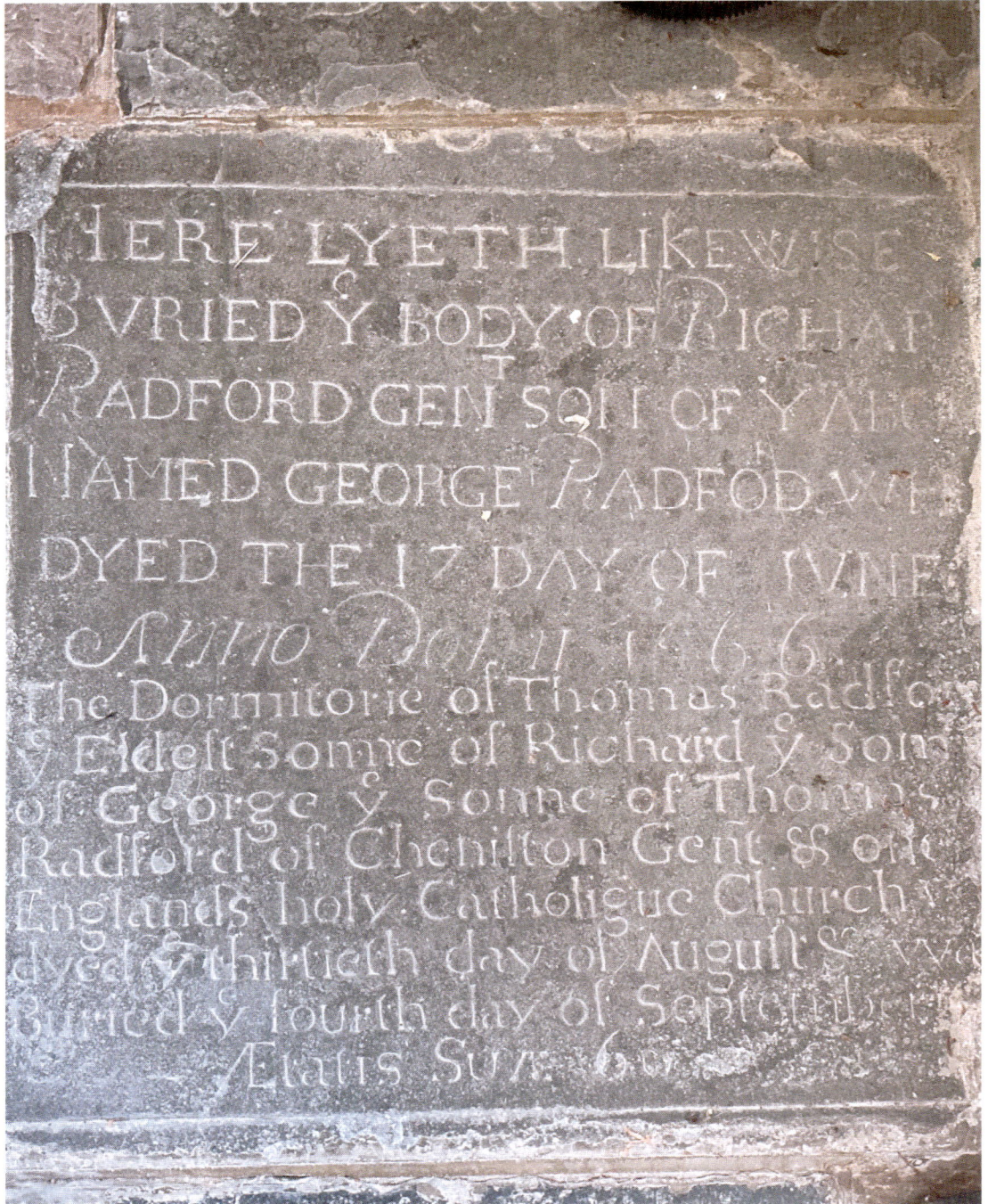

Another Radford inscription in the floor of the chapel

168

The descent of the Radford family goes back to the Radfords of the village of Oakford near Tiverton. Among their number was the lawyer and MP Nicholas Radford, whose celebrated murder and horrific disposal of his body by men of Thomas de Courtenay, 5th Earl of Devon, in the Wars of the Roses, was once described as one of the crimes of the century.

Tristram Risdon in his *Survey of the County of Devon* (1811, but compiled 1605–1632) maintains:

> 'Oliver Tracy held one fee in Winckley, in the reign of king Richard the first. He gave Radford unto Robert de Bickly, the son of Ralph Borne; the posterity of which Robert, who made their dwelling in this place, assumed the name of Radford, from whence descended Nicholas Radford, who, in the time of king Henry the sixth, dwelt at Upcott, in Cheriton [Fitzpaine] parish, unto whom Roger Prouz, of Prouz, was heir, and had his land.'

Other historical references support this, describing William de Radeford as son of Sir Robert de Bickleigh, brother to Henry and Sir William de Bickleigh, and therefore great-grandfather to John Radford of Oakford (c.1400–1460) and Nicholas Radford of Upcote, Cheriton Fitzpaine.

The earliest recorded Radford baptism in Chawleigh was that of George, son of John Radford, in 1544, and then another George, son of Thomas Radford in 1593. Thomas Radford, of Chenson in Chawleigh, married Elizabeth Broughton of Stoodleigh, and his will of 28 December 1613 leaves bequests to his wife and six children, including property in nearby Winkleigh, the original home of the de Radford family. His estate in 1614 was valued at £865 18s., equivalent to a considerable fortune today.

George Radford of Chenson, the eldest son (baptised 1593) was buried in 1626, and his will of that year made his son Thomas sole executor, with legacies to his four children (his marriage to his wife Katherine, daughter of Thomas Melhuish, in Chawleigh in 1604 had ended when she died thirteen years before). Their children, Thomas, George, Elizabeth and Richard, shared an estate of £541 7s .2d.

Thomas Westcote writes in *A View of Devonshire in MDCXXX With a Pedigree of Most of its Gentry* (1845, original manuscript 1624–1636): 'MELHUISH, of Witheridge, married and had issue Thomas and Lewis. Thomas married, first Polynor, daughter of Robert Courtenay, of Molland, esq., and had issue Robert, a daughter married to George Radford, of Chenson in Chawley, another to Edmund Snell of Chawley…'

George and Katherine's son Thomas, baptised 1606, buried 1634, married Ann, daughter of William Venner of Washfield in 1623 (Ann was later to remarry, to Philip Elston of Crediton in 1635). Thomas and Ann's only son (they also had five daughters), George, was buried in 1666, leaving money to each of his three (probably remaining) sisters, £300 each to Katherine and Elizabeth, £550 to Dorothy, and £40 'to erect a monument for me in my Isle in parish church of Chawley'.

George had married Margaret, daughter of John Bury of Colleton (Colleton Manor, also known as Colleton Barton, near Chulmleigh), in 1656. She was buried in Chawleigh on 29 October 1657, leaving one child, another Thomas. John Bury was the son of Humphrey Bury, JP, who married Gertrude (born circa 1570), daughter of John Stucley (1551–1610 or 1611) by Frances, daughter of Sir John St Leger of Monkleigh. John Bury had married Mary Arscott, daughter of Arthur Arscott of Tetcott (House) in today's district of Torridge.

The connections between local landed families of the time linked the Burys, the Stucley or Stukeley family of nearby Affeton, and the St Legers. The St Legers were a notable family in Devon (and connected with the Eggesford estate, see Chapter 1), but Sir John, a soldier, administrator and politician, died a poor man, and his son, also a soldier, died without leaving an inheritance.

Katherine Radford (daughter of Thomas and Ann), born circa 1624, married Arthur Acland (or Ackland) of Winkleigh, the wider Acland family better known today as the former owners of the National Trust's Killerton estate (and one of Devon's oldest landed families). He was described in 1648 as a 'notorious Popish delinquent'. They had at least two children, Elizabeth and Mary or Maria (the latter being a good 'Popish' name in honour of the mother of God).

Katherine's sister Elizabeth, baptised 1631, married John Stucley of Cobley (in nearby West Worlington) in 1659, and then in 1666 Robert Nutcombe of Nutcombe Manor in Clayhanger, North Devon. The last sister, Dorothy (baptised 1634), married Edward Pridham, Rector of nearby Morchard Bishop.

Richard Radford of Eggesford (baptised 1610 in Chawleigh and buried 1666), son of George Radford and Katherine (née Melhuish), left his house and two others in Chawleigh, plus property in Winkleigh, Thorverton and Oldridge, his overall estate being valued at £1250. He had married Jane Jewe of Brushford, Somerset, buried in Chawleigh in 1676. Her sons Thomas and Ambrose were named as executors in her will, and bequests made to all eight of her children, the others being George, William, Mary, Jane, Katherine and Charles.

Her son Thomas, baptised 1639, was buried intestate in 1699, his unmarried sister Jane being granted administration, along with John Butt and John Webber of Chawleigh.

George Radford, son of Richard and Jane, married Joan Lubban at Chulmleigh in 1657. He had two sons, George and Ambrose, and a daughter Mary to whom he left a house in Ashreigney. His brother Thomas Radford was one of the overseers of his will.

Ambrose Radford of Chawleigh, born 1648 and buried 1703, and another son of Richard and Jane, appears to have been a lawyer. He had married Eleanor Newcombe in 1679, and died childless. Eleanor went on to marry his friend Moses Ffitch, who also benefited by inheriting a collection of legal texts. Eleanor left property in Chawleigh to George Radford, grandson to her late husband's brother Charles.

One of Eleanor's executors was William Radford, a clerk of Nymet Rowland, with James Flexman, junior, standing as a witness. These two are part of the Radford family of Lapford, related to the Chawleigh branch.

The last mentioned child of Richard and Jane Radford, Charles, married Susannah Elworthy (a widow) in 1696. He was buried in 1704 in Chawleigh, and she in 1739, having had four children: Thomas, Jane, Richard and Mary, although Thomas had died in 1730. Mary (baptised in 1703) married farmer William Reade of Nymet Rowland in 1728.

This later Richard Radford, son of Charles and Susannah, was baptised 1701 and buried 1779. He married Margery Buttler in 1731, having four children, George, Susannah, Mary and Elizabeth, all except George baptised in East Worlington. George was buried in Chawleigh in 1786, seemingly unmarried (unless his wife had died), as administration of his will was granted to his sister Susannah. Her will describes her as a spinster. Of the other two children, Mary (baptised 1736) married Richard Dallyn or Dalling of Bishop's Tawton (near Barnstaple), and Elizabeth, baptised 1739, who married an Edworthy and had one child, Mary.

The Snell family

The Radfords were connected to the Snells by at least one marriage. The writer Fay Sampson, formerly based in Devon, has published much of her family history online (*faysampson.co.uk*), with extensive research on the Snell family in Chawleigh. Based on church inscriptions, local tax records and wills, it offers a comprehensive picture of the Snells from the sixteenth century as relatively affluent compared with most of the local population besides the aristocracy and their relatives amongst the clergy. Multiple generations of the family were connected with the village, with their presence first recorded in 1524, and prominent members commemorated in the church. They were likely to have been yeoman sheep farmers, predominantly on high ground to the south of Chawleigh, facing Dartmoor. Other occupations registered for the family were in the tanning trade (curing leather).

'EDMUND SNELL. … in the 1524 Lay Subsidy Roll … Edmund Snell is assessed for goods at £20. This is by far the highest rating in the parish. …

He does not appear in the 1544 Lay Subsidy Roll, but there is a Joan Snell widow. She, like Edmund before her, is rated at £20, as are two others, including Henry Snell, who we believe to be Edmund's grandson. This is again the highest rate for Chawleigh. Joan may be the widow of Edmund or, more probably, of his son Richard. …

There is a burial within the church of Richard Snell, who died in 1540, and his son Henry, who died in 1591. Since Edmund is the only taxpaying Snell in Chawleigh a generation before 1540, it is reasonable to assume that Richard is his son. We know from the inscription on the grave slab that Richard Snell was a benefactor of the church and it is very likely that Edmund was too. … Richard does not appear in the 1524 Lay Subsidy Roll … he was almost certainly a yeoman farmer breeding sheep. … Richard died on 5th Feb 1540 …

Inscribed on the same grave slab as Richard is a memorial to his son Henry… He died in 1591. Henry also appears on the 1544 Lay Subsidy Roll. Both Joan and Henry are rated at £20. They, with one other, are the highest rated parishioners for goods. There are, in addition, two residents of "Challegh" assessed at £2 for land. …

HENRY SNELL. … Properties known to be held by the Snells in the 16th century suggest that the farm was in the area south of the village of Chawleigh. … He appears in one record as a tanner, but it is clear from his extensive land holdings that he was also a prosperous yeoman farmer. … Henry had more than 14 children, though he does not name most of them. His eldest son and heir seems to be John Snell the elder, but he predeceased his father in 1585. This left Anthony apparently as the second son and the only one named in Henry's will.

Henry appears again in the 1569 Muster Roll for "Challey". He is the first named of five presenters. He is not listed among those who have to bear arms, so we may assume that he was then above the maximum fighting age of 60 or was unfit to bear arms. ...What is surprising is that he is not listed amongst those sufficiently affluent to be required to provide extra arms and armour.'

Compiled on behalf of the Privy Council, the Roll listed all men over sixteen, along with their equipment. The younger Snells bearing arms, most likely Henry's older sons, appear as Anthony Snell, archer; Robert Snell, harquebusier (cavalryman armed with a long gun, the harquebus); and John Snell, pikeman.

'In 1613 a terrier of the glebe lands in Chawleigh was made. It includes the following information about land owned by these sons:

"ther is certayne grounds belonging unto the psonage of Chawleighe, called the Beare about some 3 score acres, lying towards the West from the towne remote from the Towne but a lyttle, bounded on the West side by the lands of John Snell; on the North side by the lande of Anthonye Snell, ... on the South side by the lande agayne of John Snell, of Nethercote...

... on other peece of ground called Newmans pke [park], about the vallew of 12 acres; part whereof is marishe grounde, situate nere Chawleighe Beacon, bonded... on the West side by the lands of William Snell."'

On his portion of the family lands perhaps, Anthony Snell built a new house at Fiddlecott. The family held further farmland in areas including Chulmleigh, South Molton, Aishrafe (Rose Ash), Totworthie (Toatworthy) and Adgworthy (Higher Edgeworthy). His will provided generously for the poor of the parish, his widow (now left a woman of means), umpteen children from his various marriages, and godchildren, including a lamb each for five members of the extended family:

'Anthony Snell of Challey als Chauley, yeoman, made his will on 1 Mar 1613. He was buried in Chawleigh on 22 Jan 1617/8. His will was proved on 28 April 1618. He begins by giving land, some held on very long leases (up to 2000 years) to his sons William, George, Robert and Anthony. William gets half of the tenement at West Docombe in Chawleigh, held on a 1000 year lease.

George gets the remainder of Anthony's 2000 year lease on half of Wood als Woodhouse, half of East Tottley (rented out), half of Hill als East Hill (rented out), all of which are in Chawleigh, as well as parcels of the manor of Chawleigh, the other half of Wood als Woodhouse, which is leased. If George predeceases him, George's share will go to his wife or child, if is married by then, or else be divided equally between Anthony jun[ior] and Robert.

To Robert he leaves the other half of Tottley and Hill als East Hill. There is a similar provision for any wife or child if he predeceases Anthony. The implication is again that he is not yet married. Failing this, his share goes to Anthony jun[ior] and George equally.

Anthony junior's legacy is a quarter of the messuage called Higher Ford als Eastford, and other herediments in Chawleigh. If he predeceases his father without issue, these properties pass to Robert, or else to Anthony senior's right heirs.

He gives the poor of Chawleigh 40 shillings, or £2. There is a particularly large legacy of £180 to his daughter Charity. It is likely that his other daughters had already received generous marriage

THIS·WINDOW·WAS·RESTORED IN·MEMORY·OF WILLIAM·JOHN·&·LOTTIE·SNELL 1967

portions and this was to provide the same for the currently unmarried Charity. She married Raymond Sylly in Rackenford on 20 Apr 1619, a year after Anthony died, and Robert Bradford in 1626.

His son William Snell and daughter Grace Cory, children of his first marriage, get 40 shillings each, and the daughters of his son Edmund 20 shillings. He gives 12d (1 shilling) to each godchild. His wife Elizabeth receives £20 etc. and the moiety (half) of his plate, etc, in his new house of Fiddlecott.'

Fay Sampson records another of Henry's sons: 'William Snell of Fremington and Chawleigh, gent., is the first member of the family referred to as a gentleman. Fremington is on the mouth of the River Taw near Barnstaple, 18 miles from Chawleigh. … An inventory of his personal possessions listed by his executors includes a Bible and one book in Latin', so he must have been a man of education. William and his wife Margaret died in February 1604–05 when Barnstaple lay in the grip of the plague, and were buried in Chawleigh two days apart. Perhaps the pestilence had found its way to the village.

Dr George Snell, William's son, was appointed Archdeacon of Chester in 1618, where he married the daughter of the bishop. Further details of his career are registered in the records of his alma mater Caius College, Cambridge:

'In 1631 he escaped a fine for refusing knighthood (his estate being such as to justify the King in offering him that rank), by the plea that he was in holy orders, and in the same year he obtained a dispensation from Archbishop Abbot which permitted him to hold the Rectory of Waverton as well as that of Wallasey. In 1632 he resigned his Canonry in favour of a kinsman of his wife. In 1635 he was appointed Rural Dean of the Deaneries of Chester, Frodsham, Malpas, Middlewich, and Nantwich, and he also became Rural Dean of the Deanery of Bangor.'

He appears to have held all his preferments until 1646 and the victory of the Parliamentarians under Cromwell against the old order, when he was ejected and his estates seized. Thereafter he lived in poverty until 1656, his wife surviving until 1670. Her will of that year is stamped with the old family seal.

Dr Snell's sister Helen married William Tucker, whose family appears regularly in records and directories of Chawleigh folk.

Their cousin, George Snell, son of John Snell of Nethercott, is identified as a goldsmith in London – certainly a sign of the family branching out into new avenues.

The inscription to Thomas Reed in St James' Church, Chawleigh

(Photo by Jonathan Crofts)

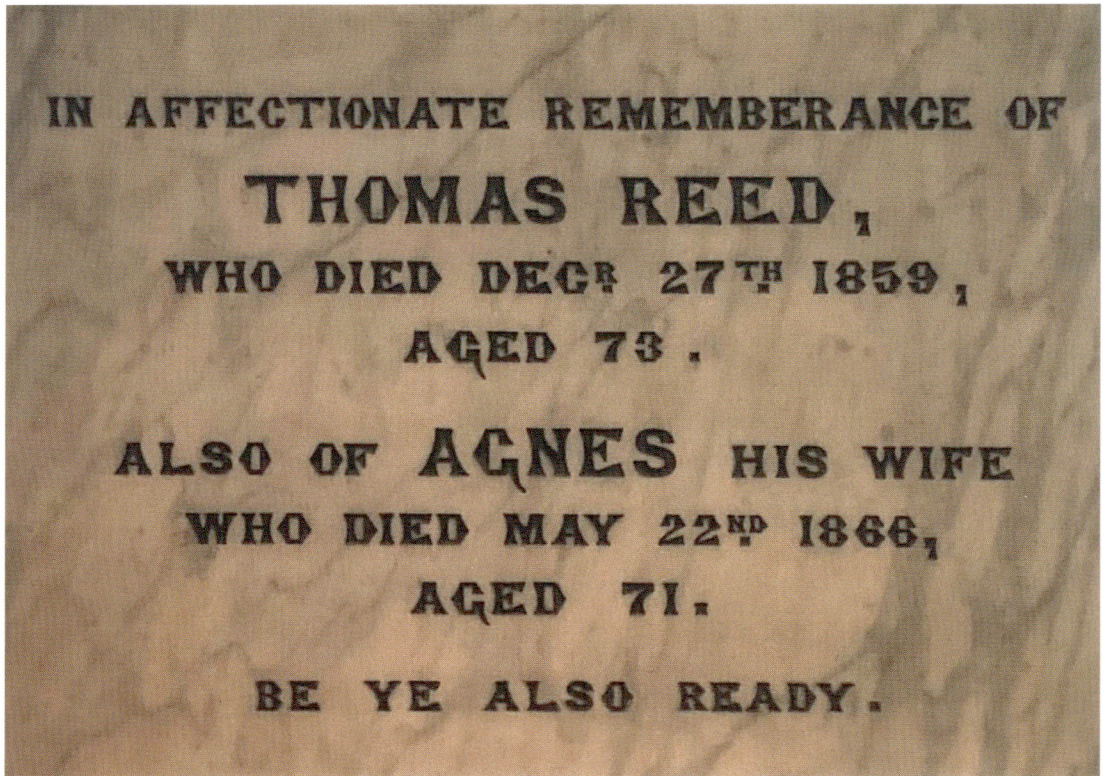

IN AFFECTIONATE REMEMBERANCE OF

THOMAS REED,

WHO DIED DEC^R 27TH 1859,

AGED 73 .

ALSO OF AGNES HIS WIFE

WHO DIED MAY 22ND 1866,

AGED 71.

BE YE ALSO READY.

The Reed family

The Reed family have been property and business owners in Chawleigh for centuries (traced back at least as far back as 1502), and are still present today, although sadly the oldest member died in her nineties in 2024. There are many references to them across Chawleigh history, and the will of a George Reed is referenced in 1662 (see Chapter 15). An inscription in the church commemorates one Thomas Reed, probably the victualler at The London Inn (now The Earl of Portsmouth) who died in 1859, followed by his wife Agnes seven years later.

Henry Reed was listed in 1850 and 1857 directories as one of four landowners of independent means, apart from the Earl of Portsmouth, along with various Reeds as farmers (see Chapters 10 and 13). In 1878-79 Messrs R Reed and T Reed are listed as two amongst five principal landowners. Henry Reed was a trustee and stand-in Chair of the Chawleigh Parish Lands Charity (see Chapter 19).

The wooden inscription to the Edworthy family in St James' Church, Chawleigh

(Photo by Jonathan Crofts)

The Reeds were significant landowners going back to at least 1613, when William Reede is listed as a benefactor for the charity (see Chapter 19). Three of them are listed alongside the Earl of Portsmouth in the *1875 Return of Owners of Land in England and Wales*, amongst eight in Chawleigh. Their acreage is inevitably dwarfed by that of the Earl (see Chapter 8).

The Edworthy family

The Edworthys in Chawleigh date back to the 1630s at least: Margaret Cash's *Devon Inventories of the 16th and 17th centuries* (1966) records the goods and chattels of the deceased yeoman John Edworthy of Chawleigh, valuing these at 'Over £203 4s. 8d'; the detail included not only livestock and corn but 'featherbedes' and 'Chamber pottes'. It was proved (probate obtained) by Roger Edworthy, Thomas Clement and William Lawrence on 3 February 1635 or 1636.

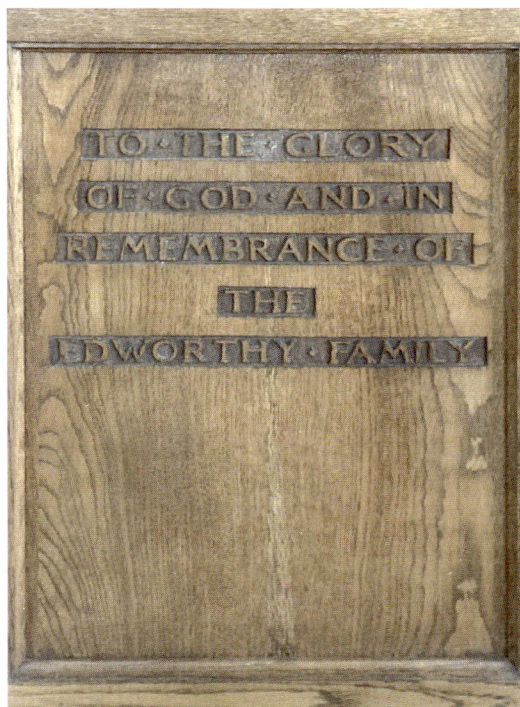

There are at least eight Edworthys recorded with sixteenth- and seventeenth-century wills in Chawleigh, and the family is also recorded in neighbouring Cheldon parish, where Ann Edworthy was churchwarden.

In the nineteenth century, the Edworthys are listed particularly in connection with roles as wheelwright and victualler at The Royal Oak. Richard Edworthy was noted in the Great Fire of 1869, struggling to extinguish the flames.

William Challice (of Leaches Farm, now Leaches House) married Harriet Edworthy in 1847 and his will was dated 1865. He died on 16 July 1885:

'I give devise and bequeath all unto my dearly beloved Wife Harriet Challice, all and every my household furniture linen and wearing apparel books plate pictures china and also all my every sum and sums of money which may be found in my house or be about my person or due to me at the time of my decease. And also all my stocks funds and securities for money book debts money on bonds bills notes or other securities and all and every other my estate and effects whatsoever and wheresoever both real and personal whether in possession or reversion remaining or expectancy unto my said wife Harriet Challice, to and for her own use and benefit absolutely.'

'Proved at Exeter the twenty first day of October 1885 by the Oath of Harriet Challice, Widow, the Relict, the sole Executrix, to whom Administration was granted… Gross value £704.16.0 Net £512'

Still at Leaches Farm, Harriet died without a will only a year later, her sister Charlotte administering the estate:

'On the twenty third day of September 1886, Letters of Administration of the personal Estate of Harriet Challice late of Chawleigh in the County of Devon, Widow, deceased, who died on the first day of September 1886, at Chawleigh aforesaid a Widow without child or parent and intestate were granted by Her Majesty's High Court of Justice in the District Registry attached to the Probate Division thereof at Exeter to Charlotte Edworthy of Salisbury in the County of Wilts, Spinster, the natural and lawful Sister and one of the next of kin of the said deceased, she having been first sworn duly to administer. …

Gross personal Estate £1047.9.8

Net £989.16.9

Reswom November 1886 £1117.5.0 gross'

There are references to many other families in the chapters of this book, and to prominent figures in the village's history. Other individuals have been just as significant in the development of this Devon community. Mutual respect and collaboration between them all were not always the case, however. Religion and local politics proved divisive in the nineteenth century, as growing education and evolving faiths set some against others in the life of the village.

CHAPTER 18

CHAWLEIGH SCHOOLS AND THE SCHOOLMASTER CONTROVERSY

In medieval times many villages benefited from a church house near the church, where church ale was brewed and village events celebrated. It is likely that the proceeds from selling church ale contributed to maintaining the church and supporting the poor. This may have been the case originally in Chawleigh, although the church house was certainly better known in later times for educational purposes rather than brewing. The hardstanding for parking vehicles in front of the church today is still registered with Devon County Council as village green or common land, and would have been the site for many of these festivities in centuries past.

Chawleigh Schools, c.1967

(Photographer unknown)

In Charles II's reign, shortly after the Restoration of the monarchy, the long-titled 'Act for the Uniformity of Publique Prayers and Administration of Sacraments & other Rites & Ceremonies and for establishing the Form of making ordaining and consecrating Bishops Preists and Deacons in the Church of England' (1662) was intended to authorise the use of a revised Book of Common Prayer. The list of schoolmasters subscribing to it, compiled around that time, included Nathaniell

Downe for Chawleigh, in 1676. Nathaniel(I) Downe died on 14 October 1702, Agnes Downe (presumably his wife) on 27 November 1715; they had three children.

G W Copeland in his 1966 paper on 'Devonshire Church Houses, pt. VI' described the building by St James' Church, which is today part private house and part Milly's Nursery, and the early days of the Chawleigh Parish Lands charity (see Chapter 19):

"'A house, called the Church House, next adjoining the churchyard, on the south side thereof – in the borough of Chawleigh", was one of the several properties conveyed by a deed dated 26 August 1775 by Christopher Northcote and Steven Cann to eight other persons. The rents and profits of the various premises, "or so much thereof as should be necessary", were applied "in and about the repairing, upholding, sustaining, maintaining, and keeping in good and decent repair the parish church of Chawleigh".

… There were also a schoolroom and a house occupied by the schoolmaster rent free. The house was repaired and converted to its present use in 1806, after having been a poor-house. "The school-room forms part of the church-house." The building is a long stone-built one south of the church and with its north side abutting into the churchyard. It has every sign of having been rebuilt or considerably altered early in the last century. The poor-house or almshouse which it became consisted of seven rooms on the upper floor.

The south side, on the village square, is of seven bays, with rectangular wooden windows glazed in patterns on irregular sexfoils. In front are two gabled porches of one stage but of unequal size. That to the west admits to the present village school, and the smaller one of the east to the former headmaster's house. This part of the building is still known locally as the Church House. The front is decorated with two wide and shallow projections below the wall-head, both on corbel-tables, interrupted by a small single pointed arch. The west projection is wider than the other. There are rectangular end chimneys, that at the west replaced by a modern gabled bell-cote. The north-east angle of the building is canted off and is surmounted by a pair of square brick stacks. The rear windows, four over five, are glazed like those in front, and the building has a chamfered plinth. The interior has been adapted and modernised.'

Local rector the Reverend Pelham Fellowes Clay, whose uncle was the 4th Earl of Portsmouth, stated in 1821 that his parish had a charity school and two private schools. The Charity Commissioners in 1823 confirmed that 'This school is maintained partly out of the Poor's rate and partly by voluntary contributions… there had been constantly since the establishment of the school, twelve children of the said poor inhabitants receiving their education there gratuitously'.

The 1850 White's *Directory of Devonshire* reveals a Free School and the Master's house vested with the trustees of the Parish Lands, and another school supported by the Rector. Richard Gough (whose son, also Richard, built the lych gate for the church, see Chapter 15) was schoolmaster and Samuel Alford schoolmaster and shopkeeper. It was Richard Gough, senior, who was at the heart of the controversy mentioned by the Reverend H J Hodgson in his notes on the church in 1923 for the Deanery. Hodgson describes the 'present Rector (Rev. W. J. Bradford)' who produced a copy of the 1857 report on Chawleigh Parish Lands including the church by Exeter architect, Mr Hayward, which highlighted the need for 'a great deal of repair and restoration'.

Hodgson goes on:

'We can find no evidence that Mr. Hayward's report was adopted. It was presented at a very unfortunate time, the whole parish was meeting with excitement over a lawsuit:– "In Chancery – The Attorney General v. Fellowes, Earl of Portsmouth." The suit, commenced 40 years previously, was, at bottom, a family dispute between the Earl and his kinsman, the Rector (Rev. Pelham Fellowes Clay) and centred around the village schoolmaster, a protégé of the Earl, but a thorn in the side of the Rector.

By the decision of the court, the Rector won on most counts, and on April 17th, 1858, a scheme for the management of the Chawleigh Church Lands Charity came into being. By this scheme, the trustees were not allowed to spend on the church more than £15 pounds per annum on its upkeep, with an additional £10 pounds for substantial repairs. The other property of the trustees was urgently in need of reparation, consequently, it was impossible to carry out any considerable repairs on the Church till many years later.'

A report in *The Western Times* (13 February 1858) summed up the longstanding legal case, which included charges against certain trustees of the Chawleigh Parish Lands Charity (see Chapter 19), as well as the Rector vs. Schoolmaster issue:

'Clause 25 of the scheme was also objected to by Mr. Hull Terrell, as far as it proposed to give the charity of Chawleigh the power of making the appointment of the parish schoolmaster, in the first instance. This section was inserted for the purpose of removing Mr. Gough, who, it appeared, was not in the good graces of the rector, and against whom, it was urged by the rector's churchwardens as supporting the views of the rector, but Mr. Gough was not a member of the Church of England, as he did not usually go to church.

To this objection Mr. Gough replied by affidavit, that he was a member of the Church of England – that he conducted his school on Church of England principles – that the only books he used in his school were those supplied by the National School Society, and that the parents of the children attending his school were at liberty to send their children on the Sunday to what place of worship they pleased, and as a confirmation of his sufficiency and adaptation to his office, there was produced a certificate, signed by the two overseers and one of the churchwardens, and by the principal inhabitants of the parish, certifying to his competency, and to their satisfaction, and to the fact that his removal would be considered by them uncalled for and improper and dangerous to the present prosperity of the school.

Mr. Gough also explained that the reason of his not attending the parish church, and of his having attended for some years past at the Independent Chapel, in Chawleigh, it was not because of his disagreeing with the doctrines of the Church of England, but on account of his dissatisfaction with the conduct of the rector of Chawleigh. In this dissatisfaction, it was stated that he was not isolated, inasmuch as the Parish Church had ceased to be frequented as formerly, and that the population had sought better instruction, having had two Dissenting Chapels erected in the parish of Chawleigh during the incumbency of the Reverend Mr. Clay.

The Judge, therefore, declined to assume for the Court of Chancery the power of appointing the Schoolmaster, and he left it to the trustees, who will doubtless continue Mr. Gough in the office which he has held for 19 years, and the Vice Chancellor also remarked that the doctrine of the Independents, at whose Chapel Mr. Gough had attended, was similar to those of the Church of England, and that that body differed from it chiefly in matters of discipline.

To the 28th clause of the scheme, which provided that the School-house might be used as a Sunday-school, and that if one was not established in it within six months by the Trustees, the Rector might use it for the purpose; it was objected that this distinction between the eleven Trustees and the Rector might produce discord, but the Vice-Chancellor decided that he did not think that such result could follow, and he accordingly retained the clause in the scheme.'

Sadly, this court decision did not serve to dispel the 'discord' within the village.

Evelyn, 5th Countess of Portsmouth, attempted to arbitrate in her letter to the Reverend Clay, her relative by marriage, on 11 October 1858, where she sought to restore:

'harmony and concord in the parish of Chawleigh… If a Sunday school should be established there on such principles that while the first great elements of our Christian Religion were taught, the prejudices of none should be hurt, I imagine no means would be more successful in healing the present unhappy dissensions in the Parish.

I hope much I may have your hearty cooperation in the undertaking, and that we may see in it the dawn of a better tune and spirit in Chawleigh. I shall be most happy to furnish the Books requisite for a Sunday School, and I now enclose for your perusal and approval some specimens of those used in all National Schools, and which I think you will agree with me are entirely free from a party tone or peculiar views, being in fact only the words of the Scriptures in simpler form. The Books with the Bible and Testament and perhaps some pictures for the little ones would I should say complete what is wanted.

I would however further propose that a Catechism Class be formed, always provided that none of those children, whose parents objected to their joining it, be required to learn it. Should you agree to this liberal arrangement, Lord Portsmouth has promised me that he will insist on Gough's regular attendance not only at the Sunday School, but also at Church afterwards, bringing as many children as possible. This of course, as Gough is still from their relative positions entirely dependent on Lord Portsmouth, from whom he receives his entire salary, should be enforced.

Both Lord Portsmouth and myself are truly anxious to see what we consider so beneficial to the Parish as a good Sunday School established in Chawleigh, and if you will cordially join us in carrying out a scheme so tolerant and just as I have described, we will do our utmost for its continuance and prosperity. While I would beg of you to meet Gough in the school in a generous spirit and courteous manner, I can assure you of our determination to see that all proper respect is shown to you, and that Gough adhered to the terms laid down…'

Despite the Countess's intervention following the pronouncement of the Court of Chancery in the previous year, the struggle within the parish had clearly not gone away. The Reverend P F Clay and Mr Henry Reed, another Trustee, summoned a Special Meeting of Trustees for 3 March 1859 in order to, amongst others, 'rescind the Resolution passed at the last Meeting "That the notice to GOUGH to quit at Lady-day be not enforced," and to propose, that he be required to give up possession of the School and Schoolhouse now occupied by him at Lady-day next.' Clearly Gough's tenure at the School was not yet fully secure.

The Schools after the Court of Chancery

Belling's 1857 *Directory of the County of Devon* noted 'The National School is near the Church and is mainly supported by the Earl of Portsmouth, and the payment of children. Number of children – boys 42; girls 38.' Richard and Rebecca Gough were shown as schoolmaster and mistress.

By 1870 the trustees were considering how to adapt the schoolhouse to the 'requirements of the New Education Bill'. By the 1870 Education Act, voluntary schools could continue unchanged, but 'school boards' were to build and manage schools where they were needed. These would be locally elected bodies with funding from local rates. Religious teaching in these board schools was to be 'non-denominational'.

Rough estimates for the space required were calculated on a Chawleigh population of 301 and 97 in Cheldon, estimating 150 children and allowing 8 square feet for each child, therefore 1200 square feet required in total. On that basis, the upstairs alterations would help provide space for 147 children. By 3 October 1870, Mr Selley the builder was submitting plans and estimates to Lord Portsmouth for both Chawleigh and East Worlington schools.

White's *Directory* maintains 'The Board Schools are the property of the feoffees of the "Church Property" who let the schools and the master's house to the School Board for a nominal rent. ... The School Board for the united district of Chawleigh and Cheldon was formed on February 19th, 1873.' In 1893 there were 120 children, with average attendance being 36 boys, 40 girls and 27 infants. The Infants Room was built in 1894, having been housed on the upper floor of the 'Big Room', which then had its floor removed.

Research by website *devonheritage.org* provides more colour in the story of Richard Gough

'One of those named for their leadership at the time of Chawleigh's great fire was Richard Gough, the schoolmaster who had been born in the village. The 1841 census shows him in office, as a bachelor aged 30, living at the home of a local woman named Rebecca Gough. By 1851, he had married Rebecca's daughter, also named Rebecca (29 in 1851), who had returned to the village as a certificated teacher and who had become the Infants' Mistress. By 1851, they had two children – Richard (3) and Helena (1).

Richard's service record ran from some time in the 1830s until his death in 1874 and must have rivalled that of John Baple. He was buried in the tiny graveyard of the Congregational Chapel opposite the school, now the Jubilee Hall. The 1891 census shows Rebecca then aged 69 living at St. Sidwell's in Chawleigh [more likely to have been Exeter]... The Chapel was adapted to other uses as a Jubilee Project in 1935 and the gravestones were cleared back and made safe so that the exact location of individual graves is no longer known. ... the gravestone of Richard Gough and his wife Rebecca – most of the inscription has weathered away but their names and the word "schoolmaster" can still be made out.'

The *devonheritage.org* website also tells the story of later schoolmaster John Baple and his wife Ellen:

'The school was to have one of Devon's longest-serving Masters – John Baple who served there from 1882 to 1924 along with his wife who was a certificated teacher and had been appointed Mistress. John Baple was born in Chawleigh in the September Quarter of 1860, the son of William Baple, a sawyer, and his wife Mary. He was to attend the same school he was later made Master of. ...

THE ELEMENTARY EDUCATION ACT, 1870.

BYE-LAWS

OF THE

SCHOOL BOARD

FOR THE UNITED SCHOOL DISTRICT OF CHAWLEIGH,

Comprising the Parishes of Chawleigh and Cheldon, North Devon.

At a Meeting of the SCHOOL BOARD of the United School District of CHAWLEIGH and CHELDON, in the County of Devon, held at the Board Room, in the Parish of Chawleigh, on Wednesday the 10th day of December, 1873, the said Board do hereby, in pursuance of the powers, vested in them under the Elementary Education Act, 1870, and subject to the approval of the Education Department, make the following Bye-laws:—

1.—The Parent of every child residing within the School District of CHAWLEIGH and CHELDON shall cause such child, not being less than five nor more than thirteen years of age, to attend a Public Elementary School, unless there be some reasonable excuse for non-attendance. Any of the following shall be a reasonable excuse, namely:

(a) That the child is under efficient instruction in some other manner.

(b) That the child has been prevented from attending school by sickness, or any unavoidable cause.

(c) That there is no Public Elementary School open which the child can attend within three miles.

2. Any child, between ten and thirteen years of age, who has been certified by one of Her Majesty's Inspectors of Schools to have reached a Standard equivalent to the Sixth Standard of the new Code, 1871, shall be altogether exempt from the obligation, under these Bye-Laws, to attend school.

3. The time during which every child shall attend school, shall, except in the cases specified in these Bye-laws, be every time and the whole time for which the school shall be open for the instruction of children of similar age.

Provided—

(a) That nothing herein contained shall prevent the withdrawal of any child from any religious observance, or instruction, inspection or examination, in religious matters.

(b) That no child shall be required to attend school on any day exclusively set apart for religious observance by the religious body to which his or her parent belongs.

(c) That no child shall be required to attend school at any time, or in any manner, contrary to anything contained in any Act for regulating the education of children employed in labour.

4.—Any parent who shall, without some reasonable excuse, neglect to cause any child to attend a school as required by these Bye-laws, shall, for every such offence, be subject to a penalty, including costs, not exceeding five shillings.

5.—These Bye-laws shall take effect from and after the day on which the same shall be sanctioned by Her Majesty, by order in Council.

Sealed with the Corporate Common Seal of the School Board of the said United School District of the Parishes of Chawleigh and Cheldon, this Fifth day of January, 1874.

The Right Honble. the EARL OF PORTSMOUTH, CHAIRMAN.

Sealed in the presence of
JOHN HANNAFORD,
CLERK.

JOHN NOTT, PRINTER, CHULMLEIGH.

The School Board bye-laws of 1870 for Chawleigh and Cheldon, requiring each child 'not being less than five nor more than 13 years of age, to attend a Public Elementary School'

The Earl of Portsmouth was the Chairman, John Hannaford the Clerk
(Photo by Jonathan Crofts, by kind permission of Jim Stevens)

The 1861 census shows Richard and Rebecca Gough as Master and Mistress of the school and they were still there in 1871 although by that time, Richard Gough was 60 and must have been thinking about retirement. The 1881 census shows George Challice in charge and since his youngest child was born in Chawleigh and was 3 years old, we can time his arrival for the mid 1870s.

… the same census shows John Baple in Exeter, where there was an excellent College for the training of teachers – St. Luke's Diocesan College. ... The appointment at Chawleigh must have been his first and last job interview for he never taught anywhere else!

In the Spring after his arrival in Chawleigh, he married Elizabeth Ellen Nott who was also a certificated teacher and eventually, she was appointed as Mistress to take charge of the infants, some of whom were barely two years old. Village schools played a very important part as child-minders in those days. A large proportion of women in Chawleigh were engaged in lace-making, working as outworkers – work that would have been impossible to do with young children present all the time.

The Baples had two children – Ellie (1884) and William Henry (1889). John Baple retired in 1924 at the age of nearly 65 after 42 years of service to his community.'

Chawleigh was known for its lace, with many of its 'lace runners' engaged in working intricate stitching onto factory-made nets. Such work needed keen vision and bright hours of daylight. The village school was a godsend, not just because it kept children out of the way, but because the lace-workers picked up a little reading and counting, essential for following a pattern.

The *Chulmleigh Deanery Magazine* of 1896 gave a flavour of Victorian education and reflects the 'excellent' progress of the Chawleigh and Cheldon United District Board School, under John Baple, quoting from H M Inspector's annual report:

'Mixed School. – "The order is excellent, and the Instruction most efficient in all respects."

Infants' Class. – "The Infants are in excellent order and thoroughly well taught."

Henrietta M. Saunders (P.T.) has obtained a second class in the Queen's scholarship Examination. She should be informed that she is now qualified under Article 50 of the Code.

The School was examined in Drawing of the 20th of May, by H. Lucas Esq., and classed "excellent".

H.M. Saunders was examined at the same time in "Model" and "Freehand" Drawing, 2nd Grade, and has been awarded a First Class Certificate for the former, and a Second for the latter by the Science and Art Department.

School Savings Bank. – Total deposits for the year £36. 2. 9d. Total standing to the credit of depositors £156.10.3d. Number of depositors 65.

Evening School Report. – "This school is very orderly and well taught; the pupils are attentive and regular and continuous in their attendance from year to year."'

The tradition of school performances was already much in evidence in 1897:

'An Entertainment was given in the schoolroom, on Friday evening, January 15th, by the scholars of the Day School to a crowded and most enthusiastic audience… Parents, teachers and children … worked together with a will, and fortunately their efforts were crowned with success, the affair having passed off without a single hitch. … At one end of the school stood a large platform… lined with children whose pretty dresses and smiling faces did not fail to attract the warmest admiration of their spectators. … Most of the singing consisted of Action Songs, rendered in capital time and tune. The recitations were chiefly in character which, on more than one occasion, fairly brought down the house.'

Such a scene is equally imaginable in schools of the twenty-first century, although perhaps today 'the singing of the National Anthem' would not bring 'the proceedings to a satisfactory close', as it did then.

Easter Monday 1897 saw the children of the schools being 'entertained at Tea by Mr. and Mrs. Baple, and very thoroughly they seemed to appreciate it. Mr. Tucker, of Leaches, kindly lent a field for the afternoon, close to the schoolrooms, where various games and races were enjoyed' – a reference to Leaches Farm, one of the closest to the school and church, the farmhouse now renamed as Leaches House. In the following June two members of families associated with Leaches were confirmed into the Church of England faith by the Bishop, along with fifteen others: James Tucker and Charlotte Eliza Challice.

The 1897 reports on the schools from H M Inspectors continued to reflect 'excellent … careful and intelligent' teaching, with the Infant Class being 'admirably taught and managed by Mrs Baple.' The schools were clearly growing, and combined with 'regular attendance', the 'Government Grants for the year considerably exceed those of any previous twelve months since the opening of the school in 1873.' Edith Margaret Webber won a two-year scholarship to a secondary school, probably going on to Edgehill College, Bideford, a Methodist school founded by the Bible Christian movement.

The monthly School Board meeting held in July 1889, reported by the *Devon and Exeter Gazette*, continued in this congratulatory theme, the recent examination 'considered highly satisfactory. The children passed ninety per cent, and the school classed as "excellent". Lucy Smith pupil teacher obtained the highest merit in addition to a first class prize at the Diocesan Inspection.' And August 1889 saw the traditional annual summer treat for the Sunday school children, in the Rectory grounds, with the much-loved tea, brass band, and dancing in the evening.

School attendance was not made compulsory in England until 1880 (for five- to ten-year-olds), although eighteen per cent of children were still missing nationally in the 1890s: even in 1901 an estimated 300,000 children were working outside school hours, and truancy remained a problem, with youngsters often required to help support the family. School fees had to be paid until 1891. In 1893 eleven-year-olds had to attend school, and those aged twelve from 1899. The 1918 Education Act made school compulsory up the age of fourteen; followed by the 1944 Act raising it to fifteen, but it was not until 1972 that a school leaving age of sixteen was mandatory.

Vocational education in Victorian Chawleigh often took the form of apprenticeships, and not always happy ones. *The Western Times* of April 1838 carried an advertisement: 'Ran away on the second of April, Robert Alford, the Parish Apprentice of Mr Robert Elworthy, of Moreton [presumably Moortown], in the parish of Chawleigh. … he is eighteen and was last seen wearing a fustian jacket,

TIVERTON STAG HUNT, DEVON

Tiverton Stag Hunt in front of Chawleigh Schoolhouse, later 20th-century jigsaw box.
The old village green area in front of the schoolhouse was still visible.

(Photo by Jonathan Crofts, by kind permission of Jim Stevens)

striped waistcoat, and corduroy trousers. [Anyone] harbouring him after this notice will be prosecuted'. The little picture accompanying the advert shows a boy in a top hat running, a bundle tied to a staff over his shoulder, and casting furtive glances behind him.

The village lacking a hall in this period, the school also served as premises for public meetings and local entertainment as well as education. *The Western Times* of 28 January 1898 reported that:

> 'The Annual Ball and Social Evening held in the schoolroom on Friday was a great success and due to the committee, Messrs Reed, Partridge (Leigh), Frederick Ford (Nethercott), and Simon Cowie (Bransgrove). The bells which had long been silent owing to sickness in the village [possibly a smallpox outbreak, which was common at that time] rang during the early part of the evening. Upwards of 80 ladies and gentlemen attended from this and neighbouring parishes of Chulmleigh, Winkleigh, Cheldon, Burrington, Worlington, Eggesford, Lapford, etc.
>
> The various rooms of the school were fitted up for the various games, etc., and the main room for dancing. Refreshments were served by Mr and Mrs Bowden. Mr Fred Lovell's band supplied the music. Carriages were ordered for 3.30 a.m. and arrived promptly after a very successful evening.'

Mr James Bowden was listed in the *Kelly's Directory* of 1889 against the Barnstaple Inn (now The Old Court House) in South Molton Street, Chulmleigh. Presumably he and his wife had offered a better deal on a fine spread for the revellers than the local hostelries.

The school was also used for the Annual Library meeting, again with tea for eighty people (*The Western Times*, 2 December 1898):

> 'All the old magazines were disposed of by casting lots which caused much amusement. An interesting programme of songs and recitations followed. Later a touching reference was made by the Rector to the cause of the unavoidable absence of Mrs Partridge of Hardings Leigh Farm who for a quarter of a century had taken a lively interest in similar gatherings connected with the library... A dance was afterwards held in the main room, to music supplied by Mr. George Challice [who had recently taken on the role of schoolmaster].'

Eventually, in 1937, the senior students were transferred to the larger school in Chulmleigh. A primary school continued in Chawleigh into the 2000s. Devon County Council reportedly invested £140,000 putting in a new (upper) floor to the school early in that decade, even though they did not own the building (it belongs to Chawleigh Parish Lands Charity). The Council went on to close the school a few years later, due to the low number of pupils. Chawleigh Parish Lands Charity continues to manage the buildings and a few other properties locally, the bitter controversy of the nineteenth century now long forgotten.

CHAPTER 19

CHARITABLE WORKS AND CONTROVERSY: CHAWLEIGH PARISH LANDS

Chawleigh Parish Lands Charity continues today, but its origins may go back as far as the sixteenth century. It has two Charitable Objects (purposes):

Church Branch: maintenance and repair of the fabric of the parish church, and subject thereto in the maintenance of the services of the church and furniture

Poors Branch: to relieve either generally or individually persons resident in the parish of Chawleigh who are in conditions of need, hardship or distress.

Not every village in the UK has a similar trust, and it sits alongside the Parish Council, the Parochial Church Council at St James' Church, Chawleigh Playing Field charity, the Jubilee Hall (village hall) charity, the WI (National Federation of Women's Institutes), and the Friendly Society, all of which have a part to play in managing village events and properties.

The Chawleigh Parish Terrier of 1613 (see Chapter 21), which lists local benefactors, includes names of those living in the 1500s, so the village has a long tradition of caring for those in need:

'The prsentment made by the Church Warden and side man of the p[ar]ish aforesaide as heere after followeth

First Wee present wheir with or p[ar]ish is Bonded, Videlizt [viz], on the East with on pcell [parcel] of Land now in the tenaure of Mrs. Stuckley, widow, on the North with the Ryver of Dart, on the West with the Ryver of Taw, on the South with the Lake which runeth between the p[ar]ish of Lapford and Chawleigh aforesaid

1613 Wee present the nams of all those p[er]sons which have geven money by their last Will to the use of the poore to continue for ever

	s.	d.		s.	d.
Henrye Row	3.	4	John Webber als. Matthew	2.	-
John Dier	6.	8	Amey Webber, vid.	20.	-
William Reede	6.	8	John Hulland	10.	-
Richard Keyne	10.	-	John Kinge	13.	4
William Fursdon	20.	-	Anise Bourtfill	5.	-
Thomas Jurdayne	20.	-	John Greenewaye	20.	-'

A report by the Charity Commissioners in 1823 cited the earliest Trust Deeds of 1775 including 'a house called the Church House, next adjoining the churchyard, on the south side thereof... there are also a schoolroom and a house occupied by the schoolmaster.'

The Commissioners also recorded local beliefs about how the charity started: 'A tradition prevails in the parish, that this charity was established by one John Hill, who is stated to have held the office of churchwarden upwards of a century ago, but we have met with no evidence of such a donation.'

John Hill of Honiley, Warwickshire, is known from the seventeenth century as the father-in-law of Sir Arthur Chichester, 1st Earl of Donegall and owner of the nearby Eggesford estate, via the Earl's first wife, Dorcas (who died in 1630). His role as benefactor remains clouded by time, however.

From around the 1740s the Commissioners started to detail the personal bequests which provided the Parish Lands trust with funds for its charitable purposes: 'the sum of £46 for the use of the parishioners' and 'the sum of £2.6.-d is stated to have been paid for bread "which was distributed as usual"'. Humphrey Aram Esq. bequeathed £40 of which the interest provided bread annually 'on the feast of Saint Thomas the apostle' (December 21st – the customary day for Christmas donations to the poor). From 1818 the bread 'was bestowed on the same class of persons usually on Good Friday'. One record shows Humphrey Aram (died circa 1771) as a Devon lawyer and landowner who lived at Chawleigh, apprenticed to Moses Fitch or Ffitch (see Chapter 17). There was also a Humphrey Henry Aram Hole, who was rector in neighbouring Chulmleigh and died in 1814.

Thomas Webber's will of 1696 provided for 10/-s. in bread to be distributed 'on Saint Thomas' day, for ever. The annuity is payable out of a garden in the parish of Pilton [now in Barnstaple], in this county, called Yeoland, the property of Miss Reid'.

Additionally, an 'annuity of 40/-s. is paid to a poor widow of this parish' from the residue of rents and profits of the estate of Mrs Gertrude Pyncombe, who stipulated that her trustees pay '10 poor men and 10 poor women, who had no relief from the parish in which they lived, and were resident in some of the parishes where her estates were situate, 40/-s. a-piece.'

Gertrude Pyncombe's works of charity are well known across Devon and Somerset. The Pyncombes of North Molton had acquired extensive lands and Gertrude, the last of them who lived circa 1670 to 1730, effectively founded a number of trusts which provided for the poor but also gave (and still give) educational grants and support for Church of England clergy. A marble mural monument from 1809 commemorates her in St Michael and All Angels Church at Poughill.

There is correspondence as late as 1937 between the then Chawleigh rector, the Reverend R F Bastow, and the Secretary of the Pyncombe Charity on the death of Mrs Ellen Jeffrey, an annuitant of Chawleigh, and the nomination of her successor: '... the person ... should be the most deserving case in the Parish who is not in receipt of Poor-law relief... If possible, will you please recommend a man to fill the vacancy as according to the Scheme there should be an equal number of men and women but at present a larger number of women are receiving the Annuity.'

The other significant gift for the parish was from the Reverend John Churchill, its rector (as well as at Eggesford), who died in 1818 and left £50, the interest for which 'should be applied for the industrious and deserving poor of the parish, either in bread, or in such manner … most conducive to the interest of religion and virtue.' The £50 was invested in the Devon and Exeter Savings Bank in the names of the Honourable Newton Fellowes, the 4th Earl of Portsmouth, and the Reverend Pelham Fellowes Clay, the new rector.

The Commissioners' report names a number of trustees who carried the responsibility for the charity's many properties at that time:

'The earliest trust deeds produced to us relating to this charity are indentures of lease and release, bearing date 25th and 26th August, 1775, whereby Christopher Northcote and Stephen Cann, described as the surviving trustees of the premises therein mentioned, conveyed to Richard Northcote, Edward Snell, William Pyke, Richard Vickery, Henry Reed, George Reed, John Cawsey, and William Snell, and their heirs, a messuage [a house with outbuildings and plot of land] and tenement, with the appurtenances, with a meadow and parcel of land, thentofore in the possession of William Passmore, and afterwards of James Passmore, George Bird and Richard Vicary; a messuage, meadow, and parcel of land, called Tussells, thentofore in the possession of George Webber, and afterwards of George Webber, his son; another messuage and tenement, thentofore in the possession of Armival Webber, and late of the said George Webber, the son; a messuage and tenement, thentofore in the possession of Annica Botefield, and afterwards of Elizabeth Hill; a messuage and tenement, thentofore in the possession of Margaret Gope, and late of Thomas Bird; a house and garden, thentofore in the occupation of William Webber, deceased, and afterwards of Richard Heywood; and a house, called the Church House, next adjoining the churchyard, on the south side thereof, all in the borough of Chawleigh…'

The report was specific about the uses to which any monies should be put:

'… to apply the rents and profits of the said premises, or so much thereof as should be necessary, in and about the repairing, upholding, sustaining, maintaining, and keeping in good and decent repair the parish church of Chawleigh …; and if any overplus should remain in the hands of the trustees … and the said parish church should be then in good and decent repair, and not want any immediate reparations, on trust, that the said trustees should … give and distribute such overplus to and amongst such poor indigent and needy persons, of the said parish of Chawleigh, as should be legally settled there, and not have monthly pay from the said parish…'

The Charity Commissioners then began to call out historic irregularities in the administration of the charity, naming various prominent individuals:

'The last appointment of trustees was made by indentures of lease and release, bearing date 19th and 20th August, 1802, whereby the said John Cawsey and Henry Reed, as the surviving trustees, conveyed the above mentioned premises to the Hon. Newton Fellowes, the Rev. John Churchill, Christopher Northcote, John Snell, John Vickery, William Snell, Henry Reed the younger, Thomas Cawsey, Henry Reed of East Torrifield [Tonifield?], and Edward Reed, and their heirs, to the use of the parties of the first and second part, upon the above mentioned trust. Of these trustees, John Cawsey, Henry Reed the elder, the Rev. John Churchill, John Snell and William Snell, have since died, and Henry Reed the younger, and Henry Reed of East Torrifield [Tonifield?], never executed the trust deed, nor does it appear that they have acted in the execution of the trusts.

… John Vickery, the lessee of the garden, No. 8 in the rental, was a trustee at the time of the demise to him and still continues so; it was, however, let to him, as the best bidder at an auction, and we are told that the present rent is its fair value. Although therefore the transaction was irregular it does not appear to have caused any loss to the charity.

… It does not appear that the trustees have strictly attended to the directions of the trust deed by rendering an account to the churchwardens and sidesman within a month after Michaelmas; but the accounts of the treasurer have been audited annually about Lady-day, the meeting of trustees for this purpose being usually attended by Mr. Fellowes, and the rector.'

The Commissioners also report on the process for letting property, and the state of repair of the buildings:

'Auctions are usually held for letting the property; but the tenement, No. 6, was let by agreement between the trustees and the tenant, in consequence of its having become vacant about four years ago, a very short time before Lady Day, so that there was not sufficient time to give notice of an auction.

The houses are repaired by the trustees with the exceptions of Nos. 3 and 9. The buildings on Nos. 2, 4 and 7, are stated to be in bad condition. The expenses of the repairs of the poor house have usually been defrayed by the parish. … The fine of £40 pounds received for the existing lease of the tenement No.9 was chiefly expended in the improvement of the schoolmaster's house. This school is maintained partly out of the poor's rates, and partly by voluntary contributions.'

Gifts to the poor of the parish in the early nineteenth century were not insubstantial, granted 'usually at the discretion of Mr. John Vickery, the treasurer', but dried up as controversy struck around 1823, resulting in a legal case ('proceedings in Chancery') against certain trustees:

'… In consequence of expensive repairs done to the houses Nos. 1 and 6, and of the distribution to the poor of considerable sums in 1816, and the years immediately preceding, which are stated to have been bestowed with a view of preventing many poor persons from forfeiting their claim to the charity, by becoming burdensome to the parish, the trustees were in advance to the charity to the amount of £144 pounds 14s. 10d. This debt has since been discharged, and the sums of £50 in 1820, £41 18s. 4½ d. in 1821, and £10 in 1822, have been paid over to the churchwardens towards the repairs of the church.

In consequence however of the proceedings in Chancery, … nothing has been given to the poor since 1818; and the trustees, for the purpose of accumulating a fund to meet the expenses of the suit, have in the year 1823, forborne to contribute any sum towards the repairs of the church.'

The impact on the main parish poor funds was clear:

'… the consequence of the cessation of the distribution to the poor has been that many of those who had previously been enabled to maintain themselves without relief from the parish have become chargeable. An increase has also necessarily taken place in the church rates.'

The controversial legal case (see Chapter 18) argued that some trustees, including the 4th Earl of Portsmouth, were not acting properly in using the charity's funds, listing multiple examples:

'In 1818, an information was filed in the court of Chancery, by the attorney-general, at the relation of Christopher Northcote, esq: one of the above mentioned trustees, against the Honourable Newton Fellowes, Edward Reed, John Vickery and Thomas Cawsey, the survivors of the acting trustees, under the trust deed of 1802.

…it is charged, that the parish of Chawleigh had been since 1787, and then were, assessed to church rates, which had been applied to keep the parish church in repair; but no part of the rents and profits of the trust lands had been paid toward such repairs, and therefore that the whole of them ought to have been applied to the relief of the poor of the said parish; that the said lands, if properly let, would produce an annual rent of £115, and upwards; that the rents had not been applied for the benefit of the poor of the said parish; but the lands had been improperly let, so as only to produce the annual rent of £87 10s.; that the defendants had applied the rents to the payment of some debts, alleged to be due to them, or some other persons, for purposes foreign to the object of the charity.'

The defendants offered financial evidence in their defence, but the legal argument against them persisted:

'…that the funds had been in various specified instances of the said accounts misapplied; that larger sums were charged as having been distributed to the poor than had in fact been so distributed; that the trustees had lands adjoining to the charity lands, and had thrown down the fences, and intermixed such lands with their own; that they had removed a stone, fixed to part of the buildings, belonging to the charity, and had converted some of the almshouses, belonging thereto, into a school-room and house for the schoolmaster, who was not an inhabitant of the said parish, and which school was not of any benefit to the parish, as the scholars educated there were not selected from the inhabitants thereof…'

The legal request was condemnatory in tone, calling for a proper financial assessment and for trustees to be replaced:

'…to ascertain the value of the lands in 1802, the boundaries of the charity estate, and the extent of the damage done by the destruction of the hedges, and the removal of the stone, before mentioned; that an account might be taken of the sums of money which the defendant sought to have received, on account of the rents and profits of the said premises, and of their application of the rents, and that they might be charged with the amount of the difference between the real annual value of the lands, and the rent at which the same had been let, and with the amount of the damage sustained by removing the boundaries; and that they might be removed from being trustees of the charity, and proper persons appointed in their stead.'

The defendants refuted the charges:

'… John Vickery, and Tos. Cawsey, in their answer, deny that the church rates had been applied to the repairs of the church, which they state to have been defrayed out of the rents and profits of the charity estates; they also deny that the said estates would produce greater rents than those for which they were then let, and that any misapplication of the rents and profits of the charity property had taken place.

…that every part thereof had been let to the highest bidder by public auction, except the tenement, No. 6, which had been let by private contract for the best rent that could be obtained; that since they had been trustees, the churchwardens had, from time to time, caused whatever repairs had been wanting in the church to be done, and had been reimbursed by the defendants out of the rents and profits of the trust estates, and that they had paid the several sums mentioned in their accounts to the churchwardens, in respect of repairs done to the church; that the sums expended by them in the repairs of the trust premises, had been beneficially laid out, and that of the sums paid by them for taxes, £68 pounds 1s. 2d. had been refunded to them in respect of the property tax; that they had never made overcharges in their accounts, nor had broken down any fences of the trust premises, with a view of intermixing the lands of the charity with their own lands, nor had removed any ancient mark or stone affixed to any part of the buildings belonging to the charity.'

The defendants claimed to have been acting in the best interests of the poor.

'…the defendants admit, that they had converted an old building, formerly an almshouse, part of the trust property, and a room near there too … into a schoolroom and dwelling for a schoolmaster and mistress, for the benefit of the children of the poor inhabitants of the said parish; that the said almshouse was not productive of any income to the charity, and that the other tenements had been occupied by a widow, under an agreement that she was to hold it for life rent free, and that the parishioners were so sensible of the necessity of establishing the said school, that in order to have the said tenement for the schoolmaster, they had agreed to provide a lodging for the said widow, and to pay for the same out of the parish rates; that such appropriation was made, with the consent of the churchwardens and parishioners, and had been of great benefit to the poor inhabitants of the said parish, and that had been constantly since the establishment of the school, 12 children of the said poor inhabitants receiving their education there gratuitously.

… We are informed, that the charge in the information of removing fences, relates to the building of a pig-stie, adjoining to the garden held by John Vickery, which the depositions on the part of the relators state to have been erected partly on the charity land, but that this is denied by affidavits on the part of the defendants.'

This part of the Commissioners' report concluded:

'At the time of our investigations (September, 1823), the master had not made his report. … it appears to us to be the interest of the parishioners of Chawleigh, and particularly of the poorer class, that the suit should be brought to a conclusion as speedily and with as little expense as possible.'

Although the Commissioners' report itself is lengthy and at times verbose, this last comment about the timing of the multi-faceted legal case with hindsight appears ironic: it took forty years for the case to be resolved.

The Case Concludes

The Western Times (13 February 1858) carried a report of the conclusion of the forty-year-old case, reminiscent of Charles Dickens' satire of the Jarndyce and Jarndyce case in his famous nineteenth-century novel *Bleak House*:

'The suit which was commenced 40 years since, on the information of a Mr. Northcote against the late Honourable Newton Fellowes, afterwards the Earl of Portsmouth, came on … a scheme for the regulation of the charity property, proposed by the Attorney General. ... The object of the scheme, was to provide for the reparation of the fabric of the church, then for the maintenance of a parish school, and lastly for five alms women. The scheme seemed to have been drawn up very much under the inspiration of the rector of Chawleigh, and it was to the clauses framed in such a spirit that the objections taken by the defendants were directed.'

The question of how trustees should be selected and constrained was settled (for now):

'By the 1st and 2nd clauses of the scheme it was proposed to appoint 12 trustees for the management of the charity, of whom the rector of Chawleigh was to be one, ex officio and the other eleven were selected from the "principal and most substantial inhabitants of the parish". The number of the trustees had been fixed at 12, and their names settled to the satisfaction of Lord Portsmouth, who was the largest landowner in the parish, and his lordship himself, and his tenants had consented to act, on the exclusion from the list of trustees of a Mr. Henry Lewis, a nominee of the rector's. By the scheme certain disqualifications for office were attached to the 11 lay trustees, from which it was proposed to free the rector. This the defendant objected to, and the Vice Chancellor decided that any trustee, clerical as well as lay, taking the benefit of the Insolvent Act should be disqualified from acting.'

The newspaper report considered the impact on the poor of the village:

'To the 38th clause, which, as originally brought in by the Attorney-General, contained a provision that the almswomen in the alms houses, were not to absent themselves for more than one day without leave, in writing, signed by the Rector of Chawleigh, or two trustees, it was objected, by the defendants, that such a restriction was harsh to poor people, who might be detained out, by illness, or by nursing their children, or grandchildren. The judge gave permission of absence for a week, without leave from anyone.'

The controversy between the rector and schoolmaster (see Chapter 18) over Church versus Chapel was reflected once more:

'By another section of the same clause, as introduced by the Attorney-General, it was provided that the almswomen were to attend the celebration of Divine Service, at the parish Church of Chawleigh, and at least every Sunday, and other holydays, unless they should be prevented by illness, &c. To this clerical section it was objected, by Mr. Hull Terrell, that some of the almswomen might be Dissenters, that there were more worshippers in the parish who were Dissenters, than who were Churchmen, and that none of the almswomen ought to be compelled to attend the ministry of a clergyman, whom the parishioners had so notoriously deserted. The Vice-Chancellor ordered this objectionable provision to be struck out.'

The Western Times attributed much of the blame for the long court case to the Reverend Clay, and no doubt these events caused considerable distress to some of the participants at the time:

'The entire scheme for management contains 39 clauses devised by the ingenuity of the Attorney-General, aided by the rector of Chawleigh, and it is rather an expensive and intricate substitute, for the common sense rules under which the charity property was managed by the principal inhabitants of the parish, before the charity was thrown into Chancery. It went there originally out of mere spite against the late honourable Newton Fellowes, in the late Mr. Northcott arising out of some matter of sporting trespass.

The suit had lasted so long that all the original parties have become freed from the jurisdiction of the Court of Chancery, and it has owed some part of its intolerable length to the circumstance that the pugnacious Mr. Northcott came to be represented by the rector of Chawleigh, the Rev. Pelham Fellowes Clay, who having been presented to the family livings of Chawleigh and Eggesford by the Portsmouth family, has shewn his clerical gratitude by blowing up the parish discord.'

Stern words indeed.

The Charity after the Court of Chancery

The years after the pronouncement by the Court of Chancery appeared at times nearly as volatile as the forty years of the legal case.

Correspondence from November 1858 shows land agent and surveyor Henry Crispin in place as 'Clerk and Receiver' of the charity, in Chulmleigh, and Mr William Croote (1776–1865) of nearby Lapford, land agent and principal agent for the Portsmouth estate, involved with receiving and passing on rents associated with the charity's properties, and making payments on its behalf. Croote, who owned Lapford Mill from the 1820s and acquired 183 acres of land and property in the parish, effectively ran the estate office from Lapford, even though the village was not largely owned by the Portsmouth estate, unlike Chawleigh.

Documents from 1859 to 1863 show how many properties belonged to the charity: Richard Passmore's house and the adjoining cottage of Edwin Hayman; Dart's Tenement (now known as Dart's Farm); Thomas Sage's house and garden; Mrs Newcombe's house and premises; the Bakehouse occupied by Mr Clarke; Alexander Tonkins and his 'gate' (possibly a tollhouse).

There was an application for an Order enabling trustees to 'carry into effect the provisions of the 20th Clause of the Scheme respecting the repairs of the Buildings belonging to the Charity, and the restorations of the Church and other works connected therewith.' This appears to be an effort to accelerate this process, rather than waiting until the next General Meeting in July to consider the matter, as previously agreed.

By July more correspondence from John Fearon, Solicitor to the Attorney General, referred the whole matter to the Charity Commissioners again.

Notice was served on 20 September 1862 to William Dart 'to quit and deliver up to the Trustees' his Garden Ground, on 25 March next. On 25 September a similar notice was served on Thomas Sage to quit his 'Dwelling House and Garden' by Lady Day 1863.

A letter from the Reverend Clay and Henry Reed of 5 February 1863 to the clerk (Henry Crispin) requested a meeting on 18 February to consider, amongst others, 'the Plan and Estimate for converting the Workshop of the Dwellinghouse formerly occupied by Thomas Edworthy into a Bakehouse'.

Although this meeting appears to have taken place, the Reverend Clay and Mr Reed were requesting another meeting only two weeks later (4 March) to 'rescind the Resolution relative to Thomas Sage's House and Garden, passed on Wednesday the 18th of February instant.' Their proposed revision was to make the tenancy period for both house and garden coincide by ending at Lady Day, but the 'increased Rent to commence at Michaelmas next'.

The draft minutes for the General Meeting of 18 July 1863 suggest that the rector, the Reverend Clay, suffering from serious illness, was replaced temporarily as chairman by Mr Henry Reed. The business of managing letting and repairs of the various properties continued regardless.

The meetings of 1864 continued in similar vein: the 2 May meeting considered how to set about 'compelling Mrs Mary Newcombe to make compensation for the waste and wilful damage committed by her on the Premises … now in her occupation', apparently related to 'certain erections … on Darts' Tenement, without … written permission'.

A letter from the Charity Commission of 8 August 1867 requests accounts from the charity, which have not been submitted 'for several past years', despite being required by law annually.

A letter from John Hannaford, local auctioneer, dated 9 January 1873, to Messrs Pearse and Crosse, solicitors in South Molton, shows that Mr Kemp and Mr Stone, trustees appointed by the court in 1858 'have become disqualified to act … in consequence of their neglecting to take any part in the proceedings of the Charity for the last two years'. Hannaford was by this stage acting for Mrs Crispin, executrix for the late clerk, Henry Crispin, recently deceased.

By 15 November 1880 accounts were produced for the costs of sale of the 'old Parsonage House' and for associated works (presumed to be on the new Rectory), for the Reverend John Vowler Tanner. A new rector was in place for a new era.

The Charity after Reverend Pelham Fellowes Clay

Charitable bequests for the benefit of the poor in Chawleigh were not restricted to earlier centuries. Victorian philanthropy was relatively commonplace amongst the middle and upper classes, an indication of social standing and ambition. Some believed it simply reflected the level of misery in contemporary society, others that it was an effective solution to the ills of the time, and was an obligation on the part of those who had worked hard and had money. Chawleigh continued to have many examples.

The 1878–79 edition of *White's History, Gazetteer & Directory of Devonshire* mentions 'the dividends of £300, left by the late Dr. May of Exeter, and invested in the 3 per cent Consols [government bonds issued by the Bank of England], are divided among the poor of the parish yearly on Dec. 4 at the discretion of the minister, churchwardens and overseers.'

Kelly's Directory for 1902 references a Dr May of Exeter who in 1876 left £100 of government stock to the Cheldon parish, thereafter providing £2.14.0d interest which was distributed yearly in the parish.

Trewman's Exeter Flying Post of 13 September 1820 records the death, aged 69, at 'Chawley Parsonage' of 'Elizabeth, wife of the Rev. James May … distinguished by an active discharge of the many and amiable duties of a wife and parent, and by the constant exercise of a truly benevolent and Christian spirit'.

Dr Herman Storm May had served in Britain's Malta garrison as Hospital Mate and then in the Peninsular War of 1812–14 (which had Britain, Spain and Portugal set against the forces under Napoleon). Dr May later lived in Exeter, and died aged about 86, his remains interred in Bath. Dr May erected a tablet in St James' Church in memory of his mother, wife of the Reverend James May, rector of Cheldon and minister of Chawleigh. Dr May's will mentions his own wife Louise, and stipulates that £300 be left to 'the Minister, Churchwardens and Overseers of the Poor', the dividends of which should benefit 'Agricultural Labourers having families of the said Parish'.

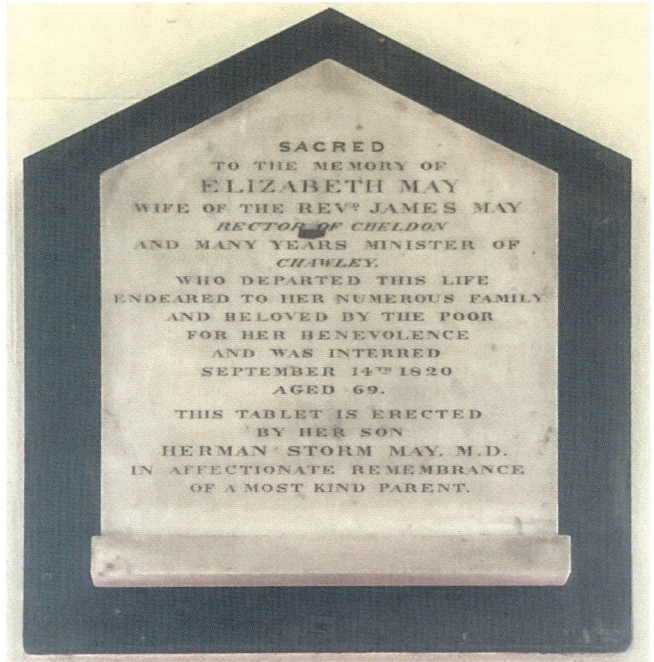

SACRED
TO THE MEMORY OF
ELIZABETH MAY
WIFE OF THE REV.d JAMES MAY
RECTOR OF CHELDON
AND MANY YEARS MINISTER OF
CHAWLEY.
WHO DEPARTED THIS LIFE
ENDEARED TO HER NUMEROUS FAMILY
AND BELOVED BY THE POOR
FOR HER BENEVOLENCE
AND WAS INTERRED
SEPTEMBER 14.th 1820
AGED 69.
THIS TABLET IS ERECTED
BY HER SON
HERMAN STORM MAY. M.D.
IN AFFECTIONATE REMEMBRANCE
OF A MOST KIND PARENT.

The tablet in St James' Church, Chawleigh, commemorating Elizabeth, mother of Dr Herman Storm May

(Photo by Jonathan Crofts)

A memorial to the family in stained glass fills the east window of St James' Church, representing the Crucifixion, Resurrection and Ascension, placed there in 1879 in memory of the Reverend James Bowen May, Edmund, and Sarah May.

The First World War and its aftermath saw the charity divesting other properties in Chawleigh. 'To be let by Tender' during the First World War were:

> 'From Xmas next a Steam Bakery, with House & Shop, situated in the village, together with Field ½ acres (more or less), now occupied by Mr. Bastow. Further particulars from C.J. Hannaford, Clerk to Chawleigh Church Lands Charity Trustees, Chulmleigh to whom Tenders must be sent on or before 31 August 1917. No tender necessarily accepted.'

A steam bakery was one that piped steam from a boiler into the oven, which kept the outer skin pliable as each loaf expanded before hardening into a good crust.

(Right)

Stained glass in the east window of St James' Church in memory of the Reverend James Bowen May, Edmund and Sarah May.

(Photo by Jonathan Crofts)

After the war, the Charity Commissioners in 1920 approved the auction sale of 'Freehold houses, Shop, Bakehouse & Gardens' in the parish. The Bakery contained '3 Bedrooms, Bakehouse with Steam Oven, Shop, Kitchen, Scullery, Wash House and small Larder' with a '3-stall Stable and Piggery' occupied by Mr J Ford. A separate 'Dwelling House and Shop' had '3 Bedrooms, Shop, Kitchen, Back Kitchen and Pantry, also a good Garden and Piggery' occupied by Mr Gove. The late 1920s then saw the charity funding most of the building of the new vestry for the church.

TO THE GLORY OF GOD
THIS ROOD SCREEN WAS RESTORED AND RENOVATED
BY THE FEOFFEES OF THE
CHAWLEIGH CHURCH LANDS CHARITY.
A.D. 1910.

E. WEBBER, J. SAUNDERS. CHURCHWARDENS. F. HUDSON. RECTOR.

The 1928 draft Charity Commission document 'Scheme for the Administration' for the charity references eleven cooptative trustees (with the Rector being the ex-officio trustee), ten of them farmers (one retired): Thomas Baker (The Barton), Isaac Saunders (Nutson), Isaac Philips (East Leigh), Frederick Butt (retired), Frank Ford (Nethercott), William Tucker (Leaches), John Webber (Burridge), Ernest Ellicott (Chenson), George Phillips (Chawleigh Week), William Reed (Fiddlecott); the eleventh was John Baple, the (by now retired) schoolmaster.

In time, the Parochial Church Council was to appoint 3 'representative' trustees, and the Parish Council similarly. Today, the charity's trustees still manage the old church house (and a few other properties) and so help preserve the heart of this ancient village. Otherwise, the oversight and management of very local issues largely rested with an elected parish council from 1894.

Brass plaque in St James' Church commemorating the 1910 restoration of the 15th-century rood screen by the Chawleigh Church Lands Charity

(Photo by Jonathan Crofts)

CHAPTER 20

CHAWLEIGH: THE VESTRY AND LOCAL GOVERNMENT

Vestry Meetings, effectively a form of local government in the nineteenth century, only lost their secular functions in 1894 when the Local Government Act created civil parishes to replace those powers of the Vestry, and parish councils were established. Vestry Meetings were chaired by the incumbent of the parish (the Rector) and were made up of (male) ratepayers of the parish. They evolved separately in each parish, and held considerable power for a rural community, including appointing Surveyors of the Highways, Overseers of the Poor and Justices of the Peace.

Decisions were not always generous: efforts were frequently made to remove 'poor persons' to other parishes where they were considered to belong, and to resist others returning to Chawleigh.

A study of the Vestry minutes in Chawleigh illustrates their diverse impacts:

24 October 1845: It was agreed that it was 'expedient' to create a new road 'from Stone Bridge houses to communicate with the new road in Stone Mill Wood'.

Ten names were also nominated 'to serve as Constables', an early form of policing to guard the peace in the village and its environs.

10 September 1846: A resolution was formed 'to repair the road on Stone Farm side, near Stone Bridge, and fence it, to preserve road and bridge from floods'.

11 February 1847: A meeting sought to 'consider the mode in which the present distress of the able bodied labourers with families shall be met, with reference to the letter received from the Board of Guardians of the Crediton Union.' Rates of 2d in the pound were to be collected by the overseers. Widespread famine in Europe after a series of failed harvests saw many rural families suffer in Devon in the Hungry Forties. Farmers unable to feed their families were often forced to put up their children as indentured labour. As apprentices, these young people were almost slave labour until they were twenty-one, with little food and no wages, but at least a roof over their heads. Ill-treated apprentices who ran away were hounded via the newspapers and received harsh penalties on recapture.

A later meeting decided that 'all persons having 3 children under 10' should receive '1s. per week, and so on for all children above 2. … All labourers to attend 24th at 5 o'clock to be examined and registered, that the money may be paid to them.'

8 April 1847: The Vestry also helped villagers find employment and funded training, carrying a unanimous motion 'to bind John Smale an apprentice to some trade (he being crippled) and that the Board of Guardians be respectfully requested to allow Seven Pounds for that purpose.' A later meeting resolved to bind him to an apprenticeship as a tailor, and a Board of Guardians to allow money not exceeding ten pounds to cover the cost.

1848: A practical appointment saw the popular schoolmaster Richard Gough appointed as 'Assistant Overseer of the Poor. Fee granted, 12 guineas, plus 6d per mile for journeys performed on parochial business.'

1849: In Chawleigh as elsewhere, parish expenditure was kept low, often by forcibly returning claimants to the care of their original community, or by encouraging their departure further afield. In the case of 'Jane and Elizabeth Tolly about to emigrate to Australia', the charity helped fund their passage: 'Board of Guardians requested to pay them a sum not exceeding one pound each to assist them.'

4 October 1849: The resolution was taken to 'stop up an old road leading from the houses near Stone Bridge to Stone Mill Road. Also to make a drain near the road in town hill and the drain over the stream crossing the road near the pond in Leaches Meadow.'

20 January 1851: Notice was to be given 'to all persons who occupy Inclosures subject to their repair in this parish "that they be immediately put in repair"'. Also parish surveyors were instructed to put roads under their direction in good repair.

1851: It was resolved 'that the churchwardens do get the North part of the roof of the Church covered with slate'.

Crimes were also recorded:

27 October 1851: The poisoning of Tailor's cow. Firing of BareHill Cottage [now Barehill Moor]. Killing and carrying of a part of Edward Reed's sheep. The Hon. N. Fellowes, Earl of Portsmouth, 'generously offered a reward of £25 upon the conviction of any offender in each of the above cases.'

10 January 1853: 'A sheep having been stolen from Richard Reed of Poundsfords in the night of 24th December or morning 25th between 5pm and 8am by persons whose shoes were bound with straw binds to avoid detection, and also another sheep stolen since from a field in the occupation of John Vickery. The Hon. N. Fellowes offers reward £50, (other farmers to add subscriptions).'

Many of the minutes continued to reflect a necessary preoccupation with the roads and infrastructure of the parish, amongst others:

11 November 1858: The proposition was made 'to alter a portion of the Parish road leading from the village of Chawleigh to the Eggesford station of the North Devon Railway'.

21 June 1859: A meeting was called 'to consider what is necessary to be done in consequence of Chawleigh Week clapper [bridge] having been driven away by the late flood. Proposed Surveyors of Highways of Chawleigh be instructed to meet the Surveyors of Chulmleigh and agreed that a Horse Girder Bridge be erected with stone piers and a proper approach to be made on the Chawleigh side, provided the parishioners of Chulmleigh agree to pay half the cost.'

1860: Public Vestry met 'to consider the case of Philip Hooper who lost his leg. Agreed that the Overseers do inquire of some Basket and Seine maker the expense of learning the business.' A seine was a woven net to catch fish, one type of basket amongst many used for agriculture and fisheries.

A map showing the approximate route of the original road (in brown) to the Stone Bridge/ Stone Mill area: it ran to the west of the modern road which now runs down to the bridge by Stone Mill, across part of today's Chawleigh Barton Woods via an area or farm then known as Myland

(By kind permission of Michael Aldridge)

1860–62: Essential road repairs saw sections let out for tender, with the stipulation that repairs be done 'with hard, well broken stone like those laid on Turnpike Roads'.

1861: The Vestry helped manage responsibilities between parish and estate landowner, as in the case of 'the hill near Myland being bad and the bridge at the bottom being narrow and much out of repair, it is expedient that the present road be diverted and a new one formed with a new bridge over the river Dart. Agent of Earl of Portsmouth stated that his lordship is willing to pay for all work except the new bridge.'

The erection of a substantial bridge to meet the proposed new route near Myland was agreed, and the Vestry offered £80 to the Earl of Portsmouth towards the work. The Earl of Portsmouth declined. A tender from Thomas and Henry Lake to the tune of £130 pounds was accepted.

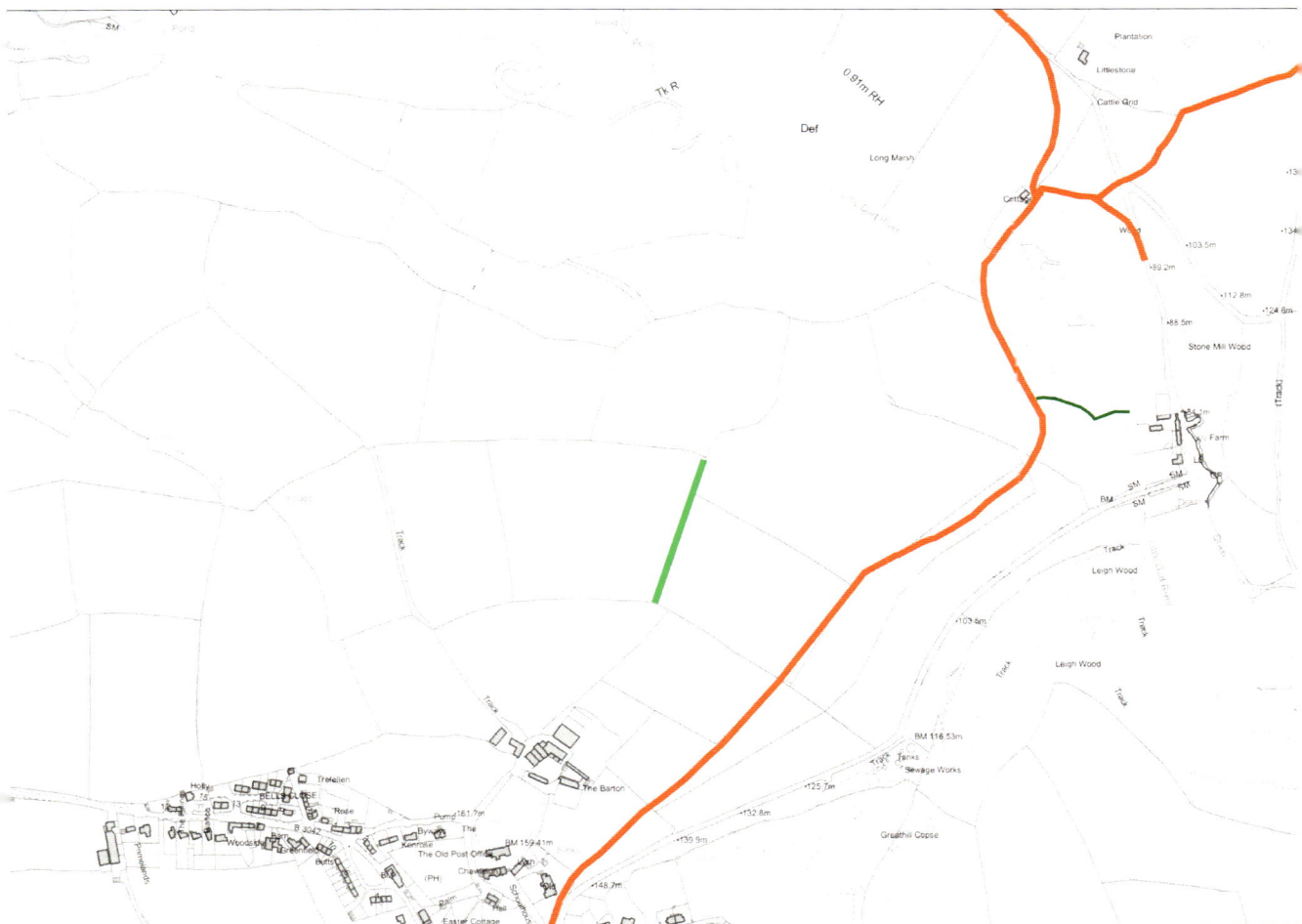

1862: It was announced that a 'new road from Leaches to Stone Mill has been made and is now a Parish Highway'.

1872: Vestry minutes recorded 'Warming Apparatus in Parish Church – money collected for the purpose'. Donations were probably given freely by parishioners otherwise accustomed to the cold as they listened to the Reverend's wise words at St James'.

July 1874: Sorrow was expressed at the death of Mr Gough, 'their late Assistant Overseer'.

The Vestry book started at Easter 1902 reveals several milestones in the twentieth-century life of the church: in 1903 the death of the Reverend John Vowler Tanner (Rector 1879–1903) was recorded; the 1917 appointment of Charles Webber as sexton (replacing John Long); a public meeting in the schoolroom in 1922 to form the Parochial Church Council (Chawleigh with Cheldon), with some members elected in their absence; in 1925 Miss Leakey of The Cottage requesting the Parish Bier, the frame used to carry the village dead to their place of burial, be removed from her property (it was then in the care of Edward Elworthy until a shed was later provided); in 1926 plans for the new vestry in the church were discussed (with objections noted as the proposed site on the north side interfered with several graves); in 1927 a site at the east end was agreed; in 1931 came the proposal to erect a churchyard shed; 1932 saw a no doubt disapproving discussion regarding children climbing up and damaging the organ.

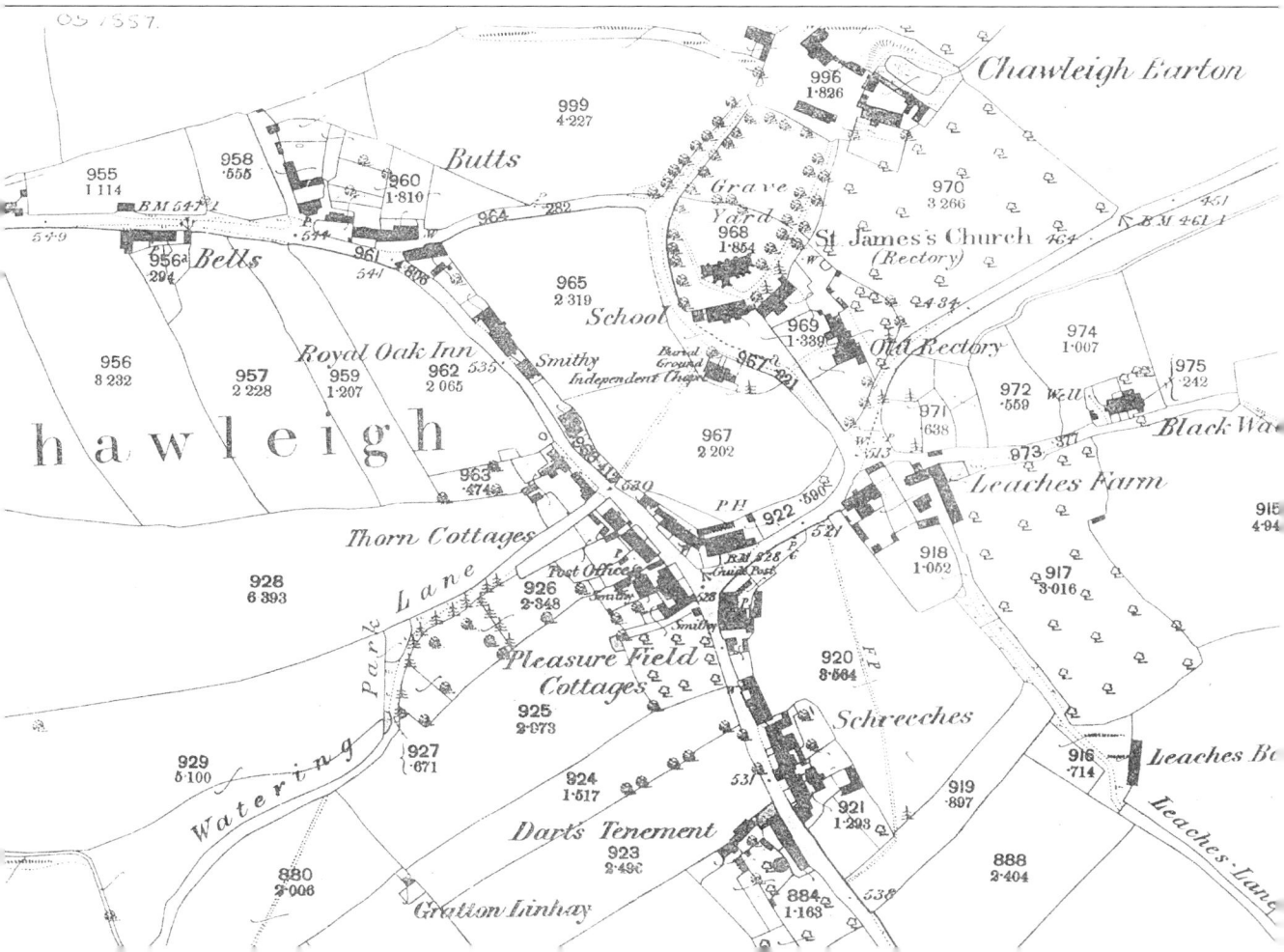

A communal village water pump in Chawleigh, still standing in 2024. Village wells and pumps were common until mains water was installed in most properties.

(Photo by Jonathan Crofts)

(Left)

Ordnance Survey map of Chawleigh, 1887, showing the positions of businesses and farms in the central part of the parish

(Courtesy of St James' Church History)

The advent of electricity in the village in the 1930s enabled Mr Clover of The Old Hall to offer to supply electricity to the church, although this was postponed for twelve months. Heating by means of a low pressure system was discussed; Reverend Bastow's arrival in 1935 meant discussions of redecoration and shifting the font to the South Door; enhancing the organ in 1937.

The arrival of the Second World War occasioned urgent discussion of blackouts for the church, the usual evening service being held at 3pm to avoid the need in the short term; blackout curtains were finally ordered in 1940. In 1942 the wartime requirement for railings and gates to be recycled into munitions and aircraft was met by an agreement to limit this to the removal of churchyard railings. (Sadly, little of the metal gathered nationally was ever turned into steel and was likely dumped or buried.)

For the second time in twenty-one years, a world war threatened the peace and security of the Chawleigh community, and the possibility of air raids threatened to put the ancient buildings at the heart of the village at risk.

CHAPTER 21

CHAWLEIGH: THE HEART OF THE OLD VILLAGE

A little apart from the inns and pubs along the main through road (see Chapter 14), the cluster of buildings around St James' Church forms the ancient centre of the village of Chawleigh. Representing the main activities within this community since earliest times, farming and worship, these older properties in the village sit above land subsequently used for forestry, Chawleigh Barton Wood, and beyond it the beautiful valley of the Little Dart, a tributary of the River Taw which rises near Rackenford to the north-east, passing near Witheridge and alongside the Worlingtons before joining the Taw.

Chawleigh Barton

Barton, a name commonly found in the West Country, means a (typically large) farm, and is derived from the Old English word *bere* meaning barley and *tun* meaning an enclosure. It was often the largest farmstead in the village where it was located. A sign perhaps of earlier status, The Barton in Chawleigh has a private gate into St James' churchyard.

Chawleigh Barton was listed by English Heritage (now Historic England) in 1986 as Grade II. It dates at least to the seventeenth century, possibly with an earlier core, and was considerably modernised in 1877, including a new frontage and the roof being raised, as shown by the stonework of the external walls. Built part in cob and rubble, with some brick details and a slate roof, the original three-room-and-through-passage plan is still evident with earlier features possibly surviving behind the Victorian plaster. The farmhouse was built facing south to catch light and heat, and has a former inner room (where people slept) at the east end. In the 1877 refurbishment, the passage was enlarged to allow the insertion of a stair.

Nineteenth-century additions along the entire rear of the building include a kitchen at the lower west end, originally the parlour, adjacent to the front door and porch, and some window openings were blocked up on this side and on one end wall, presumably as part of the renovation. Above an outer arch to the property is a Portland stone plaque bearing the Portsmouth crest and dated 1877, in the days of the 5th Earl.

The farmhouse still has a range of outbuildings to its rear, although most of its barns have been converted into separate residences. Leaches House (formerly Leaches Farm) has a similar Portsmouth crest over the porch, but The Barton also has the letters 'J S' (for John Saunders) elsewhere on the exterior.

The Post Office Directory of 1866 shows John Saunders as farmer at The Barton, William Saunders as farmer and maltster at Nutsons, and William Saunders junior as farmer at Chenson. Earlier, *White's Devonshire Directory* in 1850 shows a different J Saunders working as a shoemaker. A number of Saunders are listed in a variety of occupations, with related family graves in the churchyard.

As the Portsmouths' Devon estate began to be broken up by the 6th Earl (see Chapter 22), The Barton was one of the first properties in Chawleigh to be put up for sale: the 1908 particulars list it alongside

The front porch of Chawleigh Barton carries a 'P' and the crest of the Earl of Portsmouth carved in Portland stone

(Photo by Jonathan Crofts)

Chawleigh Barton Wood, The Old Rectory (now The Old Hall), Stone Mill, Chawleigh Week, Moor Town and Woodhouse.

Thomas Baker, the tenant farmer since 1884, is believed to have bought Chawleigh Barton Farm (and separately Chawleigh Barton Wood in 1919). His daughter Barbara married John Woollacott, who then continued to hold the farm.

Circa 1980s, The Barton, still a bigger farm, was sold off in lots, including what are now the four adjoining barn conversions. The road to the whole site still enters the outer yard of the old farm and the vestiges of the gate hinges can be seen today.

The house has a thatched cob wall which features a bee bole (Grade II and separately listed to the house). These are defined by the Bee Boles Register as 'recesses, often in a south-facing garden wall.

Each recess was large enough to hold a skep – the traditional coiled-straw hive used by beekeepers across Britain before the introduction of the modern wooden hive in the late 19th century', as described by the *evacranetrust.org*, who hold the national register. Chawleigh has at least two sets of bee boles, at The Barton and at Ford Farm (those at Ford Farm appear to date from the fifteenth or sixteenth century; those at The Barton from the seventeenth).

An oral history account included in the *Notes on the Parish of Chawleigh, Devon, and District* (collected 1958–74 by Algernon Pepperell and Miss F W Hillman, the latter a former schoolteacher in the parish) adds:

> 'Mr. William Parish (retired farm worker) says that in one of Chawleigh Barton fields there is reputed to be a "burial mound" – in "Turnip Moor" Field. Old Mr. Baker, who went to Barton in 1884, and who died in 1950, aged 94 (grandfather of Mrs. Woollacott) told him about it.'

Chawleigh Barton Wood

Stretching down from Chawleigh Barton, St James' Church and The Old Hall, below some orchards and fields, is an area of woodland, managed today as a plantation: Chawleigh Barton Wood. The earlier road from the village near Leaches House (then the Farm) down to Stone Mill at the bottom of the Little Dart valley used to run to the north of the current road, and was relocated in the 1860s.

Chawleigh Barton Wood and The Barton were sold in 1908 from what was described by the Portsmouths' agents as the 'Barton Estate'. Louis Mortimer Lee, a farmer from Crediton, is believed to have bought the wood, but in 1919 sold it on to Thomas Baker, who had once rented both the farm and its woodland.

The woods contain the site of a former rifle range, with target butts, constructed around 1921 after the First World War, for the reconstituted Territorial Force, renamed the Territorial Army. One archaeological officer has found evidence suggesting the range existed as far back as 1906.

Gordon Webber, whose father was a farmworker in Chawleigh, wrote in the Chawleigh *Dart*, the village magazine:

'By the end of the first World War 1914–1918 there was widespread unrest and anger at the huge loss of life and a war that didn't achieve much, most of the anger was directed at the Senior Army Officers but they wouldn't accept that they were to blame. After some time they hit on the idea of blaming the Private soldiers who weren't very accurate shots with their rifles. In the early 1920s the War Office decided that the TA needed more Rifle Ranges, one of these was built at Chawleigh Barton Wood, the building work was carried out by F. Hill & Sons of Chawleigh. It consisted of a large pit dug into the hillside to form the butts, the pit was over 50ft long by 6ft wide by 8ft deep, incorporated at the east end was a small store shed. The pit was walled around inside with brick at the short sides and stone at the front and back, the stonework is of a very high quality. a speciality of the Hill family.

The whole structure was roofed over with galvanised iron, now removed, 4 sets of target trains were fixed at the back, they were made by Anders McLean & Co. This meant that 4 men could shoot at the same time; the shooting position was built on land then owned by Moortown Farm, now by the Simpsons, and covered by trees. The management of the range was in the hands of the Devon TA, when the Chawleigh Home Guard was formed [in the 1940s] they used it a lot. In Barton Wood a triangular piece of woodland was marked out by three boundary stones at the angles, these are still in situ.'

The woods border on the Little Dart River, and public and permissive paths give local residents access today, along with the opportunity to appreciate the natural beauty of the trees, wildflowers, a large water lily pond, and the river itself. For sale in 2024, the sales particulars add: 'Other notable features include post WWI shooting butts and several old charcoal pads dating back to when charcoal was made. Part of Chawleigh Barton Wood is designated as Ancient woodland meaning the land has been under continuous tree cover since at least 1600 AD.'

(Left)

The front (south side) of Chawleigh Barton

(Photo by Jonathan Crofts)

(Right)

A boundary stone, above, for the Territorial Army rifle range in Chawleigh Barton Woods. Below is the mechanism for the target butts.

(Photos by kind permission of Michael Aldridge)

The Old Hall

On 25 September 1930, The Old Hall was advertised for sale, described as 'Tudor period, stone built. Panelled Entrance Hall, Tudor Hall (open to roof), carved oak screen and minstrel gallery. About 5 ½ acres. At upset price of £3,000. 3 other sitting rooms, 6 bedrooms, 2 bathrooms.' At the time it included the land opposite the Old Hall, behind today's Jubilee Hall, as well as the small area at the top of Blackwalls Lane.

A Chawleigh Parish Terrier from 1613 outlined some of the origins of the larger property now known as The Old Hall:

> 'Ther is belonging on to the psonage of Chawleighe two little Orchards, two gardens, ther is three meadowes nere the house, one lying on the South syde of the villadge, called the Morter pake [park], bounded on the West syde by a lane or thoroughfayre that leadeth unto Chumleghe Towne, on the North Syde bounded by the streat that leadeth unto the churche, the other two meadowes are joyned unto the grene on the on syde, on the other syde bounded by a waye that leadeth unto Chumleghe Town, Ther are Tenements within the pishe of Chawleghe Town some 38 or ther about, ther is certayne ground belonging unto the psonage of Chawleghe, called the Beare about some 3 score acres, lying towards the West from the towne remote from the towne but a lytle, … an other peece of ground, called Newmas pke, about the vallew of twelve acres; part whereof is marishe meadow grounde sytuate nere Chawleghe Beacon, … the grene likewise belongeth unto the psonage.

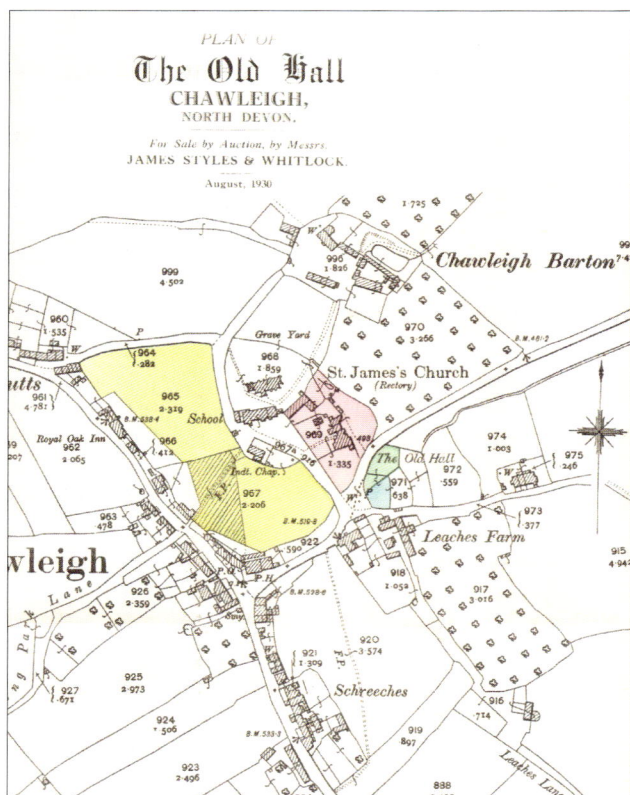

> By mee William Cogan, Clearke'

The Old Hall was formerly known as the Old Rectory and prior to that, the Rectory and the Parsonage. Long associated with St James' Church, the building was typically the home of the local rector and his family, who frequently shared this 'living' with Eggesford (see Chapters 4 and 15).

The later Chawleigh Parish Terrier of 1680 records it as having a buntinghouse, a sixteenth- and seventeenth-century term for a room or outbuilding where corn was sifted. Apart from the land now used as the village playing fields behind the Jubilee Hall, the terrier also lists separate lands on the outskirts of the main village, suggesting that the overall estate was considerable at the time:

At the Upset Price of £3,000.

North Devon
Between EXETER and BARNSTAPLE.

THE GENUINE
Tudor Period Stone-built Residence
known as

The Old Hall
CHAWLEIGH

Two miles from EGGESFORD STATION, over 500 feet above sea evel, South and West aspects, commanding magnificent views. The Residence has been beautifully restored, and retains its original character stics.

Accommodation

Panelled Entrance Hall, Noble Tudor Hall with original Oak Raftered Roof, Minstrels' Gallery, Three other Sitting Rooms, Six Bed Rooms, Two Bath Rooms.

Electric Light.   Central Heating.   Ample Water Supply.
Septic Tank Drainage.   Independent Hot Water System.   Telephone.

Stabling.   Garage.   Useful Outbuildings.

Well-timbered Grounds

Inexpensive to maintain, Garden and Meadows, in all nearly

$5\frac{1}{2}$ ACRES

HUNTING.   SHOOTING.   GOLF.

Lease of about $2\frac{1}{2}$ miles of Private Salmon and Trout Fishing (rented by Vendor), can be taken over if desired.

For Sale by Auction. by Messrs.

JAMES STYLES & WHITLOCK

At the Rougemont Hotel, Exeter
On MONDAY, 11th AUGUST, 1930
At 2.30 o'clock (unless Sold Privately).

Illustrated Particulars and Conditions of Sale from the Solicitors, Messrs. MAPLES, TEESDALE & Co., 6, Frederick's Place, Old Jewry, E.C.2, or from the Auctioneers, Messrs. JAMES STYLES & WHITLOCK,
44, ST. JAMES' PLACE, LONDON, S.W.1
Also at Rugby, Oxford, Birmingham and Chipping Norton.

Sales particulars
for The Old Hall,
Chawleigh, 1930

(By kind permission
of Tim and Helen
Robinson)

'A true and perfect terrier of the house and land belonging to the Parsonage of Chawley.

There is belonging to the Parsonage of Chawley a very good strong habitable house being built with mudd, butt mostly with stone containeing two parlors very well plancht [planked] under foot with lasted and plastered overhead, one Hall, one Kitchene, Two butteries, Two chambers very well plancht lasted and playstered overhead, one other Chamber over the greater butterie well plancht, another over the Kitchene, another over the Entry called the Buntinghouse.

One Barne, one shipping [shippon, a barn or shed for cattle], one stable and one lynney [linhay, a lean-to shed open on one or more sides], two gardens, two little orchards containeing about halfe an acre.

There are three meadowes, one being and lying on the southside of the towne, called the Mottisparke, bounded on the westside by a lane or thorowfaire that leadeth unto Chimley towne, on the northside bounded by the street that leadeth to the church. The other two meadowes are adjoyning to the Greene on the one side, on the other side by a way that leadeth unto Chimley towne. All three meadowes containeing by estimaton seaven acres.

There is also certaine other ground belonging unto the parsonage of Chawley commonly called the Beeres, containing by estimaton about three score acres, lying towards the west, from the town butt a little remote…, which said grounds are lately divided into [blank] severall fields by the husbandry of Mr. Brace, the present possessor thereof.

There is one peece of ground more, called Newname park, about the vallue of twelve acres, situate neare Chawley Beacon...

There is a Gatehouse, containing fower rooms, two upper and two lower. And the Greene before the Gatehouse, being putt into Mr Cogan's Terrier for part of the Gleabe, Anno Dni. 1613; which undoubtedly was soe, by the negligance of Mr. Brace's predecessor is for the present lost.

The Lord of the Mannor haveing seised on itt as waste ground for a faire to be held there twice in the yeare.

Walter Brace, Rector.
Robert Ford, warden.
Thomas Radford.'

The Old Rectory (as it was then known) was put up for auction in 1908 in an early sale from the Earl of Portsmouth estate, along with Chawleigh Barton and its woods. £800 was paid for the Old Rectory, 'Lot 34', without Glebe. Notes indicate it was originally sold to Lord Portsmouth circa 1878, having previously belonged to

(Right)

Ordnance Survey Devonshire Sheet XLIII. NW Surveyed: 1886 to 1887, Published: 1888 Note the new Rectory to the west – now the site of Ashley Court, home of Amber Foundation, a registered charity. At this time The Old Hall was known as the Old Rectory.

(Reproduced with the permission of the National Library of Scotland)

Chawleigh Parish Lands Charity (see Chapter 19). Much of the land originally associated with The Old Hall, formerly known as glebe land, was later owned and managed by the charity – and some still is.

Ashley Court (home today of the Amber Foundation), in Long Close, was built to replace the Old Rectory circa 1880. Today there is a newer (post-World War Two) rectory in Sunny Court, round the corner from the village shop and post office.

With a stream of owners since ceasing to be the rectory, North Devon Records Office holds undated plans for 'Alterations to the Old Hall, Chawleigh for a Rev E C de Courcy Ireland'. This likely refers to the Rev Edmond Stanley de Courcy-Ireland (1866–1955), who in 1894 married Harriet Naylor Pepper (1869–1962), with whom he had three sons. It is possible that these plans were never implemented, or that the de Courcy-Irelands never moved to the Old Hall, their intentions thwarted perhaps by the First World War or other life events.

The 1930 *Kelly's Directory* lists Robert Alexander Currie living at The Old Hall. *Kelly's* in 1935 shows Geoffrey Derrick Austin Clover (1909–1936) in residence. A Chawleigh funeral report from 4 August 1939 in the *Exeter and Plymouth Gazette* mentions a Capt. C L and Mrs Young as residents.

Leaches House (formerly Leaches Farm)

Originally one of the farmhouses within the village, Leaches House faces up towards the old schoolhouse and St James', occupying a prominent position in Chawleigh's conservation area. Its listing with English Heritage/ Historic England dates the building back to the 1600s, although the core may be earlier. Certainly the Subsidy Roll (taxation record) of 1624 shows a reference to a John Leach. The other twelve names listed are Anthony Pownsford, Robert Roberts, John Smale, Anthony Wilsdon, Anthony Snell, Thomas Webber, Katherine Mackerell (widow), Robert Hill, William Webber, Philip Searle, William Nott, and Ellinor Rashleighe.

John Leach's marriage in Chawleigh to Jane is recorded on 23 November 1624 and his burial in the churchyard on 3 November 1634. Leach was an established Devon name: the distinguished Sir Simon Leach, born in nearby Crediton in 1567 (died 1638), was Sheriff of Devon in 1624; on the death of his wife Katherine, he erected a family monument from Beer stone and local marble in St Bartholomew's Church, Cadeleigh, noted as the largest of its type in any Devon parish church. This Crediton branch was of humble origin, believed to be descended from blacksmiths, but the story is that a John Leach of Crediton bought 'iron' bars from a wreck of the Spanish Armada which turned out to be solid gold

As a taxpayer and therefore landowner, it is likely that the John Leach of Chawleigh would have been connected with the wealthy Leaches of Crediton and Cadeleigh. Speculation suggests Spanish gold may have built or purchased Leaches Farm, now Leaches House, but the truth may be lost for ever.

The History of Parliament (*historyofparliamentonline.org*) describes another Sir Simon Leach (circa 1652–1708) of Cad[e]leigh, Devon, MP for Okehampton:

'…only son of Simon Leach of Cadleigh by Bridget, daughter of Sir Bevil Granville of Stowe, Cornwall married 18 June 1673, Mary, daughter of Thomas Clifford, 1st Baron Clifford of Chudleigh.

Leach's great-grandfather and namesake, the son of a Crediton blacksmith, acquired Cadleigh about 1600 and was the first of the family to rise to prominence in Devon. Leach's father was too young to take part in the Civil War, but he married into a leading royalist family, and was arrested in January 1660 for his involvement in royalist disturbances at Exeter. He died a few months later, and Leach was one of several children given the order of the Bath at the coronation of Charles II. …

Leach was under suspicion after the Revolution, and when his brother-in-law, the 2nd Lord Clifford, was arrested in Exeter in 1692 it was announced that Leach himself was 'taken in the west'. He was not active again politically until after the death of William III. He was buried at Cadleigh on 30 June 1708, but he had sold the estate before his death, and no other member of the family sat in Parliament.'

The later Land Tax Assessment for Chawleigh of 30 June 1800 references a 'Thomas Prescott for Leaches', with the 'Sums Assessed & not Exonerated' listed as £3. 4. 7 ½d.

At some stage, the farm would have been acquired by the Portsmouth estate, and by the time of the nationwide Tithe Apportionments of 1848, Thomas Kemp is listed for Leaches and Berries, with the Honourable Newton Fellowes (4th Earl of Portsmouth) noted as the landowner. Berries is believed to have originally been the farm next door, subsumed into its neighbour, and the site of the later Leaches barns which are now private residences. A crumbling cob cottage referred to as Berries survived among the barns until the later part of the twentieth century.

After its sale into private hands, on 4 August 1939 the *Exeter and Plymouth Gazette* recorded the death of the 'well known and respected' Charles Eastman on 25 July, shortly before the start of the Second World War. He had moved to Leaches after farming at Stone Mill a few years before, and was 'at one time a member of the Methodist Church'. *The Western Times* of 30 August 1940 advertised the sale of his livestock, equipment and household furniture.

The farm was taken over by Archibald Cecil Sandy (1897–1988) for the rest of the war. Archibald fought with the Devonshire Regiment and the Royal Field Artillery in the First World War, and he and his wife Elsie (1906–1994, born Elsie May Taylor) married in 1928. They had no children but took in young evacuees from other parts of the UK during the Second World War. In 1965, they retired and put Leaches Farm up for sale, auctioned by Vick and Price of Barnstaple. Like many twentieth- and twenty-first-century owners of Leaches House, the Sandys stayed on in the village after selling the house.

According to an older Chawleigh resident, a retired farmer who used to walk from Sowdens Leigh and Mildons Leigh as a child to the village school by St James' Church, Elsie Sandy would give him sweets after school before he set off back across the fields to home. The Sandys also hosted a party every year for the children of the village.

(Coloured Pink on the Plan).

LEACHES FARM,

In the centre of the Village of Chawleigh.

A very superior HOLDING, now in the occupation of Mr. W. Tucker, comprising an area of 110a. 2r. 25p. of rich Arable, Pasture and Orchard Land. The Farm-house contains 5 Bedrooms, Box-room, Back and Front Staircases, Entrance Hall, 2 Sitting Rooms, Kitchen, Salting-house, Cellar, Dairy and Offices. The Farm Buildings are ample and commodious.

This Lot affords an excellent opportunity of acquiring a Small Estate, which is in good cultivation, remarkably well situated, being two miles from Eggesford Station, Eggesford Market and Chulmleigh.

SCHEDULE.

No. on Plan.	NAME OF FIELD.	CULTIVATION.	A.	R.	P.
972	Pond Meadow	Pasture		2	10
977	Great Hill	Pasture	4	2	7
979	Kennel	Underwood	1	3	34
978	Kennel	Pasture	4	1	31
915	Worthy	Pasture	4	3	31
917	Orchard	Orchard (not to be refilled)	3	0	3
918	Farm House, Buildings, &c.		1	0	9
916	Buildings, Barn, &c.	Buildings, Road. &c.		2	34
890	Leaches Meadow	Arable	5	2	36
914	North Lee	Arable	6	2	24
913	Waste	Waste		1	33
912	South Lee	Waste		2	19
892	South Lee	Arable	5	1	26
895	Furzey Close	Waste	1	0	23
896	Furzey Close	Arable	3	1	24
893	South Lee Orchard	Orchard	1	1	30
894	North Gratton	Arable	5	3	24
851	Lamblairs	Arable	8	3	36
898	Brake	Waste		3	11
897	Brake	Arable	3	1	11
856	South Gratton	Arable	7	0	8
852	Moor	Moor	9	2	13
853	Moor	Moor	10	2	22
833	Buckendown	Arable	6	0	3
834	Box Corner Field	Arable	7	1	7
828	By Lane	Arable	4	3	36
			110	2	25

Annual Apportioned Rent £90 2s. 0d. Commuted Tithe, £12 18s. 6d.; value for 1906, £8 17s. 4d., paid by Landlord. Land Tax and Insurance paid by Tenant The Shooting over fields number 834 and 828, is let to Mr W. Littleworth, to the 1st February next, at an annual apportioned rent of 10s. 0d., and that over the remainder of the Lot to Mr. G. A. W. Thorold at an annual apportioned rent of £3 15s. 0d., subject to six months notice to be given on any 1st August. Mr. Tucker is a Lady-day tenant subject to two years' notice.

The 1911 sales particulars, when the 6th Earl of Portsmouth put up large parts of his Devonshire estates for sale: Leaches Farm is described as 'a Small Estate'.

Several other properties were listed for sale at the same time.

The farm was later sold to the Martin family, and a second auction was to offer 'Live and Dead Farming Stock' together with 'the Large and Comprehensive Range of MODERN AGRICULTURAL IMPLEMENTS AND MACHINERY', as well as some surplus furniture and effects.

In 1986 English Heritage listed the cob- and rubble-built thatched farmhouse as Grade II, dating it back to the seventeenth century, possibly with an earlier core. The long main block of the building faces north-west on a four-room plan, with the possible former inner room (bedchamber) at the north-eastern end, although later plaster covers any early features. The old kitchen and service end was likely sited in what is now the front hall, its fireplace covered in the seventeenth century with a wooden chimneypiece, one wall taken up with a traditional oak plank-and-muntin screen, probably made in the early seventeenth century, although not necessarily originally in this position – it is not clear where the through passage originally lay. In the hall, wonderful crossbeams, some chamfered, one resting on a post with scroll-topped corners, support the ceilings. At one end, an early full-height cupboard has panelled doors on H-hinges.

At the south-western end of the house, a new kitchen with large fireplace and new or relined brick oven was probably added in the late seventeenth- to early eighteenth century and is open to the roof, showing off its A-frame trusses. A service wing, with a ground-floor cellar and dairy, was added at right angles to the rear of the original kitchen, also probably in the seventeenth century, with a salting house (to preserve meat) and still room as later additions. A long passage, its paved slab floor now covered, runs along the old rear of the house, put in under a sloping slate roof during the Portsmouth renovation to join this block with the room at the end, now a bathroom, but once an adjoining salting room used for storing meat.

The end chamber over the inner room upstairs includes some oak small-field panelling probably from the 1600s, while plaster applied in Victorian times likely conceals more. The initials T L are twice scored into the wood, most probably by Thomas Leach.

An aerial view of Leaches Farm in 1967: the four barns now known as Chestnut Court are just beyond the house, surrounding the old Berries cottage. Two of the later 20th-century houses sit on Blackwalls Lane in the background, with Blackwalls Cottages in the distance. The neighbouring plots were still undeveloped.

(Photographer unknown)

(Right)

An aerial view from the 1970s: the barns to the east still surround Berries, demolished when the barns were developed into separate residences in the 1990s.

(Photographer unknown)

In the nineteenth century the farmhouse was further gentrified with a new roof raised over the existing thatch, its centuries-old sheaves still visible in the attic space, along with trusses and beams of the original roof. Witches' marks on the chimney, attested to by the modern thatchers, were scored in to the beams and plaster to dissuade the much-feared creatures from entering. The old-fashioned mullion windows were replaced and enlarged by the Victorian Portsmouth estate to let in more daylight, and a new porch was built on to the front of the old kitchen, now the entrance hall, surmounted by a Bathstone plaque with the crest of the Earl of Portsmouth, as at Chawleigh Barton.

Today Leaches House offers its occupiers many reminders of a past way of life. In the seventeenth-century service wing and alongside the old still room (now the dining room), the old dairy is unheated, with slate shelves for keeping food and drink cool and storing jams, jellies and preserves made with produce from the orchard and kitchen garden. Pigeon holes in the outer wall on the other side of the dining room hark back to the days when the farm produced a huge variety of provisions for the family and for sale.

The thatched piggery, separately listed, retains its cob and stone walls and roof timbers, no doubt very similar to its original incarnation. Beyond it once stood another small outhouse made of cob, the building now entirely gone. The Victorian privy at the opening to the orchard still houses a double lavatory seat – his and hers perhaps, or more likely for parent and child as one hole is considerably smaller. The remaining barn of the property, Pigs Platt, housed animal pens with low dividing walls, since removed, but retains the low floor of the hayloft at one end over a workshop. Its walls show the height of the barn raised by a storey, and an original entrance onto the road blocked up.

Chawleigh, the 'hidden nook'

There is an entertaining account in Victorian times of a village walk circa 1886 in *We Donkeys in Devon* by Maria Susannah Gibbons under the intriguing pseudonym of Volo non valeo ("I was willing but unable", a motto of Castle Howard):

'Our next point was Chawleigh, a very quaint village, well worth a visit. The church more than amply repaid us for walking to it. There is a very beautiful old screen, which sadly needs restoration, as does the old lych-gate, but the church is otherwise well-restored. There are some curious old monuments which we were unable to decipher, but which no doubt have been worthy of more attention had we had time to spare. Chawleigh is one of the "hidden nooks" in Devon worth a visit. We all refreshed our inner man at the "Portsmouth Arms," a clean and comfortable little inn, where the tea, cream (such Devonshire cream), and butter, were richness itself. We gathered by the behaviour of Xenophon Edward and "Nem. Con." [presumably their horses] that the corn of which they partook was equally to their liking. And they wanted good corn, too, as any of our readers will testify who have been from Chawleigh to Chulmleigh, only two miles, it is true, but what a descent, and what an ascent! Here at the bottom of the hill, before ascending to Chulmleigh, we cross the "Little Dart," the river whose acquaintance we had made at Bickleigh. "Comparisons are odious" so we ought not to compare our two sights of the Little Dart, but we must say that both, though in different ways, were equally lovely. At Bickleigh the beauty, perhaps, is more varied and lasts longer, but the sudden view of the Little Dart Valley, as it burst unexpectedly on our eyes at the top of Chawleigh Hill, almost took away our breath, and made us feel that no words, no pencil, however gifted, could make anyone who had not seen it understand what it was. Here also, as at our other sight of the Little Dart, we were at once in thought carried back to Switzerland.'

This breathtaking 'hidden nook' of the mid-1880s was to change significantly as land ownership, social norms and government were shaken up by national politics and the new Edwardian age.

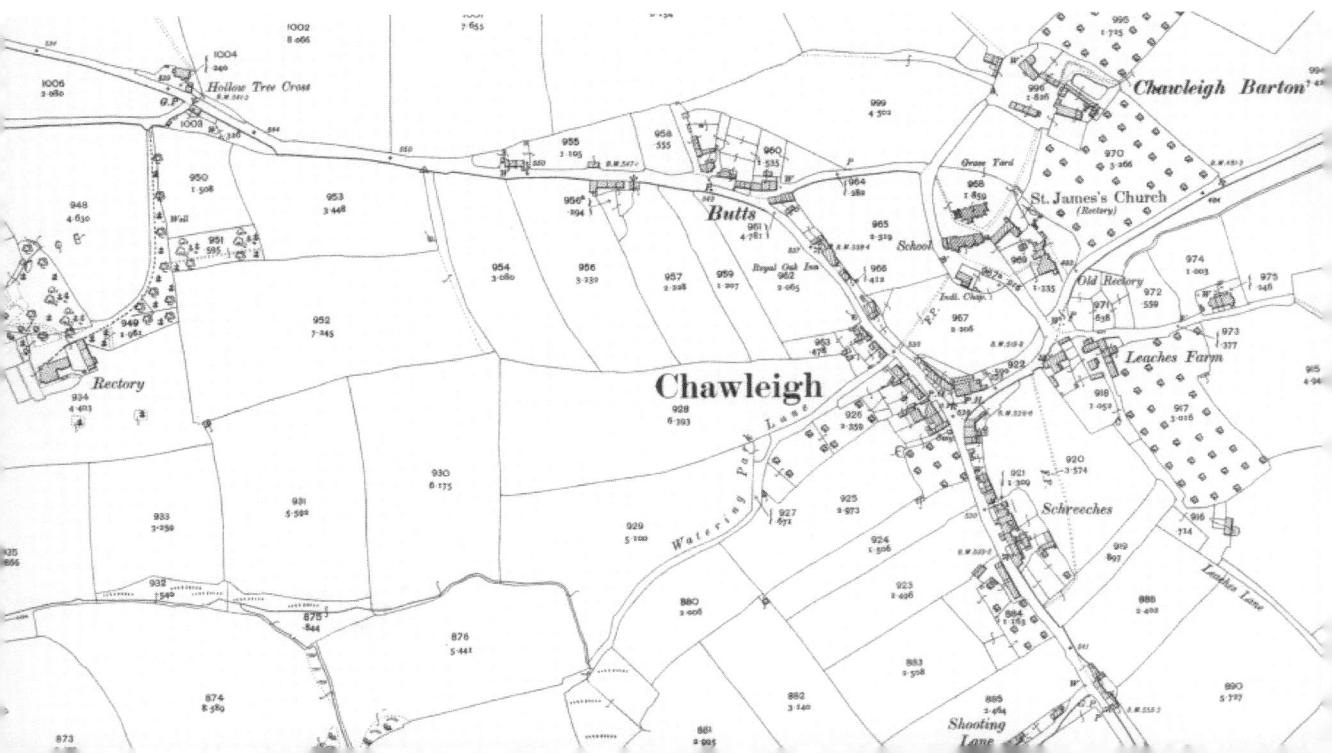

CHAPTER 22

THE DEMISE OF THE EGGESFORD ESTATE

Eggesford House. South side 1901

1901 photo of the front (south side) of Eggesford House, before it was first put up for sale

(By kind permission of Ed Howell)

(Left)

Ordnance Survey map Devon XLIII.5 Revised 1904, Published 1905, showing much of Chawleigh parish.

(Reproduced with the permission of the National Library of Scotland)

In a forerunner of sentiments over the death of Queen Elizabeth II more than a century later, the author Henry James, a visitor to Eggesford House in the time of the 5th Earl of Portsmouth and his Countess, wrote of the death of Queen Victoria in 1901: 'I mourn the safe and motherly old middle-class queen, who held the nation warm under the fold of her big, hideous Scotch-plaid shawl and whose duration has been so extraordinarily convenient and beneficent. I felt her death much more than I should have expected; she was a sustaining symbol – and the wild waters are upon us now.'

Those 'wild waters' of the Edwardian age that was to follow Victoria characterised over a decade of social upheaval at home and international tensions overseas, as the British Empire began slowly to fracture. It was in this social and political environment that the customs and structures of the Portsmouths' Devon estate began to unravel.

The 6th Earl soon appeared more interested in his political career in London and in acquiring luxury motor cars than in the rigours of country life on a sprawling estate. A report in *The Times* on 16 November 1905 mentions him as a patron of Daimler cars, 'the representative British car', alongside 'His Majesty the King' and the Prince of Wales.

Although he kept his other estates in Hampshire and Scotland, the halt in the 6th Earl's rise in national politics in 1908 (see Chapter 8) coincided with his declining interest in Devon. He had in addition funded the rebuilding of Hurstbourne Place in Hampshire together with the acquisition of the Scottish sporting estate Guisachan in 1905.

With certain mortgages outstanding from the previous Earl, July 1903 saw 750 acres of 'freehold estates, accommodation lands, and good homesteads' in West Anstey, Dulverton, Bampton and Witheridge offered by auction. These sales became almost annual. In July 1904, 1171 acres of freehold 'woodlands, residential and cottage properties and manorial rights, farm houses and homesteads' were offered for sale in North Tawton.

By 1905, the Earl was selling off parts of the estate in Burrington, Winkleigh, East Worlington, Ashreigney, Witheridge and North Tawton. In 1906, parts of Coleridge (Coldridge), East Worlington, Chawleigh, Lapford, Cheldon, Chulmleigh, Wembworthy and North Tawton were for sale.

On 24 July 1908 another auction at the Rougemont Hotel, Exeter, offered land and buildings in Chulmleigh, Cheldon, Coleridge, Dowland, East Worlington and Witheridge. The Chawleigh properties included Chawleigh Barton, Stone Mill, The Old Rectory (now The Old Hall) and other holdings. An advert from 26 July 1908 foretold: 'Sale of lands in Chawleigh, Cheldon, East Worlington and Witheridge by direction of the Earl of Portsmouth. 2,738 acres, 3r. 11p. Including fishing rights. A centre for the hunt of Sir [John] Amory's Staghounds, and the Eggesford Foxhounds, Cheriton Otter Hounds and the South Molton Harriers. Divided into 94 lots. His lordship retaining 5,000 acres.'

The Sales Particulars maintained that these comprised 'some of the best Land in the district, close to or within easy access to the Railway, and approached by good roads. The occupiers are responsible tenants

The grand interiors of Eggesford House when it was put up for sale before the First World War

(Photos by kind permission of Ed Howell)

paying moderate rentals. The premises are in good repair, and the attention of Capitalists seeking properties of this description, whether for occupation or investment, is with confidence directed to these attractive Estates.'

On 20 July 1911, J Hannaford & Son, auctioneers in Chulmleigh, led the sale of 'Freehold Estates, Cottage Residences, Accommodation Lands, Small Holdings, Coverts and Artizans' Cottages' in Coleridge, East Worlington, Lapford, Cheldon, Chulmleigh, Wembworthy, North Tawton, and Chawleigh.

This time the Sales Particulars described these as 'an exceptional opportunity for the acquirement of good agricultural and sporting Estates, which are let to responsible tenants at moderate rentals, and have in many instances been in the occupation of members of the same family for a great many years. The premises are in good repair, and meet the requirements of respective holdings which are situated close to good roads, within easy reach of the Railway, and are of a productive nature.'

The press became more outspoken as the Portsmouths disengaged from decades of involvement in Devon life and its rural economy. *The Bournemouth Graphic* wrote in 1912: 'He does not care very much for the place and spends comparatively little time there.' *The Truth* reported on 4 June 1913: 'The late Lord Portsmouth resided at Eggesford during two-thirds of the year, but his son has never cared for the place.'

Henry James's 'wild waters' of the Edwardian age were apparent throughout Britain, as country houses and their estates were dismantled physically and metaphorically. Alongside Eggesford, the 6th Earl was also selling off parts of his recently acquired Scottish estate. Asquith's Liberal government had introduced a 'People's Budget' in 1909, aimed at social reform and taxing the land of wealthy landowners, increasing death duties and taxes on the sale and ownership of property. David Lloyd George's budget had been fervently resisted by the House of Lords, which was made up of a majority of landed peers, among them the 6th Earl, prompting a constitutional crisis between the Commons and the Lords.

As *The Saturday Review of Politics, Literature, Science and Art*, Volume 114, commented in 1912: 'The sale of the Eggesford estate is another ill sign of the times. How gleeful the Government must be that they have succeeded in routing the Wallop family at length out of Devonshire! They will now no doubt be able to boast with pride that, the Prime Minister having driven the owner of Eggesford out of the Government, the Chancellor of the Exchequer has nobly completed the rout by turning him out of the West of England!'

The 1913 sale of parts of the estate offered the grand house itself. Also on offer were the Eggesford Foxhounds' Kennels, and the 'Important Fully-Licensed Hotel known as "Fox and Hounds" … a noted Fishing Centre', comprising:

The Fox and Hounds Hotel taken from the sales particulars for the Eggesford estate in 1913

(With kind permission of Ed Howell)

'10 bedrooms, Coffee Room, Bar, Club Room, Market Room, Commercial Room, Parlour, Smoke Room, Kitchen, Wash House and Out Offices. Eight-stall stable, Coach-house, Five-stall stable, Three Cattle Boxes, Pigs' House, enclosed Sheds, Harness Room, Implement Shed with Loft over, Barn and Cart Shed, and Railway Siding. Two Excellent Cottages and a Single One (in Yard). ... The Eggesford Market... comprises: Pens, Office Buildings, &c. (adjoining Railway siding).'

In Chawleigh, the sale included Southcott Farm (265 acres), 'A Small Holding known as East Hill Town' (30 acres), Nethercott Farm (308 acres), Ford Farm (53 acres), Chawleigh Week Mill and Land (104 acres), and other 'Pasture Land' and cottages.

In Eggesford, Eggesford Barton Farm (249 acres), Trenchard Farm (413 acres), Hayne Farm (282 acres), Pasture Land at Moor Town, Rose Cottage, a 'Small Holding at Four Ways'. The Eggesford Saw Mills (with 'Saw Mill worked by Turbine') also comprised a Cottage, Mill House and Sawing Shed, Timber Sheds and Cart Shed.

And in Wembworthy, Freehold Ground Rent for the Lymington Arms (then leased to Mr George Sanders since 1867), Scrabbacleave Cottage, Wembworthy Down Farm (225 acres), and Yellands (55 acres).

In Wembworthy and Winkleigh, 'The Devon Hunt Kennels and Lands adjoining' (20 acres) 'Including The Huntsman's House ... Offices, Stables for Four and Range of Kennels, Bothy Hovel and Premises. Held by the HUNT COMMITTEE at a Nominal Rent of 1s per annum for the House, Stables and Kennels, and £16 per annum for the Pasture Land...'

There were other 'arable land, small holdings, cottages and village properties (buildings, gardens, wastes etc.' also on offer.

A total of 717 acres of Woodlands and Plantation, spread across Chawleigh, Coldridge, Eggesford, Winkleigh and Wembworthy, were for sale. Rosemary Lauder in her book *Vanished Houses of North Devon* (2005) cites a newspaper account of the auction:

'The estate was sold for £85,000 to Mr. Green of Chesterfield. The rent roll was given as £3,564 19s. 10d. and the timber was valued at £40,220 11s. 1d. The Earl of Portsmouth's asking price was £100,000 but reduced the bidding until an offer of £70,000 was made. The bids rose in £1,000 to £80,000 and then slowly in £500's. The proceedings took 10 minutes. The purchaser is the senior partner of J.B. and F.W. Green, timber merchants, of Whittington, near Chesterfield. The firm have sawmills in Whittington and North Wales and have recently entered into the building trade. This estate was the fifth largest estate purchased by Mr. Green within the last 12 months or so.'

J B and F W Green still exists as a family firm in the 2020s.

As local Lapford historian David Garton has pointed out: 'The estate went under the hammer and was bought principally for its timber... At the turn of the C20, the estate had acres of ancient woodland rich with wildlife, dog mercury, bracken, gorse, broom, fox-glove and blue-bell. The trees were broad leaved, managed for their timber. After the sale of the estate the woods were denuded – stripped of good hardwood timber to help the war effort.' It was not until 1919 that the new Forestry Commission started replacing the trees (see Chapter 4).

The former Portsmouth kennels, pictured in early 2024, still used for hounds

(Photo by Jonathan Crofts)

Having acquired the timber, the Greens initiated another auction on 5 June 1914: Hannaford & Son offered 'Several Valuable and Attractive Freehold Estates, including Eggesford House & Grounds, and about 6 miles of Valuable Salmon and Trout Fishing in the River Taw, Small Holdings, Accommodation Lands, Woods, Cottage Residences, Artizans' Cottages &c., also all that Free and Fully Licenced Hotel, known as "Fox and Hounds", Eggesford ... containing about 2,763 Acres, ... actual and estimated rentals of £3,127 15 s. 4 d. in Lots.'

Significantly for the hunting community, the kennels, huntsman's house and stables – the 'Eggesford Hunt Kennels & Grass Land', Lot 51 – were sold for £1650 to Mr Luxton, member of the Eggesford Hunt Committee.

Luxton came to prominence after the 5th Earl had retired as Master of the Hunt, to be replaced by Major de Freville. De Freville however resigned after his first season, perhaps with too much interference from his predecessor, the Committee now being headed by Lord Portsmouth as Field-Master, although he died soon afterwards. Mr Preston Whyte of Leigh House, Chulmleigh, then took over and the Hunt was sustained for another two seasons. Mr H E Lambe took over in 1894 but he retired to hunt with the Blackmore Vale, leaving the Master's role vacant for the next season, and the 'country' hunted by the neighbouring packs in Mid Devon, the Tremlett and the Tiverton.

In 1896 the Hon. Lancelot Julian Bathurst took over for five seasons with an entirely new pack, living in a small cottage near Eggesford. He resigned in 1901, leaving the newly formed Committee headed by the Chairman, the Hon. John F Wallop, a brother of the 6th Earl, to approach Mr A W Luxton to be Master of the Eggesford. Mr Luxton reportedly put his 'heart and soul' into his work, supported by a Major R H Dunning of Winkleigh, as Honorary Secretary.

The hunt kennels can still be seen today, together with their sturdy Garton & King railings.

224

In the 1914 sale, the house was withdrawn at £7,000 and left empty for the duration of the war, other than a stay by German prisoners-of-war, and circa 1920 Devon County Council declined an offer to take it over as an isolation hospital.

Separately, the 6th Earl instructed Knight, Frank & Rutley to auction the 'Remaining Contents of the Mansion' on 16 and 17 July 1914, a mere eleven days before Austria-Hungary declared war on Serbia at the start of the First World War. The lamps were going out on the Portsmouth's Devonshire estate just as they were starting to all over Europe (in line with Foreign Secretary Sir Edward Grey's famous remark), shortly before everyone's lives were to be changed for ever by the conflict. Twenty-seven pages of paintings, tapestries, curtains, bedding, furniture, household objects and ornaments, and other items came under the hammer, and notes in one of the sales catalogues suggest that almost everything was sold.

On 24 August 1917, in the latter half of the First World War, J Hannaford & Sons of Chulmleigh now advertised in the *Devon and Exeter Gazette* the resale of 'the "Fox & Hounds" Hotel, Eggesford Station, on Wednesday 5th September at 2 or 2.30p.m. [as well as] several Freehold estates' including in the 'Parishes of Cheldon and Chawleigh "Mounticombe … 218.438 acres"'.

Two months later in October, Hannaford also advertised a sale by the Pyncombe Charity trustees (see Chapter 19), selling 890 acres of freehold farms, building sites and golf links in Burrington, Chawleigh (Duckham Farm), Broadwoodkelly and Ilfracombe.

With the pain of the First World War now in the past, by 6 September 1922, J Hannaford & Son were auctioning 'Part of the Eggesford Estate including a Country House, a Grass Farm, Accommodation Lands, Woodlands, Cottage Residences, Artizan's Cottages, and a fully Licenced House known as The Lymington Arms … containing about 203 acres.' The sale at the Fox & Hounds Hotel cited Charles John Hannaford as among the owners and occupiers of the remaining estate, and the Special Conditions gave him continued rights of way and drainage and fishing rights over the land to be sold; these rights were also extended to the 'Forestry Commissioners' (the Commission's Forest had been created three years previously, see Chapter 4). Bartlett, Bayliss & Co. Ltd, timber merchants, are noted as title holders amongst the vendors.

It seems the properties were not all selling or were unwanted: in June 1923, freehold properties (837 acres) were again put up for auction in Chulmleigh, Chawleigh, Kings Nympton and Wembworthy, including once more the Fox & Hounds Hotel, Eggesford Market, Stone Barton and Stone Bridge Cottage in Chawleigh and Chulmleigh (see Chapter 24).

A few years earlier, as if to confirm the dismantling of the Devon estate, Newton Wallop, the 6th Earl, passed away shortly before Christmas in 1917, with the First World War still raging, killing and maiming enormous numbers of young aristocrats and other young men across the country and the British Empire. The impact of that loss was significant for landed families, who lost not only many of their successors but also many of the 'servant class' who supported the great houses, farms and other activities on their estates. The social change accelerated by the war changed Great Britain and Ireland for ever.

As the 6th Earl and his Countess, Beatrice, had no children, the title passed to the Honourable John Fellowes Wallop of Barton House, Morchard Bishop, his brother.

The 7th Earl: John Fellowes Wallop (1859-1925)

John, Newton's brother, succeeded him as Earl in 1917, leaving Beatrice, Lady Portsmouth, with the estates, to which she was entitled for life.

Not tied to Devon in his early years, John had acted as private secretary to the Governor of Tasmania for a while. But once back, with his brother tied up with London politics, John had engaged local farmers on the estate as early as 1903 on the subject of motor vehicles replacing the horse, and the benefits of another innovation, electricity: 'Nobody dislikes the motor car more than me but I think the motor will give you the best opportunity of selling your produce … the best chance that Devon agriculture has is the introduction of electricity and motor cars.' Fearing a drop in horse prices, the farmers had responded with laughter.

John (also known as Jock) lived at Barton House, in the nearby village of Morchard Bishop, which today is still standing although divided into separate dwellings. His will describes his estate there, where he tended with care and knowledge the rare and beautiful plants and shrubs in his garden.

He was Chair of the County Main Roads Committee, and notably chaired the meeting in 1924 to approve the widening of the A377 Taw valley road from Exeter to Barnstaple.

The turnover in earls sadly accelerated in the last few decades of their time in Devon. John, the 7th Earl, died eight years after his brother in 1925, only four years older than his brother had been and still only 66. According to *The Times* on 9 September 1925, however, he had made his mark on the county:

'Lord Portsmouth was one of the most prominent public men in the West. He contested the Tavistock Division in the Liberal interest in 1900, and had since kept up his interest in politics, being chairman of the Liberal Party in the South Molton Division, and taking an active part in recent General Elections. He was vice chairman of the Devon County Council and chairman of the Devon Education Committee and of the Devon Main Roads Committee. In the latter capacity he was associated with the carrying through of the £1,000,000 road-reconstruction scheme on which the county is now engaged. He had travelled extensively in the Far East and in America. Lord Portsmouth was Hereditary Bailiff of Burley and a vice-Lieutenant and a Magistrate for Devonshire.'

Memorial to John Fellowes Wallop, 7th Earl of Portsmouth, in St Mary's Church, Morchard Bishop

(Photo by Jonathan Crofts)

The 8th Earl: Oliver Henry Wallop (1861–1943)

Oliver Henry ('O H') Wallop, third son of Isaac Newton Wallop, the 5th Earl, and Eveline, his Countess, became 8th Earl in 1925 after his two older brothers died with no children. He was born at Eggesford House, but not expecting to become Earl, he had migrated to the United States to become a rancher and stockman on a large ranch in Wyoming. Here he raised horses for polo in peacetime, and as pack horses, for transport and the cavalry in the Boer War and the First World War.

The Times's New York correspondent reported his death on 11 February 1943:

> '… the EARL OF PORTSMOUTH, who owned a large cattle ranch in Wyoming, died on Tuesday night at Colorado Springs, Colorado, at the age of 82. He became an American citizen in 1888 [other reports say 1904]. His elder son, Viscount Lymington, who succeeds as 9th Earl, was formerly Conservative M.P. for Basingstoke. He was born in 1898 and is a well-known agriculturist.'

Oliver Henry Wallop, 8th Earl of Portsmouth. 'O H' Wallop founded Canyon Ranch in the 1880s. He raised horses for polo and to supply the British Army in the First World War, as well as serving in both US state government and in the British upper chamber.

(Reproduced with kind permission of the Earl and Countess of Portsmouth)

Oliver Henry Wallop served two terms as a Republican in the Wyoming Legislature from 1908. Following his succession to the peerage in 1925, he and his wife, Marguerite Walker of Kentucky (1869–1938), arrived at the family seat in Devon, now at Barton House in Morchard Bishop. After regaining British nationality, O H became the only person thus far to have served both in the government of Wyoming as well as in the House of Lords.

The lodge at Barton House

(Photo by Jonathan Crofts)

227

Marguerite, now the 8th Countess, took on charitable roles on her arrival in Devon, and ended her days in Barton House, Morchard Bishop. On the death of his wife, the Earl put up for auction the family's last remaining estate in the West Country and returned to America. The life of Marguerite Walker Wallop was reported by *The Times* on 10 May 1938:

> 'Lady Portsmouth married her husband in 1897 when he was the Hon. Oliver Henry Wallop. … She was Dame President of the South Molton Unionist Association, president of the Morchard Bishop Nursing Association and of the Morchard Bishop Women's Institutes. Her club was the English-Speaking Union.'

Shortly before the Second World War, *The Western Times* reported the sale on 6 April 1939: 'The property, it is stated, is the last of the Portsmouth family estates in Devonshire, which in bygone days ran to some 20,000 acres, and came into their possession by marriage about 100 years ago.' Barton House was built by the Churchill family (see Chapter 5) circa 1830, and local reports suggest the Army commandeered the house during the Second World War, after which it helped to house homeless families, as did a number of large houses in that period.

Sales particulars for the Barton House Estate in 1939

(Photos by Jonathan Crofts)

The 9th Earl: Gerard Vernon Wallop (1898–1984)

Oliver and Marguerite's son, the 9th Earl, Gerard Vernon Wallop (1898–1984, born in Chicago), served on the Western Front in the First World War, and stood, as Viscount Lymington, as Conservative MP for Basingstoke from 1929 to 1934. After university at Balliol College, Oxford, he attended the Oxford School of Agriculture, and began to write and speak on the subject, an early exponent of the risks of monoculture in arable farming and of the use of agrochemicals. He married twice, in 1920 to Mary Lawrence Post, from Long Island (New York State) and, following his divorce in 1936, to Bridget Cory Crohan of Owlpen Manor in Gloucestershire.

His finances suffered from the depression in the 1930s, and he sold the Scottish estate, Guisachan, as well as the house and park at Hurstbourne Priors, which he inherited when Beatrice, his aunt and the dowager Countess, died in 1935. Concentrated now on Farleigh House as his family home and agriculturally on its estate, he helped to create Kinship in Husbandry, a precursor of the Soil Association.

In the Second World War he was Captain in the Home Guard and vice-chairman of the Hampshire War Agricultural Executive Committee. He left the Hampshire home, Farleigh Wallop, in 1952 to farm in Kenya. By the time he was in his forties, the Portsmouth connection with Devon was over and Kenya became the focus away from Hampshire.

Farleigh House in Hampshire, the later home of the Portsmouths, and the focus of the 9th Earl, Gerard Vernon Wallop

(Photo by Jonathan Crofts, by kind permission of Viscount Lymington)

'I had turned Farleigh from a bankrupt into a going concern, but I could not make more than £3000 a year after payment of taxes. So I came here to save the estate. I hope the Portsmouth continuity will be kept going in Kenya,' he said, as related on the site *europeansineastafrica.co.uk*. With a new estate of 12,000 acres, it was nearly as big as the Devon lands had been. 'By living on what I make here,' he continued, 'I am left with more money for Farleigh.

The 9th Earl's obituary in *The Times* on 1 October 1984 celebrated his farming credentials:

'In 1933 he was made a member of the Milk Marketing Board... [he] was a strong supporter of the Agricultural Marketing Act, strenuously arguing, as in his book *Horn, Hoof and Corn* (1932) for what he believed to be a potential for self-sufficiency in agriculture... He continued … to write on agriculture and *Famine in England* (1938) reiterated the belief in the ability of Britain to be self supporting and the dangers of neglecting agricultural resources in time of war... In 1943 his father died on his Wyoming cattle ranch and he succeeded him as ninth earl. In this year, also, he published *Alternative to Death* which stressed again his belief in the importance of nurturing a national life rooted in the land. In 1947–48 he was vice president and chairman of the Country Landowners Association'.

His sub-title to *Alternative to Death*, *The Relationship between Soil, Family and Community*, perhaps reflects the nineteenth-century Wallop / Portsmouth approach to the area of Devon which they held and managed for so long: a commitment to the land beneath their feet, to their (often large) families, and to the wider community living on – and living off – that land.

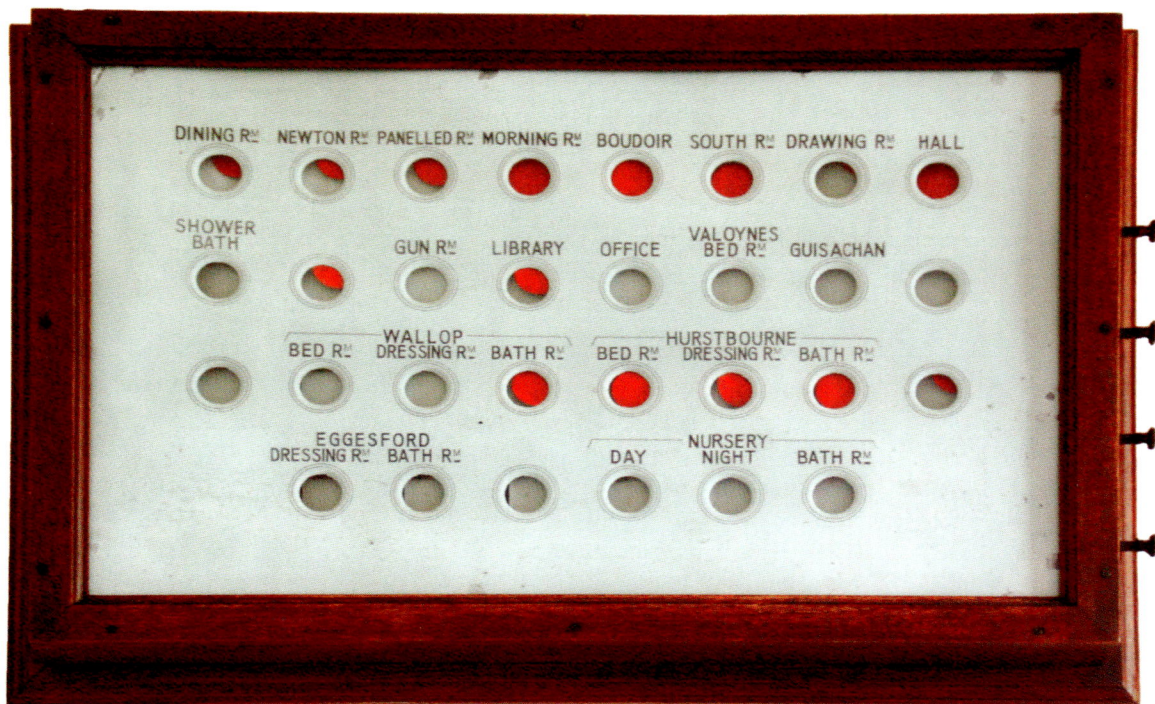

The Devon farming families of today still share and demonstrate those values, even though the land has been built on in parts, agricultural practices have moved on, and society has evolved beyond measure. The Earl of Portsmouth in Chawleigh now refers to the larger pub in the village, not the name of the landowner, and 'Portsmouth' no longer appears on title deeds across the district.

The Wallop family today and more Highclere connections

The Wallop family presence still persists in Wyoming, USA. Malcolm Wallop, grandson of Oliver Henry, the 8th Earl, born 27 February 1933, was married four times, and died in 2011. He was a US Senator for Wyoming from 1977 to 1995. In 1981 his polo ranch was put up for sale to pay death duties on the death of his father, Oliver, younger brother to the Earl of Portsmouth of the day.

His sister, Jean Margaret, married Henry Herbert, 7th Earl of Carnarvon, in 1956. Initially known as Lord Porchester, he was a childhood friend of the late Queen Elizabeth II (who called him 'Porchie' or 'Porchey') and became her horse racing manager. Elizabeth II was a house guest of the Wallops at Canyon Ranch in Big Horn, Wyoming, in 1984 during her visit to the United States with Lord and Lady Porchester. Henry succeeded as Earl of Carnarvon in 1987, inheriting the family seat, Highclere Castle: Jean Wallop thus providing a new connection between the Portsmouth (Wallop) family and the Carnarvons at Highclere (see Chapter 9). Her eldest son was godson to Queen Elizabeth II.

Malcolm Wallop's nephew is thus George Herbert, 8th Earl of Carnarvon, whose family seat, Highclere Castle, became the main filming location for the ITV television series *Downton Abbey*. Wallop's son Paul now runs the Canyon Ranch in Wyoming, while Jean's daughter, Lady Carolyn, operates a thoroughbred racing stud at Highclere, and her husband, John Warren, also became the late Queen's racing adviser.

In 2024 Gerard Vernon's grandson now holds the title of 10th Earl, his father having died before the 9th Earl. The family remain interested in their Devon history, but Chawleigh, Eggesford and the wider estate have evolved rapidly since the cataclysmic conflict of 1914–18 and their lingering departure.

(Left)

The old servants' bell board showing the rooms in Farleigh House, Hampshire, home of the 9th Earl of Portsmouth. Rooms were named after the former estates belonging to the family of Eggesford, Hurstbourne Park, and Guisachan in Scotland.

(Photo by Jonathan Crofts, by kind permission of Viscount Lymington)

CHAPTER 23

CHAWLEIGH AFTER WORLD WAR ONE

One post-war tale helps explain the origins of the track, Blackwalls Lane, which leads from Leaches House (the former Leaches Farmhouse) to a series of houses and cottages and the new Leaches Farm. Today Blackwalls Lane is an unadopted road leading to a beautiful public footpath over fields towards Hardings Leigh. According to Doreen Norton's account on the *devonheritage.org* website, written before 2006:

'John Long was one of my Grandmother's four brothers. He stayed in Chawleigh all his life and married a local girl, Bessie Webber. They had two daughters and one son who died in infancy, the two daughters being Annie and Nelly… John was a gardener at the Manse [presumably the rectory] and a bell ringer at the local church. In 1902, he bought the cottage known as "Black Walls" from the Church, and lived there until he died.

Nelly married William (Billy) Blake … Annie, who attended the Devon County Dairy School to learn butter, cheese and cream-making skills, continued to live at home with her parents, and, when her mother died, kept house for her father. Only when John Long died, did she marry Archibald (Archie) Pearce on 14 February 1953.

Archie had, for many years, been going out late at night to the other end of the village. Everyone in the village believed that he was having an affair with a married lady and that he visited her after her husband had gone to the pub for the evening! In fact he had been meeting up with Annie. None of this came to light until John Long died and they married.

Sadly, Archie died in 1966 so they only had 13 years together but Annie stayed on in the cottage. It was made up as three separate homes with "two up and two down" but she only lived in the first one. She had become quite well-known in the village and maybe, even was considered a bit eccentric.

The cottage had no electricity, the lighting was provided by oil lamps, there was no gas either and all the heating and cooking was from a Rayburn. There was not even any running water. All water came from an outside well which, in winter, had been known to freeze and there was an outside loo – both the cottage and the loo are now listed buildings!

The gardens must have been very pretty in earlier times, as it is laid out as an old cottage garden, with many rose and honeysuckle trees, a vegetable plot and a meadow at the rear.

Annie would chase anybody she did not know away from the cottage. On one occasion, she chased a lady who was trying to make a painting of the cottage, up the lane with a broom stick.

Right up to the time when she was unable to walk, she would take the footpath to Chulmleigh to do her shopping. This was a five mile walk – the very same walk my mother, as a child, would do from Chulmleigh to go to school in Chawleigh.

Eventually the cottage was sold so that Annie would have the funds to go into a nursing home in South Molton. The new owners have renovated it (it was in a very bad state of disrepair) with new thatch to the roof, replaced a chimney that had collapsed, put in main drainage, electricity, oil for cooking and heating and have made it into one cottage. In addition, they have completely stripped the walls and repainted them and in so doing have solved the mystery of the why the cottage was called "Black Walls".

They discovered, while stripping the far side wall, that the wall was covered in a thick tar-like substance which had been used to waterproof the cottage, hence "black walls". The garden has been replanted, the meadow re-seeded with wildflowers and the well covered over for safety.

And one final touch which has brought pleasure to the Long family – they have retained the sign on the side of the cottage that says "J. Long 1902" so John's memory lives on.'

(Left)

A float for Chawleigh Fair in 1923, commemorating the First World War, in front of Leaches Farmhouse: Percy Tremain stands at the head of the horse, with William Tucker (son of Charles and Jane Tucker of Leaches Farmhouse) at the rear

(Photographer unknown)

To Square Chawleigh

Conveyancing documents from 1920 show the cottage was separated into two. John Long was sold the left-hand cottage and also land known as Townhill, a small piece on the corner of Blackwalls Lane as the public road starts to descend to Stone Mill.

By 1923, listings show that the Reverend William Jocelyn Bradford, MA, was the Rector at the (newer) Rectory, resident since 1915, the living being in the gift of the Countess of Portsmouth. Donald Pell-Smith was a 'Private Resident' at Higher Ford (once the Portsmouth hunting lodge). The Eggesford Station master was now Percy Townsend, with Thomas Baker still farmer and landowner at The Barton.

J. Baple (presumably John Baple the schoolmaster, who retired in 1924) was now acting as the agent for Devon & Exeter Savings Bank, which survived from 1815 to 1975, eventually absorbed into Lloyds Bank. The original background to the bank is explained in G R Porter's *Sketch of the Progress and Present Extent of Savings' Banks in the United Kingdom* (1846):

'The Devon and Exeter Savings' Bank has been for many years placed under very zealous and able management; and, in addition to the constant services of Mr. Lee, its actuary, has received the support of considerably more than an hundred clergymen and gentlemen residing at different places within the county, who have taken pains to make known among the labouring poor in

The Portsmouth Hotel on 'The Square' in Chawleigh, probably early 1930s. The petrol station on the right advertised Pratts High Test oil, a brand which commissioned a series of highly popular pictorial road maps in that period. Note the single motor car parked up the road and the railings in front of the hotel, likely taken in the Second World War.

(By kind permission of Daphne Cockram)

(Right)

An early tractor in the fields outside Chawleigh

(Photo by kind permission of Yvonne Gerry)

234

their respective neighbourhoods the benefits to be derived from even the smallest savings, and who have, at the cost of some personal trouble, received such savings and transmitted them to Exeter for investment, an operation which, unaided, the depositors could hardly have accomplished.'

Otherwise, newly listed Ernest J Ellicott was farmer at Chenson, with Lewis Skinner now at Fiddlecott, Francis Parker at Mildons Leigh, and William Western farmer and landowner at Southcott; J. Massie & Son were a new engineering firm, and William Clark a shopkeeper. Following the various sales of parts of the Portsmouth estate, presumably, four of the farmers are also now listed as 'landowners'.

The 1930 *Kelly's Directory* lists Redvers John Bastin in the School House, Robert Alexander Currie in The Old Hall, Major Harold H Gotto at West Dockworthy, and Donald Pell-Smith still at Higher Ford. Miss Leakey is still at The Cottage, no doubt mollified by the removal of the Parish Bier in 1925. Following the foundation of the Forestry Commission in 1919 and the planting of their first trees in Eggesford Forest, Charles Adams is listed as Forester for them at Hilltown Cottage. Other new names include Arthur Gove, a carpenter, Louis Kingdon toiling in the fields at Lower Chenson, William James Slade farming at Week Mill, Charles Webber providing Sunday Newspapers, Herbert Woodman as tobacconist, and Wheaton & Son as Motor Engineers down in the Taw valley.

Kelly's in 1935 records further changes in the years leading up to the Second World War. A vestry was added to the church in 1929 'at a cost of £800, and a new organ as a memorial to the late Mr. Isaac Phillips'. It also references the Methodist Chapel (rebuilt 1922) and the old Congregational Chapel being bought by the parish for use 'as a Parish Hall' (see Chapter 16). By this time, 'Charities value £130 are derived from the parish lands:- Reverend John Churchill's Charity is £1.11.- ; Thomas Webber's Charity 10/-s; Pyncombe's Charity – £2 paid yearly to a poor widow of the parish who is not in receipt of parish relief.' The population of 1931 is recorded as '556 in civil; and 611 in ecclesiastical parish.'

Geoffrey Derrick Austin Clover (1909–1936) was in residence at The Old Hall and Major Gotto still at West Dockworthy. Llewellen Bowen was a new forester for the Commission, Mrs Eda Clark now a shopkeeper, William Jos. Ware Halse farming at Pouncers and Nicholas Prettejohn at Ford's. Herbert Petherick had taken a step up from being a blacksmith to also running a petrol station with a car for hire (probably therefore a taxi service). The Pethericks later took over the petrol pump site opposite The Earl of Portsmouth from where they ran school buses, and also, after the Second World War, the petrol and diesel garage further down the road towards Chulmleigh.

Concluding the interwar period, and coinciding with the last Portsmouth holdings in the area, the 1939 *Post Office Directory* showed a change of rector to the Reverend Richard Fraser Bastow, with Mrs Northam in the School House and Donald Pell-Smith still at Higher Ford. Russell Stephenson was now at West Dockworthy and Oscar Louis Young at The Old Hall. New names in the various trades included Lionel Bird as tobacconist, Gordon Comyn as a dentist at Sunnyside, ('Mons. 10.30 a.m.'), and Samuel Price Rowcliffe down at Saw Mills. Nine farms are listed as being over 130 acres.

In Cheldon, Lieutenant-Commander Lionel Austin Cazalet, Royal Navy (Retired), a Huguenot descendant born 1893 who served in the First World War, was given as a 'Private Resident' at Cheldon House, and there are another 4 farms listed there as over 130 acres.

The Reverend Richard Fraser Bastow (1888–1960) moved to Devon in 1920, first at Kennerleigh, serving Crediton and Woolfardisworthy East before moving to Chawleigh from 1935. He became chair of the Chawleigh Parish Council and of the Chawleigh Church Funds Charity. *The Western Times and Gazette* reported on his life and death on 7 October 1960:

> '… his greatest interest, outside the Church, lay in his small laboratory in the North Devon Rectory, where he spent most of his spare time studying diatoms. He was one of the country's greatest authorities on the subject, and among botanists, a man of international repute. He was in touch with students and experts in many parts of the world, among them a Spanish mechanic, who made his own microscope, and first wrote to Mr Bastow after reading an article by him in a learned American Journal. He was completely wrapped up in his subject, and he would never receive any payment for his writing.'

Diatoms are a unique and diverse class of algae with glass-like cell walls made of silica. An important part of the food chain, they photosynthesise like plants, and can be used as a measure of the quality of rivers and other watery environments. Reverend Bastow was clearly something of an expert, and simply for the love of it.

Bastow's Rectory (the second incarnation) to the west of the main village is now the site of Ashley Court, a home of the Amber Foundation, a registered charity aiming to 'support young people facing complex problems to transform their lives by helping them move out of homelessness and

unemployment and work towards better, brighter futures'. Amber also has centres in Wiltshire, Surrey and Kent. The Rector would surely have approved.

Another group working towards a brighter future for the community is the local branch of the Women's Institute, founded in 1934. The WI existed nationally since 1915, when wartime aspirations were to involve women more in food production and reinvigorate communities. Its leaders came out of the suffrage movement, and its founding principles were democratic, voluntary and apolitical. The Second World War saw the WI help with the evacuation of children to rural areas and increasing the knowledge of how to grow food and preserve it. More controversially in the 1940s, it passed a resolution demanding equal pay for women and men.

As the Chawleigh community magazine, *The Dart*, reported in April 2024, the branch was formed in February 1934, with a meeting held in the schoolroom:

> 'There were 24 present and after the rules and working of the Institute had been explained, Mrs E Baker proposed that a branch was formed, seconded by Mrs Evans, and carried unanimously. The meeting further decided that girls may be admitted at the age of 14, on leaving school. On a proposition by Miss Ford it was decided that the meetings be held on the first Wednesday of every month. … Mrs Bradford was elected as President, with Mrs Northam as Vice President, Miss Ford was elected as Treasurer and Miss Potter Secretary.'

In June 1934: 'Lady Portsmouth gave a talk on her recent cruises in the Mediterranean. The competition was for 3 cakes made with Homepride Flour. There were 13 entries: 1st prize was Mrs A Hill; 2nd Miss M Player.'

In July: 'An afternoon of tea and games took place in 'ideal weather' in the Rectory garden, including a treasure hunt, clock golf, posting game and a parcel game. After tea Mrs Mounsey gave a demonstration on felt slippers.'

In September: 'There was a lecture from Mrs Bell of Ashburton on the work of Dr Barnardo's Homes. Following on from this the members collected tin foil and silver paper, the sale of which helped the charity considerably. The competition was Eccles cakes made using Borwick's Baking Powder and won by Miss M Ford.'

In February 1935: 'At the end of the first year there were 40 members and the yearly subscription was 2/- (2 shillings; approx. 10p; about £9 in today's value.) … WI members from Chulmleigh and Ashreigney were invited and about 90–100 members sat down for tea at 5.30 pm. After tea a short programme of songs, duets and sketches was well rendered by members, assisted by Miss Ellicott and D Tucker. The birthday cake was made by Mrs Miller.'

Clearly not all women in Chawleigh have the time or inclination to join the WI, but the local branch, despite fluctuations in the local population, still has a healthy membership, ninety years on.

The population of Chawleigh has varied over the centuries, as inhabitants come and go, affected by feast, famine, war or the need to look for work elsewhere. It was recorded in the censuses as 755 in 1801, 705 in 1811, and 792 in 1821. Eggesford, by comparison, was recorded in *Kelly's Post Office Directory* of 1856 as 138. Census data from the Office of National Statistics in 2021 indicated a population in Chawleigh of 639, projected to rise towards 675, while Eggesford recorded 140 in 2021. Proposed new building on the edge of the village will likely draw new residents, along with the growth of nearby centres such as Crediton.

Today the heart of the village is partially protected by a designated Conservation Area, through which the administrative district of Mid Devon manages planning permission. There has been little restriction on the types of architecture to be found in the Conservation Area, which range from centuries-old cob and thatch houses like Leaches House to twenty-first-century rendered and slate-roofed bungalows. The listed buildings include the two semi-detached cottages at the far end of Blackwalls Lane, which are not part of the conservation area.

Some of the more recent architecture has not been to everyone's liking – in 1973 S H Burton wrote in his book *Devon Villages*:

'Any discomforts [of the winter lanes] are soon forgotten in Chawleigh's delightful surroundings. Well, delightful at the centre, where the cobbled triangle in front of the lovely school and school house obliterates the nastiness of some of the new buildings on the outskirts of this hilltop and street village. Chawleigh's huge churchyard is gay with snowdrops and crocuses in spring, and its beech avenue must surely whisper consolation to the occupants of this peaceful field of death. In the centre too is a lovely example of a cob cottage with those rounded corners so typical of this material. The fine church itself reflects fifteenth century confidence and wealth, when Chawleigh ("calves' clearing") had become a speculative "village borough". The gamble failed.'

In common with many English towns, cities and smaller settlements, Chawleigh is twinned with a French neighbourhood of similar size, in this case Saint-Martin-de-Mailloc, a commune in the region of Basse-Normandie in the Calvados department of northwest of France. Several decades of this entente cordiale has not dented the village's West Country rituals of apple harvests and cutting the hay, scones with a pot of tea, darts at the pub, the summer fair and horses clopping along the tracks as they have done for centuries.

Like many Devon villages today, Chawleigh is an architectural and visual mix. The Great Fire of 1869, which destroyed some twenty houses, and its mixed economic fortunes once it stopped being on the main route from London to Barnstaple, have no doubt impacted its development. It is home to many people, especially perhaps those old families whose heritage here dates back centuries. As a result, there is an abundance of stories about the buildings and the people who inhabited them.

CHAWLEIGH

Chawleigh, the village of friendship,
The village of birdsong and peace,
A village surrounded by valleys
Where troubles find happy release.
The road starts at Eggesford Station
And winds up the hill in its flight,
The picturesque roadway to Chawleigh
Whether travelled by day or by night.
The sunlight, the moonlight enfold it
As through the village it flows
Past cottages, bungalows, houses,
Past the inn where 'The Royal Oak' shows,
The church of St. James stands majestic,
A grey monument to the past,
The church bells ring out a gay message,
the music of truth that will last.
The school by the church is a picture,
The diamond-shaped panes draw the gaze
With the children unknowingly spending
What could be their happiest days.
The mediaeval house, the Old Rectory
Stands quietly proud and sedate
Looking over the years that have wandered
And the trees and the church's lych-gate.
When the skylarks are high on the meadows,
When swallows are swerving around
The month is of June and the roses
Then the brilliance of summer is found.
There is fun in the village of Chawleigh,
A procession and band lead the way
To the racing of children, and football
In the Friendly Society's day.
Most beautiful skies cover Chawleigh,
With cloud patterns only here seen
Casting soft shadows on hillsides,
The garb of a wonderful dream.
Chawleigh, the **village** of friendship,
The village of birdsong and peace,
A village surrounded by valleys
Where troubles find happy release.

oct 27th 1975

A poem by a resident of Chawleigh in 1975 characterises the affection which inhabitants typically hold for the village. Judging by the number of 'incomers' who have moved in during the early 2020s (as newcomers to Devon villages tend to be known, even if they moved in thirty years or more ago), the area still retains its appeal.

CHAPTER 24

THE PHOENIX FROM THE ASHES: EGGESFORD HOUSE TODAY

Today, from the drive approaching Eggesford House, wild deer can often be seen grazing the parkland which surrounds it, and the shapes of the remodelled building and its imposing tower loom ahead. The open parkland is surrounded by woodland, and at night the floodlit All Saints Church can be seen in the distance, where the predecessor of the house was sited.

Nikolaus Pevsner's volume on *North Devon* (1952) noted Eggesford House as being, 'Rebuilt 1830 and dismantled in 1917. It is now an extremely picturesque large ruin, standing against the sky, surrounded by the woods of the Taw valley like the best of follies. The original building on the site was Jacobean, the early Victorian one was in a Late Medieval style, embattled and turreted.'

The twentieth century saw the fall and rise of this, the second site of, Eggesford House. It was abandoned by the Portsmouth (Wallop) family before the First World War, as the 6th Earl's Devon estate was gradually offered for sale via a series of auctions, and the family largely withdrew to their Hampshire seat.

According to the 1991 sales particulars from Strutt & Parker, the house was let in 1906 to the Dowager Countess of Leitrim (other reports show her still there in 1911). Much of the estate was then sold to a timber merchant, John Green, and eventually the house was sold in 1923 to Charles Luxmoore, owner of nearby Witheridge Manor (which he had purchased from Newton Wallop in 1906).

Eggesford House as it now appears, with the approach to the front door from the right. The Lymington Wing to the left is no longer standing.

(Photo by kind permission of Ed Howell)

241

One auction in 1914 saw head gardener John Vicary buy nearby Hayne Farm and other lots. Vicary had been employed at Eggesford House since 1901, and as head gardener rented Ivy Cottage and the three-acre walled garden, which he ran as a market garden and nursery business with his sister. The sales catalogue described it as 'situated adjoining the site of the Old Mansion [the first Eggesford House] in Thorn Park… most productive and provided with a range of Glass Houses, Potting Sheds, Bothy, Stables and Stores.'

In the First World War the outbuildings of the big house were used to accommodate German prisoners-of-war. After the war the servants' wing was the last part to house anyone in that period, a forester. The towering trees which still surround the house and its parkland, despite the deforestation of the First World War, are a constant reminder that Eggesford was the location of the first plantation of the new Forestry Commission in 1919 (see Chapter 4).

Fifty years later, a new plaque mentioned Mrs Marion Roach, who participated in a commemorative planting: an earlier plaque referred to her father, Tom Brown, who is believed to be that same forester who last lived in the Portsmouths' incarnation of the house, having been involved in the Commission's first tree planting at its new Eggesford Forest.

The demolition sale of the house on 10–11 November 1927 offered 'The Materials and Fabric of the Mansion including: A large number of Oak Doors which are heavily moulded and carved. Oak and other Floors. Oak Cupboards. Oak Bookcases in the Library. Beautiful Oak Windows. The massive Staircase and about 50 tonnes of Lead on the roof and elsewhere. The Fabric of the Mansion.' The sale was on the instructions of the then owner C F C Luxmoore Esq.

The Broadwoodwidger parish website (*broadwoodwidger.com*) offers a potted history of Luxmoore's career:

'Charles Frederick Coryndon Luxmoore F.R.G.S., J.P. in 1909, born 1872. In 1897, he married his first cousin, Rosalie Maud Acworth Ommanney and they had nine children. They lived at Stafford Barton, Dolton. CFCL became famous in 1928 for his trip up the Amazon into the Brazilian jungle in an attempt to find Colonel Percy Fawcett, who had set off in 1925 with his son, Jack and his friend, Raleigh Rimmel, to search for what Fawcett termed 'The Lost City of Z'. CFCL travelled 3000 miles in his quest but was forced to abandon it some 80 miles from Fawcett's last known camp when the rainy season resulted in the rivers becoming unnavigable. Unlike Fawcett, he concluded that any attempt to hack through the jungle on foot, attempting to survive solely on its fruits, was madness. He arrived back at Stafford Barton with a range of skins and ancient artefacts and some live exotic animals, which included parrots and two jaguars. He also brought back his Brazilian interpreter, Jose. However, the latter soon returned to Brazil being unable to cope with the cold, damp weather of Devon. CFCL died in 1933, still hailed as "the great explorer". His widow continued living at Stafford Barton until her death in 1955.'

As a result of the demolition sale, there are remnants of the second Eggesford House all over Devon. Cheldon Church, just north of Chawleigh, contains a screen of ornamental ironwork, possibly unique, believed to date from the seventeenth century and originally a rack to display maces, formerly installed at the house. (Maces were heavy clubs used in battle in ancient times, but now have a happier reincarnation as fitness tools.) Luxmoore relocated fabric and joinery from Eggesford to his family home at Stafford Barton, in the village of Dolton to the west of the house, including the drawing room panelling, and took the clock from the clock tower, which local farmers had given to Lord Portsmouth as thanks for setting up the market at Eggesford Station.

Many other properties benefited from Eggesford's elegant interiors and exterior. Rosemary Lauder recounts that the Chambers family of builders from the nearby village of Winkleigh bought the shell in 1935, and used Eggesford stonework to build the village hall, together with the courtyard gates and pillars of the house. Hugh Mellor (*The Country Houses of Devon*) reports that windows were reused at Old Ford House in Tiverton.

Just like the connections and memories which the Portsmouths left across Mid and North Devon, the house too has left its own traces.

Historian Eric R Delderfield wrote in 1968: 'In nearby Chulmleigh, there are still several old folk who recall that, in the winter when it was impossible to hunt, the horses from the big house were regularly taken out for exercise. There were often as many as two score in the string and their progress through the village created as much excitement as a circus coming to town… Today… Cattle graze around and about the park that was once the setting for a noble house, but only the crows and rooks have any intimate knowledge of the shell which once abounded with gaiety and life.'

Ivy and brambles slowly took over the site, but the Reverend C A Cardale's prediction circa 1975 that 'No doubt in time as with the first site only level ground will mark the site of the house' (see Chapter 3) was to prove incorrect.

The Eggesford Hunt continued beyond the departure of the Portsmouth family: this image shows the Hunt's Puppy Show on 28 April 1925

(Photo by kind permission of Ed Howell)

The ruins remained largely untouched until the 1990s. According to Rosemary Lauder's 2005 account of the *Vanished Houses of North Devon*, in 1991 the then owners put the house and 83 acres on the market. There was planning permission to convert the stable block into three dwellings, and to turn 'the major portion of the house as built in 1828 to form a substantial country house in a superb position.'

The Times on 15 February 1992 depicted the ruins as 'Heap of the Week' and it captivated a London-based architect who went on to commit the following decades to its reincarnation. Ed and Jo Howell bought the Eggesford site from the Chambers, some sixty years after their own purchase. According to Ed, the family had established a trust for the site and other nearby land, to benefit future generations but not dispose of the assets; the listing of the house ruins in the 1980s encouraged the trustees to sell, however, rather than carry the liabilities of maintaining extensive buildings which would only deteriorate over time.

After the purchase, the Howells lived first in the stables (which they converted into a cottage and office) while Ed's vision for the house was gradually realised. Glass and other contemporary materials have transformed the house into a unique home, including a roof garden with views of the surrounding woodland and open park, the Taw valley, and All Saints Church in the distance.

The ruins of Eggesford House, described as 'Heap of the Week' by *The Times* in the 1990s

(Below)

Photo from the 1991 sales particulars

(All images by kind permission of Ed Howell)

Ground floor

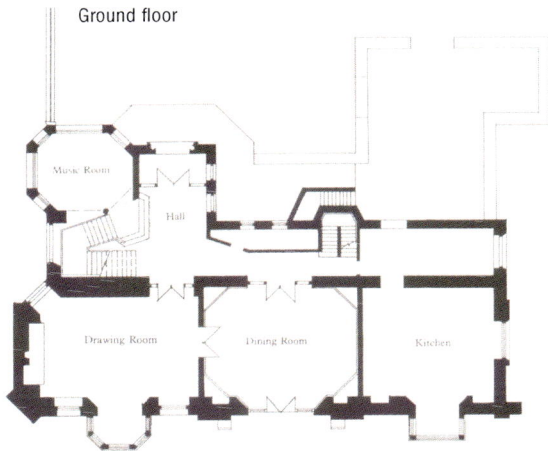

First floor

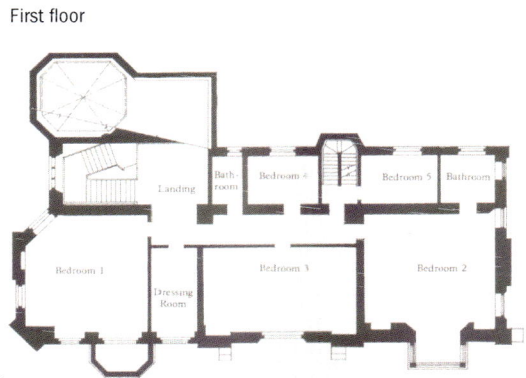

(Above)

Plans from the 1991 sales particulars

(Below)

Aerial photo of renovation building works in the 1990s
(All images by kind permission of Ed Howell)

The spacious interior feels modern yet acknowledges its past. Over thirty years the Howells have welcomed descendants of past owners into their home, intrigued by its history as well as its space and location.

Architectural historian James Rothwell wrote in 2007 for the *Society of Architectural Historians of Great Britain*:

> '… a modern house has … been skilfully inserted within the surviving walls of the main block by architect Ed Howell for himself and his wife Jo. Whilst creating something unashamedly contemporary they have worked with and preserved what survived of the old. Where walls or other elements of the structure had completely disappeared their replacements are modern, where they survived they were repaired and reused but the temptation to go further and restore has been wisely resisted. The symbol of this approach is the great granite lintel which must have proved too heavy to move beyond a few yards from the front door when extracted from the building in the 1920s and there it still lies 80 years later, so much a part of Eggesford that it has been included in a recent portrait of Mr Howell.

The principal sequence of spaces, along the south-east front, have been brought back into use as living rooms and a kitchen, all thrown together with wide

Eggesford House, east side, before its most recent reincarnation by the Howells

(Photos by kind permission of Ed Howell)

246

Eggesford House today, east side, 2020s

arches opened up between them and striated stone floors laid throughout. They are still approached through the now skeletal porch and the stair hall beyond. The latter had lost its rear wall entirely and the timber-clad and glass structure has risen to take its place, enclosing the staircase which when completed will rise along the lines of the original. A quarter landing gives access to the communication gallery which fulfils the same purpose as it did in the 19th century though now the walls, rather than being covered in dark flock paper, are the rubble-stone and brick left exposed when the plaster deteriorated and now painted a clean white.

The Howells have constructed their house within the shell of the Lee building and the Lymington wing, added to the north by the 5th Earl later in the 19th century, remains ruinous. It was probably designed by Clark and Holland of Newmarket who worked elsewhere on the estate for the Earl, including the rebuilding of East Worlington church in 1879. They may also have been responsible for the clock tower, added between 1880 and 1888 and fitted up in the latter year with a clock given to the Earl by local farmers. The clock went to Stafford Barton but the tower remained and was the only part of the building which retained its roof throughout the 20th century. Although the walls are of local stone, concrete was used instead of undressed stone for the window and door surrounds and for the spiral stair.'

(Left)

One innovation, the modern roof terrace at Eggesford House, with fine views to the Taw valley, the Church, and the countryside beyond

(Above)

The view through to the sitting room and one of its bay windows from the hallway of Eggesford House, as redesigned by architect Ed Howell

(Left)

The sitting room at Eggesford House today, redesigned by architect Ed Howell

(Photos by Ed Howell)

The Gardens today

In 2019 the authoritative Devon Gardens Trust (*devongardenstrust.org.uk*) surveyed Eggesford House gardens as part of their Research and Recording Project, which aims to update the *Devon Gazetteer of Parks and Gardens of Local Historic Interest* created after 1998. The site report references the 'early medieval Heywood and Eggesford castles … possibly as picturesque incidents on the drive around the estate' (see Chapter 1).

It confirms that 'panoramic views from the house have been restored', and the 'nearby cottage, a possible cottage orné, now known as Heyswood House, is in separate ownership' (see Chapter 5). Of the main house garden, it continues: 'Vestiges of the pleasure garden remain with a terrace lawn leading out to the ha-ha. The original garden was not extensive or ornate, and few shrubs and a few roses remain. The park still has significant specimen trees and the surrounding woodlands are extensive. Much of the previous landscape is in the hands of Forestry England.'

1880 Ordnance Survey map, 1st Edition showing Eggesford House and grounds (Reproduced with the permission of the National Library of Scotland, as featured in the 1913 Eggesford Sales Catalogue)

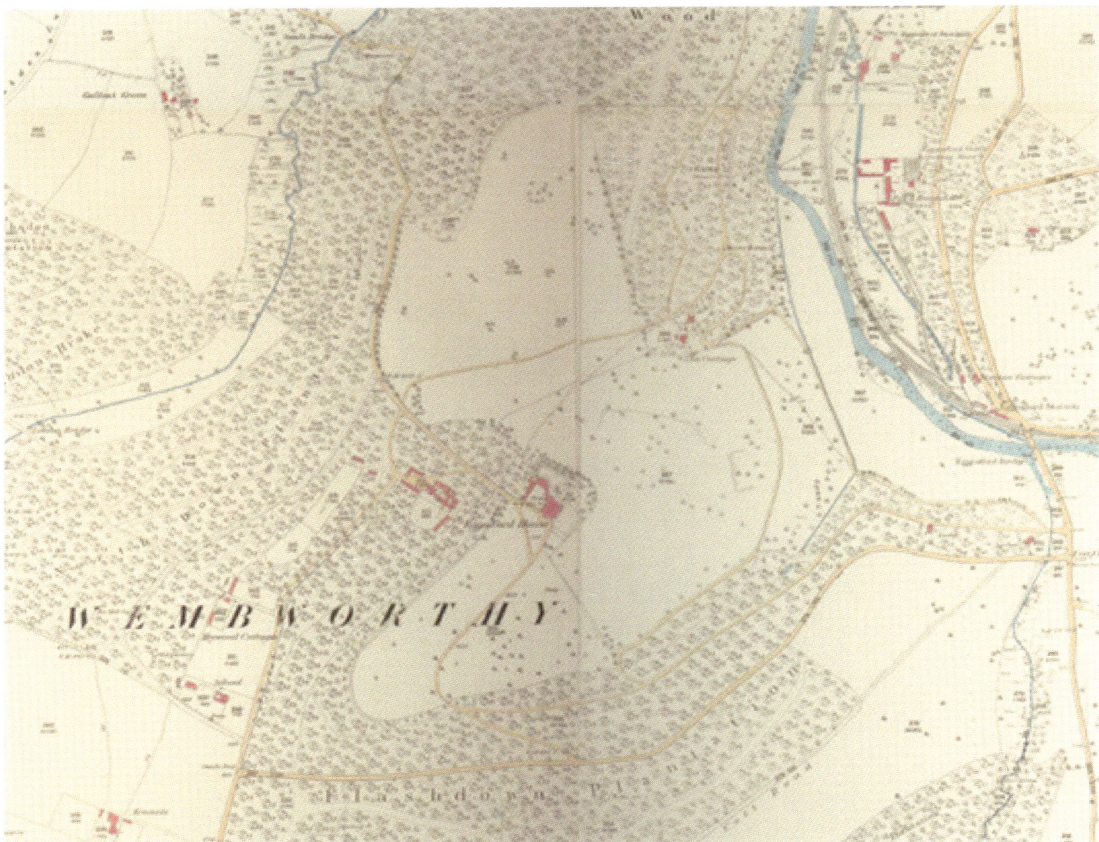

The original Cottage
on the Eggesford estate,
now The Lodge

(Photo from the sales
catalogue of 1913 by
kind permission of
Ed Howell)

The walled kitchen garden was originally associated with the earlier house down by the church, and is shown in the 1805 Ordnance Survey Drawing Map 36 (Crediton). 'The tithe map shows 2 ponds to the south on the edge of Upper Thorn Park, at differing levels and in different fields, hidden in trees, and may have provided water for the walled kitchen garden and house.'

W Croote Junior, for a period land agent for the estate, drew up plans in 1835 for landscape improvements: the proposed changes included roads and tracks and a new site for the kitchen garden:

'A pinetum and arboretum were proposed for the woodland between the early medieval Heywood and Eggesford castles, with extra interconnecting tracks to extend the already plentiful rides around the circular and oval earthworks. The Cottage (originally a small 3-room building, possibly a cottage orné) is shown facing south within woodland, with a new lower level approach road to replace the original, and a new sweeping track leading up to the main house.'

The 1840 Tithe map showed the entrance changed 'and the sweeping new entrance ride constructed'. Devon Gardens Trust continues:

'It was still in use when the property was purchased in 1991 and led up from what is now the B3042, passing The Lodge, now Woodlands, shown as the Lodge on the 1835 plan and later called Ivy Cottage on the 1913 sale map (on the 1887 OS map and probably earlier ones, there is a further Lodge at the bottom of the drive, now known as The Lodge), ending with a turning circle in front of the house. This drive still exists but half way along reduces to a track, with the tarmac road bearing right and on to Heyswood (not Heywood) House, originally known as The Cottage.

The main entrance now utilises the entrance opposite Flashdown (from the Parsonage on the 1835 map) and the original rear drive, which leads from the top un-named road past the Wembworthy Centre and Heywood House, turning right along a track through a plain stone pillared entrance. The track continues to the north-west aspect of the house, passing the stable block, now in a ruinous state, and The Little Cottage, a renovated portion of the outbuildings.'

Although the new kitchen garden was never constructed, Newton Fellowes' interests appeared to include horticulture as well as more traditional country pursuits: the *Exeter and Plymouth Gazette* (22 June 1844) reported that the 28th Exhibition of the North Devon Horticultural Society included 'three splendid specimens of *Fuchsia exoniensis* furnished by Messrs Lucombe and Pince & Co., a very curious specimen of a seedling white single rose from the garden of Hon. Newton Fellowes at Eggesford raised by his gardener, Mr Griffin, from a plant of the Asiatic Mountains.'

When the house was put up for sale in 1913, the catalogue described the gardens as 'not extensive, but are tastefully laid out in terraces, flower and rose gardens and lawns, relieved by clumps of beautiful flowering shrubs'. According to the Devon Gardens Trust report, contemporary photographs show 'a large turfed turning circle in front of the porch, with gravel paths and flat lawns to the south and west'.

'To the north west of the porch, between the house and tower, the current owners have restored walling and grown hedging… The covered well in the centre, with a large underground cistern for rain water, is still present. The haha, as shown in the 1835 Haywood [sic] map, is still mostly present and bounds the north-west lawn.

The parkland within the current boundary, south of the house, now extends to 12 ½ hectares but has a number of mature trees, including a *Pinus radiata* (Monterey Pine), *Aesculus hippocastanum* (Horse Chestnut), *Cedrus atlantica* (Atlas cedar), *Cedrus libani* (Cedar of Lebanon), and *Juglans regia* (Common Walnut)… The woodland surrounding the parkland extends to 31 hectares, including a section of Flashdown Plantation.'

The kitchen gardens of the first house down by the church became a garden centre. *The Western Morning News* of 8 September 1950 recorded the freehold market garden and house comprising 1 ½ acre walled garden, two acres of orchard and 3 acres of pasture to be sold. Several owners later, Mr and Mrs Burks bought it in 1981 and then sold to Alison and Derrick Dyer some ten years later. The bothy was turned into living accommodation and the glasshouses removed, and a commercial garden centre emerged which finally closed in September 2018.

The novelist Henry James, a visitor to Eggesford in the time of the Portsmouths (see Chapter 9), wrote in his preface to *The Aspern Papers*, published in 1888:

'I delight in a palpable imaginable visitable past — in the nearer distances and the clearer mysteries, the marks and signs of a world we may reach over to as by making a long arm we grasp an object at the other end of our own table. The table is the one, the common expanse, and where we lean, so stretching, we find it firm and continuous.

That, to my imagination, is the past fragrant of all, or of almost all, the poetry of the thing outlived and lost and gone, and yet in which the precious element of closeness, telling so of connections but tasting so of differences, remains appreciable.

We are divided, of course, between liking to feel the past strange and liking to feel it familiar; the difficulty is, for intensity, to catch it at the moment when the scales of the balance hang with the right evenness.'

Nearly 140 years later, this collection of stories and connections between Eggesford, Chawleigh and the Portsmouth family and their estate in Devon, written to reflect the motto of the Portsmouths, *En Suivant la Vérité*: *By Following the Truth*, can also help find the balance perhaps for that shared past to be more 'palpable, imaginable, visitable'.

Perhaps all this will help us to understand ourselves and our homes and communities a little better, for now and for the future.

The Portsmouth (Wallop family) coat of arms and motto, taken from Vol. V of Arthur Collins's *The Peerage of England* (1779)

(Photo by Jonathan Crofts)

AFTERWORD

All houses wherein men have lived and died
Are haunted houses. Through the open doors
The harmless phantoms on their errands glide,
With feet that make no sound upon the floors.

We meet them at the door-way, on the stair,
Along the passages they come and go,
Impalpable impressions on the air,
A sense of something moving to and fro.

There are more guests at table than the hosts
Invited; the illuminated hall
Is thronged with quiet, inoffensive ghosts,
As silent as the pictures on the wall.

The stranger at my fireside cannot see
The forms I see, nor hear the sounds I hear;
He but perceives what is; while unto me
All that has been is visible and clear.

We have no title-deeds to house or lands;
Owners and occupants of earlier dates
From graves forgotten stretch their dusty hands,
And hold in mortmain still their old estates.

From *Haunted Houses* (1858)

by American poet
Henry Wadsworth Longfellow (1807–1882)

ACKNOWLEDGEMENTS AND SOURCES

Many people have contributed in some way to the creation of this book, and I am very grateful to all of them. Documented sources are also listed below, and where online sources have been used, care has been taken to validate their authenticity, as information is often duplicated online and is not always accurate. Inevitably, historical information does at times conflict, whatever the source.

I am indebted, in no particular order, to:

Julian Fellowes, with whom I once worked, creator of *Downton Abbey*, for his support and interest, and for writing the Foreword

Annabel, Lady Portsmouth, for her support and guidance

Monty and the late Joy James, for encouragement and for making available Monty's own extensive research on the history of Chawleigh, together with that of Algernon Pepperell and Miss F W Hillman, collected between 1958–74

Ed and Jo Howell of Eggesford House, for their general support, reference sources, and photographs of the house, then and now (including *Some Notes on the Family of Fellowes from The Family & Descendants of William Fellowes of Eggesford* by the Reverend Edmund Horace Fellowes, Oxley & Son, 1910, and various sales catalogues for Eggesford House)

Joanne Court and her husband Peter of The Old Glebe, Eggesford, for providing the wide-ranging Eggesford research by Nigel Wright, the former owner, including the Taw Valley Local History Archive, 1986–87

Daphne Cockram and Yvonne Gerry for sharing their books and photographs of Chawleigh history

St James' Church, Chawleigh, for the loan of their folders on church and village history

Henry and Tom Martin, and Sue Chapman, for their knowledge of Leaches House and Farm, and Henry for his history of the Chawleigh Friendly Society and his photos

Jim Stevens, former postman, for his knowledge and collections on Chawleigh

James and Jan Bulmer of Higher Ford House, for their support, and information on the Portsmouths' hunting lodge

Nathalie Baron and Ian Brown of Chawleigh Barton

Tim and Helen Robinson of The Old Hall, Chawleigh

Michael Aldridge for photos and information on Chawleigh Barton Woods

Alison Deveson, author of *En Suivant La Vérité: A History of the Earls of Portsmouth and the Wallop Family* (Portsmouth Estates, 2008); Alison has a Carnarvon family / Highclere connection too – as a librarian, she catalogued the whole of the library there, which can be seen from time to time on screen in *Downton Abbey*

The staff at Farleigh House at Farleigh Wallop, Hampshire, during our research visit there

Henry Parker of Downes House, Crediton, for information on his ancestral home and the Redvers Buller family

Sir Hugh Stucley of Affeton Castle and Hartland Abbey for information on the Stucley family

James Rothwell, MA, FSA, National Decorative Arts Curator for The National Trust, for the use of his notes for the *Society of Architectural Historians of Great Britain* (2007)

Dr Elizabeth Foyster for her support and for making available information from her book on John Charles Wallop, 3rd Earl of Portsmouth: *The Trials of the King of Hampshire* (Oneworld, 2016)

Writer Fay Sampson, formerly based in Devon, for information on the Snell family *faysampson.co.uk*

Bideford Railway Heritage Centre, *bidefordrailway.co.uk*

British Library Newspapers (The British Newspaper Archive)

broadwoodwidger.com for information on Charles Luxmoore

The staff at the Devon Heritage Centre in Exeter (South West Heritage Trust)

devonheritage.org created by the late Muriel and Richard Brine

devonhistorysociety.org.uk a registered charity that promotes the study of all aspects of Devon's history

europeansineastafrica.co.uk for information on the Wallop family in Kenya

exeterfoundry.org.uk for the history of Garton & King Ltd

genuki.org.uk a charitable trust, the virtual reference library of genealogical information, UK and Ireland

The staff at Hampshire Archives in Winchester

Historic England, *historicengland.org.uk*

Historic Houses, *historichouses.org*

History of Parliament, *historyofparliamentonline.org*

David Garton of the Lapford History website, (*lapfordhistory.co.uk*)

Lloyds Banking Group Archives via *archiveshub.jisc.ac.uk*

The National Archives, *nationalarchives.gov.uk*

naval-history.net for information on HMS *Eggesford*

The staff at the North Devon Record Office in Barnstaple

spreytonvillage.co.uk for information on George Lambert, MP

Alan Rosevear, *turnpikes.org.uk*

westleighparish.org for information on the Christies of Tapeley Park

Annie Rushton for her immaculate cover design, and Alison Gardner for her magnificent page design

And last but not least my wife and editor Monica Byles for her support and encouragement, research, painstaking checking and editing, and her unending enthusiasm for this project

And for providing photographs and other images: Viscount Lymington and the Earl and Countess of Portsmouth; Devon History Society; Forestry England; Gamble & Gunn (Hat Makers & Dealers), gambleandgunn.com; The Lewis Walpole Library, Yale University, US; National Library of Scotland; National Portrait Gallery London; Natural History Museum, London; South Molton Museum; South West Heritage Trust

Reference texts:

The Architect: A Weekly Illustrated Journal of Art, Civil Engineering and Building, vol. II (Gilbert Wood & Co., July–December 1869)

The Lost Houses of Eggesford, Matthew Axe, Lesley Chapman and Sharon Miller (Eggesford Gardens Ltd, 1995)

Devonshire characters and strange events, Sabine Baring-Gould (John Lane 1908)

An Old English Home and Its Dependencies, Sabine Baring-Gould (1898)

Billing's Directory and Gazetteer of the County of Devon, Martin Billings (Steam-Press Offices, 1857)

Roodscreens and Roodlofts, Frederick Bligh Bond and Reverend Dom Bede Camm (Pitman & Sons Ltd, 1909)

The Brownings' Correspondence, browningscorrespondence.com

Eveline, Countess of Portsmouth: A Recollection, Lady Winifred Burghclere (John Murray, 1907)

Devon Villages, S H Burton (Hale, 1973)

All Saints, Eggesford, guide by Reverend C A Cardale (c.1975)

Notes on Eggesford House, Reverend C A Cardale (c.1975)

Lady Almina and the Real Downton Abbey, Fiona, Countess of Carnarvon (Hodder & Stoughton, 2011)

Devon and Cornwall Record Society, New Series, vol. 11, *Devon Inventories of the Sixteenth and Seventeenth Centuries* ed. Margaret Cash (Devonshire Press, 1966)

Digging up the Dirt in Eggesford, Lesley Chapman and Sharon Miller (1996)

History of the Family of Chichester from A.D. 1086–1871, Including the Descents of the Various Branches Settled at Raleigh, Youlston, Arlington, Widworthy, Calverleigh, Hall, and Elsewhere in Devonshire; also of the Chichesters, Marquesses of Donegal, and Barons Templemore, Sir Alexander Palmer Bruce Chichester, Alexander Spicer (John Camden Hotten, 1871)

The Visitation of the County of Devon in the Year 1564, with Additions from the Earlier Visitation of 1531, ed. Frederic Thomas Colby, DD (W. Pollard, 1881)

Report of the Commissioners Concerning Charities; Containing that Part which Relates to the County of Devon,, vol. III, Chawleigh (1923)

Country Life magazines, *countrylife.co.uk*

Tarka Line Walks, Peter Craske (Crimson Publishing, 2013)

Melinda Creech blog on Robert Browning (Armstrong Browning Library & Museum, Baylor University, Texas, USA) *blogs.baylor.edu/armstrongbrowning/2014/01/06/browning-at-downton-abbey-the-rest-of-the-story/*

Notes on Devon's Churches, Beatrix F Cresswell (1919, written and compiled by Deanery)

Parochial and Manorial Chapels in Devon, Beatrix F Cresswell (1920)

A Memoir of the Reverend John Russell Of Tordown, E W L Davies (Richard Bentley & Son, 1883)

West Country Historic Houses and their Families, Eric R Delderfield (David & Charles, 1968)

Devon and Cornwall Notes and Queries, vol. 25, H P R Finberg, 'The Place-names of Devon' (1952–53)

Devon & Cornwall Notes & Queries, vol. 27, C D Radford, 'The royal descent from Edward I of the Radford families' (1956–58)

Devon & Cornwall Notes & Queries, vol. 28, C D Radford, 'Radfordiana Devoniensis' (1959–61)

Devon & Cornwall Notes & Queries, vol. 29, Reverend H Fulford Williams (1964)

Devon Buildings Group's newsletter of October 1988

Site Report: Eggesford House, Devon Gardens Trust (2019)

Transactions of the Devonshire Association: G W Copeland, 'Devonshire Church-Houses, Part VI' (1966, *devonassoc.org.uk*)

Transactions of the Devonshire Association, Reverend O J Reichel, 'The Hundred of North Tawton' (c.1807)

Transactions of the Devonshire Association, vol. 30

Transactions of the Devonshire Association, vol. 35, Reverend T W Whale, 'Analysis of the Exeter Domesday in Hundreds' (1903)

Transactions of the Devonshire Association, vol. 35, Reverend W Wykes-Finch, 'The Ancient Family of Wyke of North Wyke, Co. Devon' (1903)

Transactions of the Devonshire Association, vol. 95, E T Vachell, MA, 'Eggesford and Heywood Castles' (1963)

Transactions of the Devonshire Association, vol. 124, Peter Christie, 'The True Story of the North Devon Savages' (1992)

We Donkeys in Devon, Volo non valeo / Maria Susannah Gibbons (Henry S Eland, 1886)

Dictionary of Irish Biography, www.dib.ie

The Dictionary of National Biography (1912)

Letters of Mrs Millicent Garrett Fawcett L LD, Manchester Archives and Local Studies

Various books on Devon parishes, C A T Fursdon, 1920s–1930s

Indian Biographical Dictionary, C Hayavadana Rao (1915)

Inquisitions and assessments relating to Feudal Aids, 1284–1431 (HMSO, 1899)

Horse & Hound magazine, *horseandhound.co.uk*

Devon, W G Hoskins (Phillimore, 2011; First Edition, Collins, 1954)

Appendix to the Reports of the Select Committee of the House of Commons on Public Petitions (Session 1846)

The Toll-houses of North Devon, Tim Jenkinson & Patrick Taylor (Polystar Press, 2010)

Devon Tollhouses: A Gazetteer, John Kanefsky (Exeter Industrial Archaeology Group, 1976)

Kelly's Directory, various dates

Return of Owners of Land, ed. John Lambert (HMSO & Eyre & Spottiswoode, 1875)

Devon Families, Rosemary Lauder (Halsgrove, 2002)

Vanished Houses of North Devon, Rosemary Lauder (North Devon Books, 2005)

Magna Britannia, Devonshire, vol. 6, Daniel and Samuel Lysons (Thomas Cadell, 1822)

The Country Houses of Devon, Hugh Meller (Black Dog Press, 2015)

A Series of Picturesque Views of Seats of Noblemen and Gentlemen of Great Britain and Ireland, vol. 6, ed. Reverend Francis Orpen Morris (William Mackenzie, 1880)

Ecclesiastical Antiquities of Devon, Dr George Oliver (W C Featherstone, 1840)

The Church in Devon 400–1560, Nicholas Orme (Impress Books, 2013)

The Victoria History of the Counties of England: Devonshire, William Page (Constable, 1906)

Domesday Book data, Hull University, Professor John Palmer, George Slater, via *opendomesday.org*

Notes on the Parish of Chawleigh, Devon, and District, Algernon Pepperell and Miss F W Hillman (collected 1958–74)

The Buildings of England: North Devon, Nikolaus Pevsner (Penguin, 1952)

Thomas Hardy: His Life and Friends, F B Pinion (Palgrave Macmillan, 1992)

Collections Towards a Description of the County of Devon, Sir William Pole (J Nichols, 1791)

The History of Devonshire, Reverend Richard Polwhele (Cadell, Johnson, and Dilly, 1797)

Sketch of the Progress and Present Extent of Savings' Banks in the United Kingdom, G R Porter (1846)

Post Office Annual Directory, various dates

The Chorographical Description or Survey of the County of Devon, Tristram Risdon ('with considerable additions', Rees & Curtis, 1811; originally compiled, 1605–1632)

Travels in Georgian Devon: The Illustrated Journeys of the Reverend John Swete, 1789–1800 – 4 vols, eds. Margery M Rowe and Todd Gray (Devon Books, 1997–2000)

The Saturday Review of Politics, Literature, Science and Art, vol. 114 (John W Parker & Son, 1912)

The Palgrave Encyclopedia of Victorian Women's Writing, ed. Lesa Scholl and Emily Morris (Palgrave Macmillan, 2022)

Illustrations of Devon History, R R Sellman (Methuen, 1962)

The Life of Herbert Henry Asquith, Lord Oxford and Asquith, J A Spender and Cyril Asquith (Hutchinson & Co., 1938)

British Sport and Sportsmen, 'The Sportsman' (British Sport and Sportsmen, 1908)

Exon: The Domesday Survey of South-West England, ed. P A Stokes, Studies in Domesday, gen. ed. J Crick (London, 2018), *www.exondomesday.ac.uk*

Affeton Castle: A Lost Devon Village, John H A Stucley (1967)

The Foxhounds of Great Britain and Ireland, Their Masters and Huntsmen, Sir Humphrey F de Trafford (Walter Southwood & Co., 1905)

Sufferings of the Clergy in Devon and Cornwall during the Grand Rebellion, Dr John Walker (1714)

The Wallop Family and Their Ancestry, V J Watney (Johnson, 1928)

'Dearest Emmie': Thomas Hardy's Letters to his First Wife, ed. Carl J Weber (Palgrave Macmillan, 1963)

A View of Devonshire in MDCXXX, with a Pedigree of Most of its Gentry, Thomas Westcote (William Roberts, 1845; original manuscript, 1624–1636)

The Western Morning News, 28 November 1963: 'The Glory that was Eggesford'

History, Gazetteer, and Directory of Devonshire, William White (Robert Leader, 1850)

Imperial Gazetteer of England and Wales: Embracing Recent Changes in Counties, Dioceses, Parishes, and Boroughs: General Statistics: Postal Arrangements: Railway Systems, &c.; and Forming a Complete Description of the Country, John Marius Wilson (A Fullarton & Co., 1870–72)

A History of Devonshire with Sketches of its Leading Worthies, R N Worth (Elliot Stock, 1886)

The Author

Jonathan Crofts lived in southwest London from 1993, but since 2021 has split his time between Devon and London.

After leaving Bristol University with a degree in Modern Languages, he embarked on a career in theatre and television, including sixteen years at the BBC, and latterly working all over the world as a consultant with media and broadcast organisations. His time in TV drama production included filming at locations similar to Eggesford House, and once with actor and writer Julian Fellowes in the BAFTA award-winning *Our Friends In The North*.

Jonathan has followed local history over the last thirty years through reading, talks, walks and visits, as well as his own research and photography, and published his first book on his London neighbourhood, *Meadows Mansions and Munitions*, in 2021.

His wife Monica Byles has spent nearly forty years in book publishing, both fiction and non-fiction, and has guided and supported Jonathan in the production of this latest book, including the final edit. Her own family have resided in or had links with Devon since the Norman Conquest.

In 2021 Jonathan and Monica moved into their four-hundred-year-old farmhouse in Chawleigh. Intrigued by the Portsmouth 'P' and crest over their front door, the story of the house emerged on closer research, alongside the history of their village and the aristocratic Portsmouth estate and family which once owned it.

In 2024 Jonathan became a trustee of the Friends of the historic All Saints Church in Eggesford, FEAST. They succeeded in the 1990s in keeping open the Church, threatened with closure by the Church of England, with its fine monuments and fascinating history, and FEAST still works today to preserve and enhance the building and the beautiful site for the benefit of the public.

The book is a tribute to the people of Chawleigh, Eggesford, and the wider estate over the last five centuries.